A GRIPPING ACCOUNT OF TERROR,
BETRAYAL, POLITICAL INTRIGUE,
AND UNTHINKABLE CHOICES

SON OF HAMAS

MOSAB HASSAN YOUSEF

WITH RON BRACKIN

SALTRIVER®

AN IMPRINT OF TYNDALE HOUSE PUBLISHERS, INC.

Visit Tyndale's exciting Web site at www.tyndale.com.

TYNDALE is a registered trademark of Tyndale House Publishers, Inc.

SaltRiver and the SaltRiver logo are registered trademarks of Tyndale House Publishers, Inc.

Son of Hamas: A Gripping Account of Terror, Betrayal, Political Intrigue, and Unthinkable Choices

Library of Congress Cataloging-in-Publication Data

Yousef, Mosab Hassan.
  Son of Hamas : a gripping account of terror, betrayal, political intrigue, and unthinkable choices / Mosab Hassan Yousef, with Ron Brackin.
    p. cm.
  Includes bibliographical references.
  ISBN 978-1-4143-3307-6 (hc)
    1. Yousef, Mosab Hassan. 2. Christian converts from Islam—Israel—Biography. I. Brackin, Ron.
II. Title.
  BV2626.4.Y68A3 2010
  248.2'46092—dc22
  [B]   2009046326

ISBN 978-1-4143-3668-8 (International Trade Paper Edition)

Printed in the United States of America

16 15 14 13 12 11 10
8   7   6   5   4

To my beloved father and my wounded family
To the victims of the Palestinian-Israeli conflict
To every human life my Lord has saved

My family, I am very proud of you; only my God can understand what you have been through. I realize that what I have done has caused another deep wound that might not heal in this life and that you may have to live with its shame forever.

I could have been a hero and made my people proud of me. I knew what kind of hero they were looking for: a fighter who dedicated his life and family to the cause of a nation. Even if I was killed, they would have told my story for generations to come and been proud of me forever, but in reality, I would not have been much of a hero.

Instead, I became a traitor in the eyes of my people. Although I once brought pride to you, I now bring you only shame. Although I was once the royal prince, I am now a stranger in a foreign country fighting against the enemy of loneliness and darkness.

I know you see me as a traitor; please understand it was not you I chose to betray, but your understanding of what it means to be a hero. When Middle Eastern nations—Jews and Arabs alike—start to understand some of what I understand, only then will there be peace. And if my Lord was rejected for saving the world from the punishment of hell, I don't mind being a reject!

I don't know what the future holds, but I do know that I am not afraid. And now I want to give you something that has helped me to survive so far: all the guilt and shame I have carried for all these years is a small price to pay if it saves even one innocent human life.

How many people appreciate what I have done? Not so many. But that's okay. I believed in what I did and I still believe, which is my only fuel for this long journey. Every drop of innocent blood that has been saved gives me hope to carry on to the last day.

I paid, you paid, and yet the bills of war and peace continue to come. God be with us all and give us what we need to carry this heavy weight.

With love,
Your son

CONTENTS

Map of Israel and the Occupied Territories *ix*
A Word from the Author *xi*
Preface *xiii*

CHAPTER 1: Captured *1*
CHAPTER 2: The Ladder of Faith *5*
CHAPTER 3: Muslim Brotherhood *13*
CHAPTER 4: Throwing Stones *21*
CHAPTER 5: Survival *31*
CHAPTER 6: A Hero's Return *39*
CHAPTER 7: Radical *45*
CHAPTER 8: Fanning the Flames *49*
CHAPTER 9: Guns *61*
CHAPTER 10: The Slaughterhouse *67*
CHAPTER 11: The Offer *77*
CHAPTER 12: Number 823 *87*
CHAPTER 13: Trust No One *95*
CHAPTER 14: Riot *105*
CHAPTER 15: Damascus Road *113*
CHAPTER 16: Second Intifada *125*
CHAPTER 17: Undercover *135*
CHAPTER 18: Most Wanted *147*
CHAPTER 19: Shoes *155*
CHAPTER 20: Torn *165*

CHAPTER 21: The Game *173*

CHAPTER 22: Defensive Shield *185*

CHAPTER 23: Supernatural Protection *193*

CHAPTER 24: Protective Custody *201*

CHAPTER 25: Saleh *211*

CHAPTER 26: A Vision for Hamas *223*

CHAPTER 27: Good-Bye *233*

Epilogue *243*

Postscript *247*

The Players *253*

Glossary *257*

Time Line *261*

Endnotes *263*

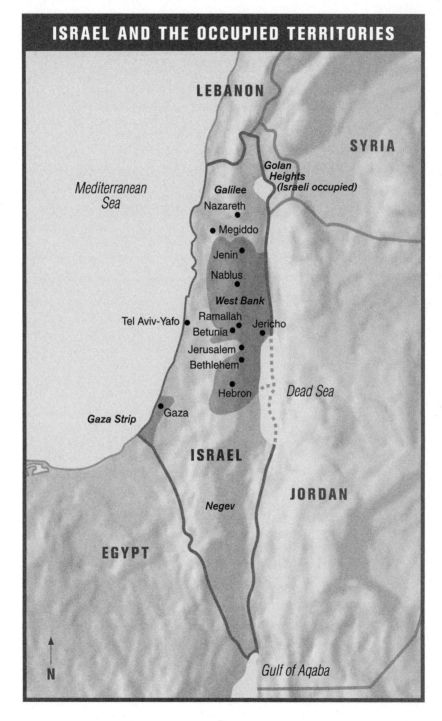

A WORD FROM THE AUTHOR

TIME IS SEQUENTIAL—a thread spanning the distance between birth and death.

Events, however, are more like a Persian carpet—thousands of richly colored threads woven into intricate patterns and images. Any attempt to place events into purely chronological order would be like pulling the threads loose and laying them end to end. It might be simpler, but you would lose the design.

The events in this book are my best recollections, sorted out from the maelstrom of my life in the occupied territories of Israel and woven together as they occurred—consecutively and concurrently.

To provide you with reference points and to sort out the Arabic names and terms, I have included a brief time line in the appendices, along with a glossary and a list of players.

For security reasons, I have intentionally omitted much of the detail from the accounts of sensitive operations conducted by the Israel Security Agency, the Shin Bet. The information revealed in this book in no way jeopardizes the ongoing global war on terrorism in which Israel plays a leading role.

Finally, *Son of Hamas,* like the Middle East, is a continuing story. So I invite you to keep in touch by visiting my blog at http://www.sonofhamas.com, where I share my insights on breaking regional developments. I also post updates on what the Lord is doing with the book and in my family and where he is leading me today.

—*MHY*

PREFACE

PEACE IN THE MIDDLE EAST has been the holy grail of diplomats, prime ministers, and presidents for more than five decades. Every new face on the world stage thinks he or she is going to be the one to resolve the Arab-Israeli conflict. And each one fails just as miserably and completely as those who have come before.

The fact is, few Westerners can come close to understanding the complexities of the Middle East and its people. But I do—by virtue of a most unique perspective. You see, I am a son of that region and of that conflict. I am a child of Islam and the son of an accused terrorist. I am also a follower of Jesus.

Before the age of twenty-one, I saw things no one should ever see: abject poverty, abuse of power, torture, and death. I witnessed the behind-the-scenes dealings of top Middle Eastern leaders who make headlines around the world. I was trusted at the highest levels of Hamas, and I participated in the so-called Intifada. I was held captive in the bowels of Israel's most feared prison facility. And as you will see, I made choices that have made me a traitor in the eyes of people I love.

My unlikely journey has taken me through dark places and given me access to extraordinary secrets. On the pages of this book

I finally reveal some of those long-hidden secrets, exposing events and processes that to this point have been known only by a handful of shadowy individuals.

The uncovering of these truths will likely send shock waves through parts of the Middle East, but I hope it will also bring comfort and closure to the families of many victims of this unending conflict.

As I move among Americans today, I find that many of them have a lot of questions about the Arab-Israeli conflict, but very few answers and even less good information. I hear questions like:

- "Why can't people just get along in the Middle East?"
- "Who is in the right—the Israelis or the Palestinians?"
- "To whom does the land really belong? Why don't Palestinians just move to other Arab countries?"
- "Why doesn't Israel give back the land and property it won in the 1967 Six-Day War?"
- "Why are so many Palestinians still living in refugee camps? Why don't they have their own state?"
- "Why do Palestinians hate Israel so much?"
- "How can Israel protect itself from suicide bombers and frequent rocket attacks?"

These are good questions, all of them. But none of them touch on the real issue, the root problem. The current conflict stretches all the way back to the animosity between Sarah and Hagar described in the first book of the Bible. To understand the political and cultural realities, however, you really don't have to look much further than the aftermath of World War I.

When the war ended, the Palestinian territories, national home of the Palestinian people for centuries, fell under the mandate of Great Britain. And the British government had an unusual notion for the area, which it stated in the Balfour Declaration of 1917: "His Majesty's Government view with favour the establishment in Palestine of a national home for the Jewish people."

Encouraged by the British government, hundreds of thousands of Jewish immigrants, mostly from Eastern Europe, flooded into the Palestinian territories. Clashes between Arabs and Jews were inevitable.

Israel became a state in 1948. However, the Palestinian territories remained just that—nonsovereign territories. Without a constitution to maintain some semblance of order, religious law becomes the highest authority. And when everyone is free to interpret and enforce the law as he sees fit, chaos ensues. To the outside world, the Middle Eastern conflict is simply a tug-of-war over a small stretch of land. But the real problem is that no one yet has understood the real problem. And as a result, negotiators from Camp David to Oslo confidently continue to splint the arms and legs of a cardiac patient.

Please understand, I did not write this book because I think I'm smarter or wiser than the great thinkers of the age. I am not. But I believe that God has given me a unique perspective by placing me on multiple sides of an apparently insoluble conflict. My life has been partitioned like the crazy little piece of real estate on the Mediterranean known as Israel by some, Palestine by others, and the occupied territories by still others.

My purpose in the pages that follow is to set the record straight on some key events, lay bare some secrets, and if all goes well, leave you with hope that the impossible can be accomplished.

Chapter One

CAPTURED
1996

I STEERED MY LITTLE WHITE SUBARU around a blind corner on one of the narrow roads that led to the main highway outside the West Bank city of Ramallah. Stepping lightly on the brake, I slowly approached one of the innumerable checkpoints that dot the roads running to and from Jerusalem.

"Turn off the engine! Stop the car!" someone shouted in broken Arabic.

Without warning, six Israeli soldiers jumped out of the bushes and blocked my car, each man carrying a machine gun, and each gun pointed directly at my head.

Panic welled up in my throat. I stopped the car and threw the keys through the open window.

"Get out! Get out!"

Wasting no time, one of the men jerked open the door and threw me to the dusty ground. I barely had time to cover my head before the beating began. But even as I tried to protect my face, the heavy boots of the soldiers quickly found other targets: ribs, kidneys, back, neck, skull.

Two of the men dragged me to my feet and pulled me to the checkpoint, where I was forced onto my knees behind a cement barricade. My hands were bound behind my back with a sharp-edged plastic zip tie that was cinched much too tight. Somebody blindfolded me and shoved me into the back of a jeep onto the floor. Fear mingled with anger as I wondered where they were taking me and how long I would be gone. I was barely eighteen years old and only a few weeks away from my final high school exams. What was going to happen to me?

After a fairly short drive, the jeep slowed to a halt. A soldier pulled me from the back and removed my blindfold. Squinting in the bright sunlight, I realized that we were at Ofer Army Base. An Israeli defense base, Ofer was one of the largest and most secure military facilities in the West Bank.

As we moved toward the main building, we passed by several armored tanks, which were shrouded by canvas tarps. The monstrous mounds had always intrigued me whenever I had seen them from outside the gates. They looked like huge, oversized boulders.

Once inside the building, we were met by a doctor who gave me a quick once-over, apparently to make sure I was fit to withstand interrogation. I must have passed because, within minutes, the handcuffs and blindfold were replaced, and I was shoved back into the jeep.

As I tried to contort my body so that it would fit into the small area usually reserved for people's feet, one beefy soldier put his boot squarely on my hip and pressed the muzzle of his M16 assault rifle into my chest. The hot reek of petrol fumes saturated the floor of the vehicle and forced my throat closed. Whenever I tried to adjust my cramped position, the soldier jabbed the gun barrel deeper into my chest.

Without warning, a searing pain shot through my body and made my toes clench. It was as if a rocket were exploding in my skull. The force of the blow had come from the front seat, and I realized that one of the soldiers must have used his rifle butt to hit me in the head. Before I had time to protect myself, however, he hit me again, harder this time and in the eye. I tried to move out of reach but the soldier who had been using me for a footstool dragged me upright.

"Don't move or I *will* shoot you!" he shouted.

But I couldn't help it. Each time his comrade hit me, I involuntarily recoiled from the impact.

Under the rough blindfold, my eye was beginning to swell closed, and my face felt numb. There was no circulation in my legs. My breathing came in shallow gasps. I had never felt such pain. But worse than the physical pain was the horror of being at the mercy of something merciless, something raw and inhuman. My mind reeled as I struggled to understand the motives of my tormentors. I understood fighting and killing out of hatred, rage, revenge, or even necessity. But I had done nothing to these soldiers. I had not resisted. I had done everything I was told to do. I was no threat to them. I was bound, blindfolded, and unarmed. What was inside these people that made them take such delight in hurting me? Even the basest animal kills for a reason, not just for sport.

I thought about how my mother was going to feel when she learned that I had been arrested. With my father already in an Israeli prison, I was the man of the family. Would I be held in prison for months and years as he had been? If so, how would my mother manage with me gone too? I began to understand how my dad felt—worried about his family and grieved by the knowledge that we were worrying about him. Tears sprang to my eyes as I imagined my mother's face.

I also wondered if all my years of high school were about to be wasted. If I indeed was headed for an Israeli prison, I would miss my final exams next month. A torrent of questions and cries raced through my mind even as the blows continued to fall: *Why are you doing this to me? What have I done? I am not a terrorist! I'm just a kid. Why are you beating me like this?*

I'm pretty sure I passed out several times, but every time I came to, the soldiers were still there, hitting me. I couldn't dodge the blows.

The only thing I could do was scream. I felt bile rising in the back of my throat and I gagged, vomiting all over myself.

I felt a deep sadness before losing consciousness. Was this the end? Was I going to die before my life had really even started?

Chapter Two

THE LADDER OF FAITH
1955–1977

MY NAME IS MOSAB HASSAN YOUSEF.

I am the oldest son of Sheikh Hassan Yousef, one of the seven founders of the Hamas organization. I was born in the West Bank village of Ramallah, and I am part of one of the most religious Islamic families in the Middle East.

My story begins with my grandfather, Sheikh Yousef Dawood, who was the religious leader—or imam—for the village of Al-Janiya, located in the part of Israel that the Bible calls Judea and Samaria. I adored my grandfather. His soft, white beard tickled my cheek when he hugged me, and I could sit for hours, listening to the sound of his sweet voice chanting the *adhan*—the Muslim call to prayer. And I had plenty of opportunities to do so since Muslims are called to pray five times every day. Chanting adhan and the Qur'an is not an easy thing to do well, but when my grandfather did it, the sound was magical.

When I was a boy, some chanters bothered me so much that I wanted to stuff rags in my ears. But my grandfather was a passionate man, and he carried his listeners deep into the meaning of the adhan as he sang. He believed every word of it.

About four hundred people lived in Al-Janiya in the days when it was under Jordanian rule and Israeli occupation. But the residents of this little rural village had little use for politics. Nestled into the gently rolling hills a few miles northwest of Ramallah, Al-Janiya was a very peaceful and beautiful place. Its sunsets tinted everything in hues of rose and violet. The air was clean and clear, and from many of the hills' peaks you could see all the way to the Mediterranean.

By four o'clock every morning, my grandfather was on his way to the mosque. When he finished morning prayers, he would take his little donkey to the field, work the soil, tend his olive trees, and drink fresh water from the spring that flowed down the mountain. There was no air pollution because only one person in Al-Janiya had a car.

When he was at home, my grandfather welcomed a steady stream of visitors. He was more than the imam—he was everything to the people in that village. He prayed over every newborn baby and whispered the adhan in the child's ear. When someone died, my grandfather washed and anointed the body and wrapped it in winding clothes. He married them, and he buried them.

My father, Hassan, was his favorite son. Even as a young boy, before it was required of him, my father went regularly with my grandfather to the mosque. None of his brothers cared anything about Islam like he did.

At his father's side, Hassan learned to chant the adhan. And like his father, he had a voice and a passion that people responded to. My grandfather was very proud of him. When my father was twelve years old, my grandfather said, "Hassan, you have shown that you are very interested in God and Islam. So I am going to send you to Jerusalem to learn sharia." Sharia is Islamic religious law that deals with daily life, from family and hygiene to politics and economics.

Hassan knew and cared nothing about politics or economics. He simply wanted to be like his father. He wanted to read and chant the Qur'an and to serve people. But he was about to learn that his father was much more than a trusted religious leader and beloved public servant.

Because values and traditions have always meant more to the Arab people than government constitutions and courts, men like my grandfather often became the highest level of authority. Especially in areas where secular leaders were weak or corrupt, the word of a religious leader was considered law.

My father was not sent to Jerusalem simply to study religion; his father was preparing him to rule. So for the next few years, my father lived and studied in the Old City of Jerusalem beside Al-Aqsa Mosque—the iconic golden-domed structure that visually defines the profile of Jerusalem in the eyes of most of the world's people. At the age of eighteen, he completed his studies and moved to Ramallah, where he was immediately employed as imam of the mosque in Old Town. Filled with passion to serve both Allah and his people, my father was eager to begin his work in that community, just as his father had done in Al-Janiya.

But Ramallah was not Al-Janiya. The former was a bustling city. The latter was a sleepy little village. The first time my father entered the mosque, he was shocked to find only five old men waiting for him. Everyone else, it seemed, was in the coffeehouses and pornographic theaters, getting drunk and gambling. Even the man who chanted the adhan for the mosque next door had run a microphone and cord from the minaret, so he could continue the Islamic tradition without interrupting his card game.

My father's heart was broken for these people, though he wasn't sure how he would ever reach them. Even his five old men admitted they only came to the mosque because they knew they were going to die soon and wanted to go to heaven, but at least they were willing to listen. So he worked with what he had. He led these fellows in prayer, and he taught them the Qur'an. In a very short amount of time, they grew to love him as if he were an angel sent from heaven.

Outside the mosque, it was a different story. For many, my father's love for the god of the Qur'an only highlighted their own casual approach to the faith, and they were offended.

"Who is this child doing the adhan?" people scoffed, pointing to my baby-faced father. "He doesn't belong here. He is a troublemaker."

"Why is this little guy embarrassing us? Only old people go to the mosque."

"I would rather be a dog than be like you," one of them shouted in his face.

My father quietly endured the persecution, never shouting back or defending himself. But his love and compassion for the people would not let him give up. And he continued to do the work he had been called to do: urging the people to return to Islam and Allah.

He shared his concerns with my grandfather, who quickly realized that my father had even greater zeal and potential than he had originally thought. My grandfather sent him to Jordan for advanced Islamic study. As you will see, the people he met there would ultimately change the course of my family's history and even affect the history of conflict in the Middle East. But before I continue, I need to pause briefly to explain a few important points of Islamic history that will help you understand why the countless diplomatic solutions that have been put forward have uniformly failed and can offer no hope for peace.

Between 1517 and 1923, Islam—personified by the Ottoman Caliphate—spread from its base in Turkey across three continents. But after a few centuries of great economic and political power, the Ottoman Empire became centralized and corrupt and began its decline.

Under the Turks, Muslim villages throughout the Middle East were subject to persecution and crushing taxation. Istanbul was simply too far away for the caliph to protect the faithful from abuses by soldiers and local officials.

By the twentieth century, many Muslims were becoming disillusioned and began to look for a different way of life. Some embraced the atheism of the recently arrived communists. Others buried their problems in liquor, gambling, and pornography, much of which was introduced by Westerners who were lured to the area by mineral wealth and growing industrialization.

In Cairo, Egypt, a devout young primary schoolteacher named Hassan al-Banna wept for his countrymen who were poor, jobless, and godless. But he blamed the West, not the Turks, and he believed that the only hope for his people, especially the youth, was a return to the purity and simplicity of Islam.

He went to the coffeehouses, climbed up on tables and chairs, and preached to everyone about Allah. Drunkards mocked him. Religious leaders challenged him. But most of the people loved him because he gave them hope.

In March 1928, Hassan al-Banna founded the Society of the Muslim Brothers, popularly known as the Muslim Brotherhood. The goal of the new organization was to rebuild society according to Islamic principles. Within a decade, every province in Egypt had a branch. Al-Banna's brother established a chapter in the Palestinian territories in 1935. And after twenty years, the Brotherhood numbered about half a million in Egypt alone.

Members of the Muslim Brotherhood were largely drawn from the poorest and least influential classes—but they were fiercely loyal to the cause. They gave out of their own pockets to help their fellow Muslims, as called for in the Qur'an.

Many people in the West who stereotype all Muslims as terrorists don't know about the side of Islam that reflects love and mercy. It cares for the poor, widows, and orphans. It facilitates education and welfare. It unites and strengthens. This is the side of Islam that motivated those early leaders of the Muslim Brotherhood. Of course, there is also the other side, the one that calls all Muslims to jihad, to struggle and contend with the world until they establish a global caliphate, led by one holy man who rules and speaks for Allah. This will be important for you to understand and to remember as we go along. But back to our history lesson. . . .

In 1948, the Muslim Brotherhood attempted a coup against the Egyptian government, which the Brotherhood blamed for the nation's growing secularism. The uprising was interrupted before it could get traction, however, when the British Mandate ended and Israel declared its independence as a Jewish state.

Muslims throughout the Middle East were outraged. According to the Qur'an, when an enemy invades any Muslim country, all Muslims are called as one to fight to defend their land. From the viewpoint of the Arab world, foreigners had invaded and now occupied Palestine, home of the Al-Aqsa Mosque, Islam's third holiest place on earth after Mecca and Medina. The mosque was built on the site from which it was believed that Mohammad had traveled with the angel Gabriel to heaven and spoken with Abraham, Moses, and Jesus.

Egypt, Lebanon, Syria, Jordan, and Iraq immediately invaded the new Jewish state. Among the ten thousand Egyptian troops were thousands of Muslim Brotherhood volunteers. The Arab coalition, however, was outnumbered and outgunned. Less than a year later, the Arab troops had been driven out.

As a result of the war, about three-quarters of a million Palestinian Arabs fled or were expelled from their homes in the territories that became the State of Israel.

Although the United Nations passed Resolution 194, which stated in part that "refugees wishing to return to their homes and live at peace with their neighbours should be permitted to do so" and that "compensation should be paid for the property of those choosing not to return," this recommendation was never implemented. Tens of thousands of Palestinians who fled Israel during the Arab-Israeli War never regained their homes and land. Many of these refugees and their descendants live in squalid refugee camps operated by the United Nations (UN) to this day.

When the now-armed members of the Muslim Brotherhood returned from the battlefield to Egypt, the suspended coup was on again. But news of the overthrow plan leaked out, and the Egyptian government banned the Brotherhood, confiscated its assets, and imprisoned many of its members. Those who escaped arrest assassinated Egypt's prime minister a few weeks later.

Hassan al-Banna, in turn, was assassinated on February 12, 1949, presumably by the government secret service. But the Brotherhood was not crushed. In just twenty years, Hassan al-Banna had shaken Islam out of its dormancy and created a revolution with armed fighters. And for the next few years, the organization continued to add to its numbers and its influence among the people, not only in Egypt but also in nearby Syria and Jordan.

By the time my father arrived in Jordan in the mid-1970s to continue his studies, the Muslim Brotherhood there was well established and beloved by the people. Its members were doing everything that was on my father's heart—encouraging renewed faith among those who had strayed from the Islamic way of life, healing those who were hurt, and trying to save people from the corrupting influences in society. He believed these men were religious reformers to Islam, as Martin Luther and William Tyndale were to Christianity. They only wanted to save people and improve their lives, not to kill and destroy. And when my father met some of the early leaders of the Brotherhood, he said, "Yes, this is what I have been looking for."

What my father saw in those early days was the part of Islam that reflects love and mercy. What he didn't see, what he perhaps has never yet allowed himself to see, is the other side of Islam.

Islamic life is like a ladder, with prayer and praising Allah as the bottom rung. The higher rungs represent helping the poor and needy, establishing schools, and supporting charities. The highest rung is jihad.

The ladder is tall. Few look up to see what is at the top. And progress is usually gradual, almost imperceptible—like a barn cat stalking a swallow. The swallow never takes its eyes off the cat. It just stands there, watching the cat pace back and forth, back and forth. But the swallow does not judge depth. It does not see that the cat is getting a little bit closer with every pass until, in the blink of an eye, the cat's claws are stained with the swallow's blood.

Traditional Muslims stand at the foot of the ladder, living in guilt for not really practicing Islam. At the top are fundamentalists, the ones you see in the news killing women and children for the glory of the god of the Qur'an. Moderates are somewhere in between.

A moderate Muslim is actually more dangerous than a fundamentalist, however, because he appears to be harmless, and you can never tell when he has taken that next step toward the top. Most suicide bombers began as moderates.

The day my father first put his foot on the bottom rung of the ladder, he could never have imagined how far from his original ideals he would eventually climb. And thirty-five years later, I would want to ask him: Do you remember where you started? You saw all those lost people, your heart broke for them, and you wanted them to come to Allah and be safe. Now suicide bombers and innocent blood? Is this what you set out to do? But speaking to one's father about such things is not done in our culture. And so he continued on that dangerous path.

Chapter Three

MUSLIM BROTHERHOOD
1977–1987

WHEN MY FATHER RETURNED to the occupied territories after his studies in Jordan, he was filled with optimism and hope for Muslims everywhere. In his mind he saw a bright future brought about by a moderate manifestation of the Muslim Brotherhood.

Accompanying him was Ibrahim Abu Salem, one of the founders of the Muslim Brotherhood in Jordan. Abu Salem had come to help breathe life into the stagnated Brotherhood in Palestine. He and my father worked well together, recruiting young people who shared their passion and forming them into small activist groups.

In 1977, with only fifty dinars in his pocket, Hassan married Ibrahim Abu Salem's sister Sabha Abu Salem. I was born the following year.

When I was seven years old, our family moved to Al-Bireh, the twin city of Ramallah, and my father became imam of Al-Amari refugee camp, which was established within Al-Bireh's municipal borders. Nineteen camps dotted the West Bank, and Al-Amari had been established in 1949 on about twenty-two acres. By 1957, its weathered tents had been replaced by wall-to-wall, back-to-back concrete houses. Streets were the width of a car, their gutters flowing with raw sewage like rivers of sludge. The camp was overcrowded; the water, undrinkable. One lone tree stood at the center of the camp. The refugees depended on the United Nations for everything—housing, food, clothing, medical care, and education.

When my father went to the mosque for the first time, he was disappointed to find only two rows of people praying, with twenty men in each row. Several months after he began to preach in the camp, however, people filled the mosque and overflowed into the streets. In addition to his devotion to Allah, my father had a great love and compassion for the Muslim people. And in return, they, too, grew to love him very much.

Hassan Yousef was so likable because he was just like everyone else. He did not think of himself as higher than those he served. He lived as they lived, ate what they ate, prayed like they prayed. He didn't wear fancy clothes. He drew a small salary from the Jordanian government—barely enough to cover his expenses—which supported the operation and maintenance of religious sites. His official day off was Monday, but he never took it. He didn't work for wages; he worked to please Allah. For him, this was his holy duty, his life's purpose.

In September 1987, my father took a second job teaching religion to the Muslim students who attended a private Christian school in the West Bank. Of course, that meant we saw less of him than before—not because he didn't love his family but because he loved Allah more. What we didn't realize, however, was that a time was coming in the days ahead when we would hardly see him at all.

While my father worked, my mother carried the burden of raising the children alone. She taught us how to be good Muslims, waking us for dawn prayer when we were old enough and encouraging us to fast during the Islamic holy month of Ramadan. There were now six of us—my brothers Sohayb, Seif, and Oways; my sisters Sabeela and Tasneem; and myself. Even with my father's income from two jobs, we barely had enough money to pay the bills. My mother worked hard to stretch every dinar until it snapped.

Sabeela and Tasneem started helping my mother with the chores when they were very young. Sweet and pure and beautiful, my sisters never complained, even though their toys were covered with dust because they didn't have time to play with them. Instead, their new toys were kitchen utensils.

"You do too much, Sabeela," my mother told my oldest sister. "You need to stop and rest."

But Sabeela just smiled and continued working.

My brother Sohayb and I learned very early how to build a fire and use the oven. We did our share of cooking and washing dishes, and we all looked after Oways, the baby.

Our favorite game was called Stars. My mother wrote our names on a sheet of paper, and every night before bedtime, we gathered in a circle so she could award us "stars" based on what we had done that day. At the end of the month, the one who had the most stars was the winner; it was usually Sabeela. Of course, we had no money for actual prizes, but it didn't matter. Stars was more about earning our mother's appreciation and honor than anything else, and we always waited eagerly for our little moments of glory.

The Ali Mosque was just half a mile away from our house, and I felt very proud to be able to walk there by myself. I desperately wanted to be like my father, just as he had wanted to be like his father.

Across the street from Ali Mosque loomed one of the largest cemeteries I had ever seen. Serving Ramallah, Al-Bireh, and the refugee camps, the cemetery was five times as big as our entire neighborhood and was surrounded by a two-foot-high wall. Five times a day, when the adhan called us to prayer, I walked to and from the mosque past thousands of graves. For a boy my age, the place was unbelievably creepy, especially at night when it was totally dark. I couldn't help imagining the roots of the big trees feeding on the buried bodies.

Once when the imam called us to noon prayer, I purified myself, put on some cologne, dressed in nice clothes like my father wore, and set off for the mosque. It was a beautiful day. As I neared the mosque, I noticed that more cars than usual were parked outside, and a group of people were standing near the entrance. I removed my shoes like I always did and went in. Just inside the door was a dead body, wrapped in white cotton in an open box. I had never seen a corpse before, and even though I knew I shouldn't stare, I couldn't take my eyes off him. He was wrapped in a sheet, with only his face exposed. I watched his chest closely, half expecting him to start breathing again.

The imam called us to line up for prayer, and I went to the front with everyone else, though I kept glancing back at the body in the box. When we finished our recitations, the imam called for the body to be brought to the front to receive prayer. Eight men lifted the coffin to their shoulders, and one man shouted, *"La ilaha illallah! [There is no God but Allah!]"* As if on cue, everyone else began shouting as well: *"La ilaha illallah! La ilaha illallah!"*

I put on my shoes as quickly as I could and followed the crowd as it moved into the cemetery. Because I was so short, I had to run between the legs of the older guys just to keep up. I had never actually been inside the cemetery, but I reasoned that I would be safe since I was with so many other people.

"Do not step on the graves," someone shouted. "It is forbidden!"

I carefully made my way through the crowd until we arrived at the edge of a deep, open grave. I peered to the bottom of the eight-foot hole where an old man was standing. I had heard some of the kids in the neighborhood talk about this man, Juma'a. They said he never attended mosque and did not believe in the god of the Qur'an, but he buried everybody, sometimes two or three bodies a day.

Isn't he afraid of death at all? I wondered.

The men lowered the corpse into Juma'a's strong arms. Then they handed him a bottle of cologne and some green stuff that smelled fresh and nice. He opened the winding sheet and poured the liquid over the body.

Juma'a turned the body onto its right side, facing Mecca, and built a little box around it with pieces of concrete. As four men with shovels filled in the hole, the imam began to preach. He began like my father.

"This man is gone," he said as the dirt fell onto the dead man's face and neck and arms. "He left everything behind—his money, building, sons, daughters, and wife. This is the destiny of each of us."

He urged us to repent and stop sinning. And then he said something I had never heard from my father: "This man's soul will soon return to him and two terrible angels named Munkar and Nakir will come out of the sky to examine him. They will grab his body and shake him, asking, 'Who is your God?' If he answers incorrectly, they will beat him with a big hammer and send him down into the earth for seventy years. Allah, we ask you to give us the right answers when our time comes!"

I stared down into the open grave, horrified. The body was nearly covered by now, and I wondered how long it would be before the interrogation would begin.

"And if his answers are not satisfactory, the weight of the dirt above him will crush his ribs. Worms will slowly devour his flesh. He will be tormented by a snake with ninety-nine heads and a scorpion the size of a camel's neck until the resurrection of the dead, when his suffering may earn Allah's forgiveness."

I couldn't believe all this was happening right by my house every time they buried someone. I had never felt good about this cemetery; now I felt even worse. I decided that I needed to memorize the questions, so when the angels interrogated me after I died I would be able to answer correctly.

The imam said that the examination would begin as soon as the last person left the cemetery. I went home, but I could not stop thinking about what he had said. I decided to head back to the cemetery and listen for the torture. I went around the neighborhood, trying to get my friends to come with me, but they all thought I was crazy. I would have to go alone. All the way back to the cemetery, I trembled with fear. I couldn't control it. Soon I found myself standing in an ocean of graves. I wanted to run, but my curiosity was stronger than my dread. I wanted to hear questions, screaming—anything. But I heard nothing. I moved closer until I touched a headstone. Only silence. An hour later, I was bored and went home.

My mother was busy in the kitchen. I told her that I had gone to the cemetery where the imam said there would be torture.

"And . . . ?"

"And I went back after the people left the dead man, but nothing happened."

"Torture can only be heard by animals," she explained, "not humans."

For an eight-year-old boy, that explanation made perfect sense.

Every day after that, I watched as more bodies were brought to the cemetery. After a while, I actually began to get used to it and started hanging around just to see who had died. Yesterday, a woman. Today, a man. One day, they brought two people in, and then a couple of hours later, they brought someone else. When no one new came, I walked among the tombs and read about the people already buried there. Dead a hundred years. Dead twenty-five. What was his name? Where was she from? The cemetery became my playground.

Like me, my friends were afraid of the cemetery at first. But we dared each other to go inside the walls at night, and since none of us wanted to be seen as cowards, we all eventually overcame our fears. We even played soccer in the open spaces.

As our family grew, so did the Muslim Brotherhood. Before long, it had transitioned from an organization of the poor and refugees to include educated young men and women, businessmen, and professionals who gave out of their own pockets to build schools and charities and clinics.

Seeing this growth, many young people in the Islamic movement, particularly those in Gaza, decided that the Brotherhood needed to take a stand against the Israeli occupation. We have taken care of society, they said, and we will continue to do that. But will we accept occupation forever? Doesn't the Qur'an command us to drive out the Jewish invaders? These young men were unarmed, but they were tough and hard and spoiling for a fight.

My father and the other West Bank leaders disagreed. They were not ready to repeat the mistakes of Egypt and Syria, where the Brotherhood had attempted coups and failed. In Jordan, they argued, our brothers do not fight. They participate in elections and have a strong influence on society. My father did not oppose violence, but he didn't think his people were in any position to take on the Israeli military.

For several years, the debate within the Brotherhood continued and the grassroots pressure for action increased. Frustrated with the inaction of the Muslim Brotherhood, Fathi Shaqaqi had founded Palestinian Islamic Jihad in the late 1970s. But even so, the Muslim Brotherhood was able to maintain its nonviolent stance for another decade.

In 1986, a secret and historic meeting took place in Hebron, just south of Bethlehem. My father was there, though he didn't tell me about it until many years later. Contrary to some inaccurate historical accounts, the following seven men were present at this meeting:

- a wheelchair-bound Sheikh Ahmed Yassin, who would become the spiritual leader of the new organization
- Muhammad Jamal al-Natsheh from Hebron
- Jamal Mansour from Nablus
- Sheikh Hassan Yousef (my father)

- Mahmud Muslih from Ramallah
- Jamil Hamami from Jerusalem
- Ayman Abu Taha from Gaza

The men who attended this meeting were finally ready to fight. They agreed to begin with simple civil disobedience—throwing stones and burning tires. Their objective was to awaken, unify, and mobilize the Palestinian people and make them understand their need for independence under the banner of Allah and Islam.[1]

Hamas was born. And my father climbed a few more rungs toward the top of the ladder of Islam.

Chapter Four

THROWING STONES

1987–1989

HAMAS NEEDED A MOVE—any move—that could serve as a justification for an uprising. That move came in early December 1987, even though it was all a tragic misunderstanding.

In Gaza, an Israeli plastics salesman named Shlomo Sakal was stabbed to death. Just a few days later, four people from Gaza's Jabalia refugee camp were killed in a routine traffic accident. Word spread, however, that they had been killed by Israelis in revenge for Sakal's murder. Riots broke out in Jabalia. A seventeen-year-old threw a Molotov cocktail and was shot dead by an Israeli soldier. In Gaza and the West Bank, everyone took to the streets. Hamas took the lead, fueling the riots that became a new style of fighting in Israel. Children threw stones at Israeli tanks, and their pictures appeared on the covers of magazines throughout the international community the same week.

The First Intifada had begun, and the Palestinian cause became world news. When the intifada started, everything changed at our cemetery-playground. Every day, more bodies were arriving than ever before. Anger and rage stalked hand in hand with grief. Palestinian crowds began to stone Jewish people who had to drive past the cemetery to get to the Israeli settlement a mile away. Heavily armed Israeli settlers killed at will. And when Israel Defense Forces (IDF) arrived on the scene, there was more shooting, more wounding, more killing.

Our house was right in the center of all the chaos. Many times, the water storage tanks on our roof were shredded by Israeli bullets. The dead bodies the masked *feda'iyeen,* or freedom fighters, brought to our cemetery were no longer only old people. Sometimes they were still-bleeding corpses on stretchers, not washed, not wrapped in winding sheets. Each martyr was buried immediately so no one would be able to take the bodies, steal the organs, and return the corpses to their families stuffed with rags.

There was so much violence that I actually became bored during those rare seasons when things were quiet. My friends and I started throwing stones too—to stir things up and to be respected as fighters in the resistance. We could see the Israeli settlement from the cemetery, high up on top of the mountain, surrounded by a high fence and guard towers. I wondered about the five hundred people who lived there and drove new cars—many of them armored. They carried automatic weapons and seemed to be free to shoot anyone they wanted. To a ten-year-old kid, they seemed like aliens from another planet.

One evening just before sunset prayer, some friends and I hid by the road and waited. We decided to aim at a settlers' bus because it was a bigger target than a car and would be easier to hit. We knew the bus came every day at the same time. As we waited, the familiar strains of the imam chanted over the loudspeakers, *"Hayya 'alās-salāh* [Make haste toward worship]."

When we finally heard the low rumble of a diesel engine, we each picked up two stones. Though we were hidden and couldn't see the street, we knew exactly where the bus was by the sound. At just the right moment, we jumped up and let our ammunition fly. The unmistakable sound of stone striking metal assured us that at least a few of our projectiles had found their target.

But it wasn't the bus. It was a big military vehicle filled with edgy, angry Israeli soldiers. We quickly ducked back into our hiding place in the ditch as the vehicle came to a stop. We couldn't see the soldiers, and they couldn't see us. So they just started shooting into the air. They continued to fire aimlessly for a couple of minutes, and ducking low, we quickly made our escape into a nearby mosque.

Prayer had already begun, but I don't think anybody there was really focused on what they were saying. Everyone was listening to the stutter of automatic weapons just outside and wondering what was going on. My friends and I slipped into line in the last row, hoping no one would notice. But when the imam had finished his prayers, every angry eye turned toward us.

Within seconds, IDF vehicles began screeching to a halt in front of the mosque. Soldiers poured into the room, forcing us all outside and ordering us to lie facedown on the ground as they checked our IDs. I was the last one out and terrified that the soldiers knew I was responsible for all the trouble. I thought surely they would beat me to death. But no one paid any attention to me. Maybe they figured a kid like me wouldn't have had the nerve to throw rocks at an IDF vehicle. Whatever the reason, I was just glad they weren't targeting me. The interrogation went on for hours, and I knew that many of the people there were angry at me. They may not have known exactly what I had done, but there could be no doubt that I had triggered the raid. I didn't care. I was actually exhilarated. My friends and I had challenged the might of the Israeli arm and come out unscathed. The rush was addictive, making us even bolder.

A friend and I hid again another day, this time closer to the road. A settler car came, and when I stood up, I threw a stone as hard as I could. It hit the windshield, sounding like a bomb exploding. It didn't break the glass, but I could see the driver's face, and I knew he was terrified. He drove another forty yards or so, hit the brakes, and then threw his car into reverse.

I ran into the cemetery. He followed but stayed outside, steadying his M16 against the wall and scanning the graves for me. My friend had run off in the opposite direction, leaving me on my own against an angry, armed Israeli settler.

I lay quietly on the ground between the graves, knowing the driver was just waiting for me to lift my head over the low tombstone. Finally, the tension was too much; I couldn't keep still any longer. I jumped up and ran as hard and fast as I could. Fortunately, it was getting dark, and he seemed afraid to enter the cemetery.

I hadn't gone very far when I felt my feet fall out from underneath me. I found myself at the bottom of an open grave that had been prepared for the next person to die. Would that be me? I wondered. Above me, the Israeli sprayed the cemetery with bullets. Stone fragments rained into the grave.

I crouched there, unable to move. After about half an hour, I heard people talking, so I knew he had gone and it was safe to climb out.

A couple of days later, as I was walking along the road, the same car passed me. There were two guys in it this time, but the driver was the same. He recognized me and quickly jumped out of the car. I tried to run again, but this time I wasn't so lucky. He caught me, slapped me hard across the face, and dragged me back to the car. No one said a word as we drove up to the settlement. Both of the men seemed nervous and gripped their guns, turning from time to time to look at me in the backseat. I wasn't a terrorist; I was just a scared little kid. But they acted like big-game hunters who had bagged a trophy tiger.

At the gate, a soldier checked the driver's ID and waved him through. Didn't he wonder why these guys had a little Palestinian kid with them? I knew I should be scared—and I was—but I couldn't help but stare at my surroundings. I had never been inside an Israeli settlement before. It was beautiful. Clean streets, swimming pools, a gorgeous view of the valley from the mountaintop.

The driver took me to the IDF base inside the settlement, where the soldiers took my shoes and made me sit on the ground. I thought they were going to shoot me and leave my body in a field somewhere. But when it started getting dark, they told me to go home.

"But I don't know how to get home," I protested.

"Start walking, or I will shoot you," one of the men said.

"Could you please give me my shoes?"

"No. Just walk. And the next time you throw a stone, I will kill you."

My house was more than a mile away. I walked all the way back in my socks, gritting my teeth as the rocks and gravel dug into the soles of my feet. When my mother saw me coming, she ran down the sidewalk and hugged me tight, nearly squeezing the breath right out of my lungs. She had been told that I was kidnapped by Israeli settlers, and she was afraid they would kill me. Over and over, she scolded me for being so foolish, all the while kissing my head and holding me tightly against her chest.

One might think I had learned my lesson, but I was a dumb little kid. I couldn't wait to tell my cowardly friends about my heroic adventure. By 1989, it was a normal occurrence for Israeli soldiers to knock on our door and push their way into our home. They always seemed to be looking for somebody who had thrown stones and fled through our backyard. The soldiers were always heavily armed, and I couldn't understand why they cared so much about a few rocks.

Because Israel controlled the borders, it was nearly impossible for Palestinians to get weapons in the First Intifada. I don't ever remember seeing a Palestinian with a gun during this time—only stones and Molotov cocktails. Nevertheless, we had all heard the stories of the IDF firing into unarmed crowds and beating people with clubs. Some reports said that as many as thirty thousand Palestinian children were injured badly enough to require medical treatment. It just didn't make sense to me.

One night, my father was especially late coming home. I sat by the window, watching for his little car to turn the corner, my stomach rumbling with hunger. Though my mother urged me to eat with the younger children, I refused, determined to wait for my dad. Finally, I heard the engine of his old car and shouted that Dad was home. My mother immediately started filling the table with steaming dishes and bowls.

"I am so sorry to be late," he said. "I had to travel out of town to resolve a dispute between two families. Why didn't you eat?"

He changed his clothes quickly, washed his hands, and came to the table.

"I'm starving," he said with a smile. "I haven't eaten a thing all day." This was not unusual because he could never afford to eat out. The delicious aroma of my mother's stuffed zucchini filled the house.

As we settled in and began to eat, I felt a rush of admiration for my father. I could see the exhaustion on his face, yet I knew how much he loved what he did. The grace he showed toward the people he served was matched only by his devotion to Allah. As I watched him talking with my mother and my brothers and sisters, I thought about how different he was from most Muslim men. He never thought twice about helping my mother around the house or taking care of us children. In fact, he scrubbed his own socks in the sink every night, just so my mother would not have to deal with them. This was unheard of in a culture where women considered it a privilege to scrub their husbands' legs after a long day.

Now as we went around the table, each of us took turns telling our father all about what we were learning at school and what we had been doing with our time. Since I was the oldest, I let the little ones talk first. But just when it was my turn to speak, I was interrupted by a knock at the back door. Who could be visiting at this time? Maybe somebody had a big problem and had come to ask for help.

I ran to the door and opened the small window that served as a peephole. I did not recognize the man.

"*Abuk mawjood?*" he asked in fluent Arabic, meaning, "Is your father here?" He was dressed like an Arab, but something about him did not seem right.

"Yes, he is," I said. "Let me call him." I did not open the door.

My father had been standing behind me. He opened the door, and several Israeli soldiers came into our home. My mother quickly put a scarf on her head. Being uncovered in front of the family was okay, but never in front of others.

"Are you Sheikh Hassan?" asked the stranger.

"Yes," my father said, "I am Sheikh Hassan."

The man introduced himself as Captain Shai and shook my father's hand.

"How are you?" the soldier asked politely. "How is everything? We are from the IDF, and we would like you to come with us for five minutes."

What could they want with my father? I searched his face, trying to read his expression. He smiled kindly at the man, with no hint of suspicion or anger in his eyes.

"Okay, I can go with you," he said, nodding at my mother as he walked toward the door.

"Wait here at home and your father will be back shortly," the soldier said to me. I followed them outside, scanning the neighborhood for more soldiers. There were none. I sat down on the front steps to wait for my father to return. Ten minutes passed. An hour. Two hours. Still he did not come back.

We had never spent the night without our father before. Even though he was busy all the time, he was always home in the evening. He woke us for dawn prayer every morning, and he was the one who took us to school every day. What would we do if he didn't come home tonight?

When I came back inside, my sister Tasneem was asleep on the couch. The tears were still wet on her cheeks. My mother tried to busy herself in the kitchen, but as the hours dragged on, she became more and more agitated and upset.

The next day, we went to the Red Cross to see if we could get any information about my father's disappearance. The man at the desk told us that he had definitely been arrested but that the IDF would not give the Red Cross any information for at least eighteen days.

We went back home to count off the two and a half weeks of waiting. During all that time, we heard nothing. When the eighteen days were up, I went back to the Red Cross to see what they had learned. I was told they had no new information.

"But you said eighteen days!" I said, struggling to fight back the tears. "Just tell me where my father is."

"Son, go home," the man said. "You can come back next week."

I did go back, again and again for forty days, and each time I received the same answer: "There is no new information. Come back next week." This was very unusual. Most of the time, families of Palestinian prisoners learned where their loved one was being held within a couple of weeks of detention.

When any prisoner was released, we made a point of asking him if he had seen my father. They all knew he had been arrested, but no one knew anything else. Even his lawyer knew nothing because he was not allowed to visit him.

We learned only later that he had been taken to Maskobiyeh, an Israeli interrogation center, where he was tortured and questioned. The Shin Bet, Israel's internal security service, knew my father was at the top level of Hamas and assumed that he knew everything that went on or was planned. And they were determined to get it out of him.

It wasn't until many years later that he told me what really happened. For days, he was handcuffed and hung from the ceiling. They used electric shock on him until he passed out. They put him in with collaborators, known as "birds," hoping he would talk to them. When that failed, they beat him some more. But my father was strong. He remained silent, never giving the Israelis any information that could hurt Hamas or his Palestinian brothers.

Chapter Five

SURVIVAL

1989–1990

THE ISRAELIS THOUGHT if they captured one of the leaders of Hamas, things would get better. But during the time my father was in prison, the intifada only became more violent. In late 1989, Amer Abu Sarhan of Ramallah had seen all the Palestinian deaths he could take. Since no one had guns, he grabbed a kitchen knife and stabbed three Israelis to death, in effect launching a revolution. This incident marked the start of a significant escalation of violence.

Sarhan became a hero to the Palestinians who had lost friends or family members, whose land had been seized, or who had any other reason to want revenge. They were not terrorists by nature. They were just people who had run out of hope and options. Their backs were to the wall. They had nothing left and nothing to lose. They cared nothing for the world's opinion or even their own lives.

For us kids in those days, going to school became a real problem. It was not uncommon for me to walk out of school to find Israeli jeeps driving up and down the streets, announcing an immediate curfew through loudspeakers. Israeli soldiers took curfews very seriously. These were not like curfews in American cities, where authorities call a teenager's parents if he's caught driving around after 11 p.m. In Palestine, if a curfew had been declared and you were on the street for any reason, you were shot. No warning, no arrest. They just shot you.

The first time a curfew was called while I was at school, I didn't know what to do. I had a four-mile walk ahead of me and knew there was no way I could make it home before curfew. The streets were already empty, and I was scared. I couldn't stay where I was, and even though I was just a kid trying to get home from school, if the soldiers saw me, I knew they would shoot me. A lot of Palestinian kids got shot.

I began to dodge from house to house, creeping through backyards and hiding in bushes along the way. I tried to avoid barking dogs and men with machine guns as best I could, and when I finally turned the corner onto our street, I was so thankful to see that my brothers and sisters had already made it home safely.

But curfews were just one change we dealt with as a result of the intifada. On many occasions, a masked man would show up at school and tell everybody that a strike had been called and to go home. The strikes, called by one of the Palestinian factions, were designed to hurt Israel financially by reducing the sales tax revenue the government collected from store owners. If the stores were not open, the owners would have to pay less tax. But the Israelis were not stupid. They just started arresting shopkeepers for tax evasion. So who was hurt by the strikes?

On top of that, the various resistance organizations were incessantly fighting with one another for power and prestige. They were like kids scrapping over a soccer ball. Nevertheless, Hamas was steadily growing in power and had begun to challenge the dominance of the Palestine Liberation Organization (PLO).

The PLO had been founded in 1964 to represent the Palestinian people; its three largest member organizations include: Fatah, a left-wing nationalist group; the Popular Front for the Liberation of Palestine (PFLP), a communist group; and the Democratic Front for the Liberation of Palestine (DFLP), also communist in ideology.

The PLO demanded that Israel return all of the land that had belonged to the Palestinian territories prior to 1948 and grant Palestine the right to self-determination. To this end, it fought a global campaign of public relations, guerrilla warfare, and terrorism from its base, first in neighboring Jordan, then in Lebanon and Tunisia.

Unlike Hamas and Islamic Jihad, the PLO was never an inherently Islamic organization. Its groups were made up of nationalists, not all of them practicing Muslims. In fact, many of them did not believe in God. Even as a young boy, I saw the PLO as corrupt and self-serving. Its leaders sent people, many of whom were just teenagers, to carry out one or two high-profile terrorist attacks a year in order to justify fund-raising for the struggle against Israel. The young feda'iyeen were little more than fuel to stoke the fires of anger and hatred and to keep the donations flowing into the personal bank accounts of PLO leaders.[2]

In the initial years of the First Intifada, ideological differences kept Hamas and the PLO on very separate paths. Hamas was largely animated by religious fervor and the theology of jihad, while the PLO was driven by nationalism and the ideology of power. If Hamas called a strike and threatened to burn the stores of anyone who stayed open, PLO leaders across the street threatened to burn the stores of anyone who closed.

What the two groups shared, however, was a deep hatred for what they labeled "the Zionist entity." Finally, the two organizations agreed that Hamas would have its strike on the ninth of every month, and Fatah—the PLO's largest faction—would have its strike on the first. Whenever a strike was called, everything stopped. Classes, commerce, cars—everything. Nobody worked, earned, or learned.

The whole West Bank was shut down, with masked men demonstrating, burning tires, writing graffiti on walls, and shutting down businesses. But anyone could put on a ski mask and say they were PLO. No one ever really knew who was under the masks; everybody was simply driven by individual agendas and personal vendettas. Chaos reigned.

And Israel took advantage of the confusion. Since anyone could be an intifada fighter, Israeli security troops put on masks and infiltrated the demonstrations. They could walk into any Palestinian city in the middle of the day and pull off amazing operations dressed as masked feda'iyeen. And since no one could be certain who any particular masked man was, people did what they were told rather than risk a beating, having their business burned, or being called an Israeli collaborator, which often resulted in a hanging.

After a while, the chaos and confusion even reached the point of silliness. Once or twice when an exam was scheduled, my fellow students and I persuaded older kids to come to school wearing masks and say there was a strike. We thought it was fun.

In short, we were becoming our own worst enemies.

Those years were especially hard for our family. My father was still in prison, and the endless succession of strikes kept us kids out of school for nearly a full year. My uncles, religious leaders, and everyone else, it seemed, decided it was their job to discipline me. Because I was the firstborn son of Sheikh Hassan Yousef, they held me to very high standards. And when I didn't meet their expectations, they beat me. No matter what I did, even if I went to the mosque five times a day, it was never good enough.

Once I was running in the mosque, just playing with a friend, and the imam chased me down. When he caught me, he lifted me over his head and threw me to the floor onto my back. It knocked the breath out of me, and I thought I was going to die. Then he kept punching me and kicking me. Why? I really wasn't doing anything that any of the other kids weren't doing. But because I was the son of Hassan Yousef, I was expected to be above that.

I was friends with a boy whose father was a religious leader and big shot in Hamas. This man used to encourage people to throw stones. But while it was okay for other men's sons to get shot at for pelting settlers with rocks, it was not okay for his only son. When he found out we had been throwing stones, he called us to his place. We thought he wanted to talk to us. But he ripped the cord out of a space heater and started to whip us with all his might until we bled. He broke up our friendship in order to save his son, though my friend would eventually leave home, hating his father more than the devil.

Apart from trying to keep me in line, no one helped our family while my father was in prison. With his arrest, we lost the extra income he earned teaching at the Christian school. The school promised to hold his job for him until his release, but in the meantime, we did not have enough money to buy what we needed.

My father was the only one in our family with a driver's license, so we couldn't use our car. My mother had to walk long distances to go to the market, and I often went along to help her carry the parcels. I think the shame was worse than the want. As we went through the market, I crawled under the carts to pick up broken, rotting produce that had fallen on the ground. My mother negotiated a lower price for these unappetizing vegetables nobody else wanted, telling the vendors we were buying them to feed livestock. She still has to negotiate for everything to this day because my father has been in prison thirteen times—more times than any other Hamas leader. (He is in prison as I write this.)

I think maybe no one helped us because everybody believed that our family had plenty of money. After all, my father was a prominent religious and political leader. And people undoubtedly trusted that our extended family would help us. Surely Allah would provide. But our uncles ignored us. Allah did nothing. So my mother took care of her seven children alone (our little brother Mohammad had arrived in 1987).

Finally, when things got really desperate, my mom asked a friend of my father's for a loan—not so she could go shopping and buy clothes and cosmetics for herself, but so she could feed her children at least one meal a day. But he refused her. And instead of helping us, he told his Muslim friends that my mother had come to him begging for money.

"She has a salary from the Jordanian government," they said, judging her. "Why is she asking for more? Is this woman taking advantage of her husband's imprisonment to become rich?"

She never asked for help again.

"Mosab," she said to me one day, "what if I make some baklava and other homemade sweets and you go and sell them to the workers in the industrial area?" I said I would be glad to do anything to help our family. So every day after school, I changed my clothes, filled a tray with my mother's pastries, and went out to sell as many as I could. I was shy at first, but eventually I went boldly to every worker and asked him to buy from me.

One winter day, I left as usual to sell my pastries. But when I got to the area, I found that it was empty. No one had come to work that day because it was so cold. My hands were freezing, and it had started to rain. Holding the plastic-covered tray over my head as an umbrella, I noticed a car containing several people parked on the side of the street. The driver spotted me, opened his window, and leaned out.

"Hey, kid, what have you got?"

"I have some baklava," I said, walking over to the car.

Looking inside, I was shocked to see my uncle Ibrahim. His friends were shocked to see Ibrahim's nephew all but begging on a cold, rainy day, and I was ashamed to be an embarrassment to my uncle. I didn't know what to say. They didn't either.

My uncle bought all the baklava, told me to go home, and said he would see me later. When he arrived at our house, he was furious with my mother. I couldn't hear what he said to her, but after he left, she was crying. The next day after school, I changed and told my mom I was ready to go back out to sell pastries.

"I don't want you to sell baklava anymore," she said.

"But I'm getting better every day! I am good at it. Just trust me."

Tears came into her eyes. And I never went out again.

I was angry. I didn't understand why our neighbors and family wouldn't help us. And on top of that, they had the nerve to judge us for trying to help ourselves. I wondered if the real reason they would not lend a hand to our family was that they were afraid of getting into trouble themselves if the Israelis thought they were helping terrorists. But we weren't terrorists. Neither was my father. Sadly, that would change too.

Chapter Six
A HERO'S RETURN
1990

WHEN MY FATHER WAS FINALLY RELEASED, our family was suddenly treated like royalty after being shunned for a year and a half. The hero had returned. No longer the black sheep, I became the heir apparent. My brothers were princes, my sisters princesses, and my mother was the queen. No one dared to judge us anymore.

My father got his job back at the Christian school, in addition to his position at the mosque. Now that he was home, my father tried to help my mom around the house as much as possible. This eased the workload we kids had been carrying. We certainly weren't rich, but we had enough money to buy decent food and even an occasional prize for the winner of Stars. And we were rich in honor and respect. Best of all, my father was with us. We didn't need anything else.

Everything quickly returned to normal. Of course, *normal* is a relative term. We still lived under Israeli occupation with daily killing in the streets. Our house was just down the road from a cemetery gorged with bloody corpses. Our father had horrifying memories of the Israeli prison where he had been incarcerated for eighteen months as a suspected terrorist. And the occupied territories were degenerating into little more than a lawless jungle.

The only law respected by Muslims is Islamic law, defined by *fatwas,* or religious rulings on a particular topic. Fatwas are intended to guide Muslims as they apply the Qur'an to daily living, but because there is no central unifying rule maker, different sheikhs often issue different fatwas about the same matter. As a result, everyone is living by a different set of rules, some much more strict than others.

I was playing indoors with my friends one afternoon when we heard screaming outside. Yelling and fighting were nothing new in our world, but when we ran outside, we saw our neighbor, Abu Saleem, waving a big knife around. He was trying to kill his cousin, who was doing his best to avoid the shiny blade as it slashed through the air. The entire neighborhood tried to stop Abu Saleem, but this man was huge. He was a butcher by trade, and I once watched him slaughter a bull in his backyard, which left him covered from head to foot in sticky, steaming blood. I couldn't help but think about what he had done to that animal as I watched him running after his cousin.

Yes, I thought to myself, *we are truly living in a jungle.*

There were no police to call, no one in authority. What could we do but watch? Fortunately, his cousin ran away and did not return.

When my father came home that night, we told him what had happened. My father is only five foot seven and not what you would call athletic. But he went next door and said, "Abu Saleem, what's going on? I heard there was a fight today." And Abu Saleem went on and on about wanting to kill his cousin.

"You know that we are under occupation," my father said, "and you know that we don't have time for this foolishness. You've got to sit down and apologize to your cousin, and he has to apologize to you. I don't want any more problems like this."

Like everyone else, Abu Saleem respected my father. He trusted in his wisdom, even in matters such as this. He agreed to work things out with his cousin, and then he joined my father in a meeting with the other men in the neighborhood.

"Here is the situation," my father said quietly. "We don't have a government here, and things are getting completely out of control. We can't keep fighting each other, shedding the blood of our own people. We are fighting in the streets, fighting in our homes, fighting in the mosques. Enough is enough. We are going to have to sit down at least once every week and try to solve our problems like men. We don't have police, and we don't have room for anybody to kill anybody. We have bigger problems to deal with. I want your unity. I want you to help each other. We need to be more like a family."

The men agreed that what my father was proposing made sense. They decided to meet together every Thursday night to discuss local issues and resolve any conflicts they might be having with one another.

As imam of the mosque, it was my father's job to give people hope and help them resolve their problems. He was also the closest thing they had to a government. He had become just like his father. But now he also spoke with the authority of Hamas—with the authority of a sheikh. A sheikh has more authority than an imam and is more like a general than a priest.

Since my father had come home three months before, I had tried to spend as much time as I could with him. I was now president of the Islamic student movement in our school, and I wanted to know all I could about Islam and the study of the Qur'an. One Thursday evening, I asked if I could join him at the weekly neighborhood meeting. I was nearly a man, I explained, and I wanted to be treated as such.

"No," he said, "you stay here. This is for men. I will tell you later what went on."

I was disappointed, but I understood. None of my friends were allowed to attend the weekly meetings either. At least I would be privy to what happened at the meeting once my father returned home.

So he left for a couple of hours. While my mother prepared a delicious fish dinner, somebody knocked at the back door. I opened the door just wide enough to peek through and saw Captain Shai, the same man who had arrested my father nearly two years earlier.

"Abuk mawjood?"

"No, he's not here."

"Then open the door."

I didn't know what else to do, so I opened the door. Captain Shai was polite, just as he had been the first time he came for my father, but I could tell he didn't believe me. He asked if he could look around, and I knew I didn't have a choice but to let him. As the soldier began to search our house, moving from room to room, looking in closets and behind doors, I wished that somehow I could keep my father from coming home. We didn't have a cell phone back then, so I couldn't warn him. But the more I thought about it, I realized that it wouldn't have mattered if we had. He would have come home anyway.

"Okay, everybody stay quiet," Captain Shai said to a group of soldiers who had been stationed outside. They all ducked down behind bushes and buildings, waiting for my dad. Feeling helpless, I sat down at the table and listened. After a while, a loud voice shouted, "Stop right there!" Then came the sound of movement and men talking. We knew this couldn't be good. Would my father have to go back to prison?

Within minutes, he slipped back inside, shaking his head and smiling apologetically at each of us.

"They are taking me back," he said, kissing my mother and then each one of us. "I don't know how long I will be gone. Be good. Take care of one another."

Then he put on his jacket and left as his fried fish grew cold on his plate.

Once again we were treated like refugees, even by the men in the neighborhood he had tried to protect from themselves and others. Some people would ask about my father with feigned concern, but it was clear to me they really didn't care.

Although we knew my father was being held in an Israeli prison, no one would tell us which one. We spent three months looking for him in every prison, until we finally heard that he was being held in a special facility where they interrogate only the most dangerous people. *Why?* I wondered. Hamas had made no terrorist attacks. It wasn't even armed.

Once we found out where my father was being held, the Israeli officials allowed us to visit him once a month for thirty minutes. Only two visitors could go in at once, so we took turns going with our mother. The first time I saw him, I was surprised to see that he had let his beard grow long, and he looked exhausted. But it was so good to see him, even like that. He never complained. He only wanted to know how everything was for us, asking us to tell him all the little details of our lives.

During one visit, he handed me a bag of candies. He explained that the prisoners were given one piece every other day, and instead of eating his, he had saved every piece so he could give them to us. We cherished the wrappers until the day he was released again.

Finally, that longed-for day came. We weren't expecting him, and when he walked through the door, we all clung to him, afraid we might be dreaming. Word of his arrival spread quickly, and for the next six hours, people poured into our house. So many came to welcome him that we drained our storage tanks trying to give everyone a drink of water. I felt proud as I watched the obvious admiration and respect the people had for my father, but at the same time, I was angry. Where had all these people been while he was gone?

After everyone had left, my father said to me, "I am not working for these people, for their praise, or for them to take care of me and my family. I am working for Allah. And I know that you all are paying as heavy a price as I am. You, too, are servants of Allah, and you must be patient."

I understood, but I wondered if he knew just how bad things were when he wasn't here.

As we were talking, there was another knock at the back door. The Israelis arrested him again.

Chapter Seven
RADICAL
1990–1992

IN AUGUST 1990, while my father was in prison for the third time, Saddam Hussein invaded Kuwait.

Palestinians went crazy. Everybody ran out into the streets, cheering and looking for the missiles that would surely rain down on Israel. Our brothers were finally coming to our rescue! They were going to hit Israel hard, in the heart. Soon, the occupation would be over.

Expecting another poison gas attack like the one that had killed five thousand Kurds in 1988, the Israelis distributed gas masks to every citizen. But Palestinians received only one gas mask per household. My mother had one, but the seven of us had no protection. So we tried to be creative and make our own masks. We also bought nylon sheets and taped them to the windows and doors. But in the morning, we woke to find that the humidity had caused all the tape to peel off.

We were riveted to the Israeli TV channel, and we cheered with each warning of incoming missiles. We climbed up to the roof to watch the Scuds from Iraq light up Tel Aviv. But we saw nothing.

Maybe Al-Bireh is not the best place to get a good view, I reasoned. I decided to go to my uncle Dawood's house in Al-Janiya, where we would be able to see all the way to the Mediterranean. My younger brother Sohayb came with me. From my uncle's roof, we saw the first missile. Actually it was just the flame, but still, it was an awesome sight!

When we heard the news that about forty Scuds had reached Israel and that only two Israelis had been killed, we were sure the government was lying. As it turned out, it was true. When the Iraqis jerry-rigged the missiles to make them travel farther, they sacrificed power and accuracy.

We stayed at my uncle Dawood's house until the UN forces drove Saddam Hussein back to Baghdad. I was angry and bitterly disappointed.

"Why is the war finished? Israel is not finished. My father is still in an Israeli prison. The Iraqis have got to keep launching missiles!"

Indeed, all Palestinians were disappointed. After decades of occupation, a real war had finally been called, with devastating warheads being fired at Israel. And yet, nothing had changed.

———

Following my father's release after the Persian Gulf War, my mother told him that she wanted to sell her dowry gold to buy a piece of land and get a loan to build a house of our own. We had been renting up to this point, and whenever my father was away, the owner cheated us and became rude and abusive to my mother.

My father was moved that she was willing to part with something so precious, but he was also concerned that he might not be able to keep up the loan payments since he could be arrested again at any time. Nevertheless they decided to chance it, and in 1992, we built the house where my family still lives today in Betunia, by Ramallah. I was fourteen.

Betunia seemed to be less violent than either Al-Bireh or Ramallah. I attended the mosque near our new house and got involved in a *jalsa*, a group that encouraged us to memorize the Qur'an and taught us principles that leaders claimed would lead to a global Islamic state.

A few months after we moved, my father was arrested again. Often, he was not even charged with anything specific. Because we were under occupation, emergency laws allowed the Israeli government to arrest people merely because they were suspected of being involved with terrorism. As a religious—and by default, political— leader, my father was an easy target.

It seemed this was becoming a pattern—and though we didn't realize it at the time, this pattern of arrest, release, and rearrest would continue for many years to come, putting increasing strain on our family each time. Meanwhile, Hamas was growing more violent and aggressive as the younger Hamas men pressured the leadership to push even harder.

"The Israelis are killing our children!" they cried. "We throw stones, and they shoot us down with machine guns. We are under occupation. The United Nations, the whole international community, every free man in the world recognizes our right to fight. Allah, himself, may his name be praised, requires it. Why do we wait?"

Most attacks in those days were personal, not organizational. Hamas leaders had no control over members who had their own agendas. My father's goal was Islamic freedom, and he believed in fighting Israel in order to achieve freedom. But for these young men, fighting became its own goal—not a means to an end, but an end in itself.

As dangerous as the West Bank had become, Gaza was even more so. Due to geography, Gaza's dominant influence was the fundamentalist Muslim Brotherhood in Egypt. And overcrowding only made things worse. Gaza was one of the most densely populated pieces of real estate on earth—really not much more than a 139-square-mile refugee camp packed with more than a million people.

Families hung real estate documents and door keys on their walls as silent evidence and daily reminders that they had once owned homes and beautiful farms—property that had been taken by Israel as spoils of past wars. It was an ideal environment for recruiting. The refugees were motivated and available. They were persecuted not only by Israelis but also by Palestinians—their own people—who viewed them as second-class citizens. In fact, they were considered invaders themselves, since their camps had been built on their neighbors' lands.

Most of the impatient young Hamas activists were from the refugee camps. Among them was Imad Akel. The youngest of three sons, Imad was studying to be a pharmacist when he must have finally had his fill of injustice and frustration. He got hold of a gun, killed several Israeli soldiers, and took their weapons. As others followed his example, Imad's influence grew. Operating independently, Imad established a small military cell and moved to the West Bank, which offered more targets and more room to move around. I knew from the conversations among the men in town that Hamas was very proud of him, although he was not at all accountable to the organization. Nevertheless, the leaders did not want to mix what he was doing with Hamas's other activities. So they added the military wing, the Ezzedeen Al-Qassam Brigades, and made Imad its leader. He was soon the most wanted Palestinian in Israel.

Hamas was now armed. As guns quickly replaced stones, graffiti, and Molotov cocktails, Israel had a problem it had never encountered before. It was one thing to deal with PLO attacks from Jordan, Lebanon, and Syria, but now the attacks were coming from inside its own borders.

Chapter Eight
FANNING THE FLAMES
1992–1994

ON DECEMBER 13, 1992, five Al-Qassam members kidnapped Israeli border policeman Nissim Toledano near Tel Aviv. They demanded that Israel release Sheikh Ahmed Yassin. Israel refused. Two days later, Toledano's body was discovered, and Israel launched a massive crackdown on Hamas. Immediately, more than sixteen hundred Palestinians were arrested. Then Israel decided to secretly deport 415 leaders of Hamas, Islamic Jihad, and the Muslim Brotherhood. Among them were my father, who was still in prison, and three uncles.

I was only fourteen years old at this time, and none of us knew that this was happening. As the news leaked out, however, we were able to piece together enough details to figure out that my father was probably among the large group of teachers, religious leaders, engineers, and social workers who had been handcuffed, blindfolded, and loaded onto buses. Within hours of the story breaking, lawyers and human rights organizations began to file petitions. The buses were halted as the Israeli High Court convened at 5 a.m. to consider the legal challenges. And throughout the following fourteen hours of debate, my father and the other deportees were kept on the buses. Blindfolds and handcuffs remained in place. No food. No water. No bathroom breaks. In the end, the court backed the government, and the buses resumed their trek north. We later learned that the men were then driven to a snow-covered no-man's-land in southern Lebanon. Although we were in the middle of a bitter winter, they were dumped there with no shelter or provisions. Neither Israel nor Lebanon would allow relief agencies to deliver food or medicine. Beirut refused to transport the sick and injured to its hospitals.

On December 18, the UN Security Council adopted Resolution 799, calling for the "safe and immediate return" of the deportees. Israel refused. We had always been able to visit my dad when he was in prison, but since the Lebanese border was closed, we had no way to see him in exile. A couple of weeks later, we finally saw him on television for the first time since his deportation. Apparently, Hamas members had named him secretary-general of the camp, second only to Abdel Aziz al-Rantissi, another Hamas leader.

Every day after that, we watched the news, hoping to catch another glimpse of my father's face. From time to time, we would see him with a bullhorn delivering instructions to the deportees. When spring came, he even managed to send us mail and photographs taken by reporters and members of relief organizations. Eventually, the deportees gained access to cell phones, and we were able to talk to him for a few minutes every week.

Hoping to generate global sympathy for the deportees, the media interviewed their family members. My sister Tasneem brought tears to the eyes of the world as she cried "*Baba! Baba!* [Daddy! Daddy!]" on camera. Somehow, our family became the unofficial representatives of all the other families. We were invited to attend every protest, including the ongoing demonstration in front of the Israeli prime minister's office in Jerusalem. My father told us he was very proud, and we did take some comfort in the support we received from people all over the world, even Israeli peacemakers. About six months later, we heard the news that 101 deportees were going to be allowed to come home. Like all the families, we desperately hoped my father would be among them.

He wasn't.

The next day, we visited with the heroes who had returned from Lebanon to see if we could find out any news about my father. But they could tell us only that he was doing well and would be home soon. About three more months passed before Israel agreed to allow the remaining deportees to return home. We were overjoyed at the prospect.

On the designated day, we waited impatiently outside the Ramallah prison where the remaining deportees were to be released. Ten came out. Twenty. He wasn't with them. The last man passed by, and the soldiers said that was all. There was no sign of my father and no word of his whereabouts. The other families joyously took their loved ones home, and we were left standing outside alone in the middle of the night with no idea where my father was. We went home discouraged, frustrated, and worried. Why hadn't he been released with the rest of the prisoners? Where was he now?

The next day, my father's attorney called to tell us that my father and several other deportees had been returned to prison. Apparently, he said, the deportation had proved counterproductive for Israel. During their exile, my father and other Palestinian leaders had been all over the news, earning the world's sympathy because the punishment was perceived as excessive and an abuse of their human rights. Throughout the Arab world, the men were seen as heroes of the cause, and as such, they became far more important and influential.

The deportation also had another unintended but disastrous effect for Israel. The prisoners had used their time in exile to forge an unprecedented relationship between Hamas and Hezbollah, the main Islamic political and paramilitary organization in Lebanon. This connection carried major historical and geopolitical ramifications. My father and other Hamas leaders often snuck out of the camp to avoid the media in order to meet with Hezbollah and Muslim Brotherhood leaders, something they could never do inside the Palestinian territories.

While my father and the others had been in Lebanon, the most radical Hamas members were still free and becoming more furious than ever. And as these radicalized new men filled the temporary leadership roles within Hamas, the gap between Hamas and the PLO widened.

About that time, Israel and Yasser Arafat entered into secret negotiations, which resulted in the 1993 Oslo Accords. On September 9, Arafat wrote a letter to Israeli prime minister Yitzhak Rabin in which he officially recognized "the right of the State of Israel to exist in peace and security" and renounced "the use of terrorism and other acts of violence."

Rabin then formally recognized the PLO as "the representative of the Palestinian people," and President Bill Clinton lifted the ban on American contact with the organization. On September 13, the world stared in amazement at a photograph of Arafat and Rabin shaking hands at the White House. A poll at that time showed that the vast majority of Palestinians in the West Bank and Gaza supported the terms of the Accords, also known as the Declaration of Principles (DOP). This document led to the creation of the Palestinian Authority (PA); called for the withdrawal of Israeli troops from Gaza and Jericho; granted autonomy to those areas; and opened the door for the return of Arafat and the PLO from exile in Tunisia.

But my dad was against the DOP. He didn't trust Israel or the PLO and therefore put no trust in the peace process. Other Hamas leaders, he explained, had their own reasons for opposing it, including the risk that a peace accord might actually stick! Peaceful coexistence would mean the end of Hamas. From their perspective, the organization could not thrive in a peaceful atmosphere. Other resistance groups also had a stake in the continuation of conflict. It's hard to achieve peace in a place where so many have different goals and interests.

So the attacks continued:

- An Israeli man was stabbed to death on September 24 by a Hamas feda'iyeen in an orchard near Basra.
- The Popular Front for the Liberation of Palestine and Islamic Jihad claimed responsibility for the deaths of two Israelis in the Judean desert two weeks later.
- Two weeks after that, Hamas shot and killed two IDF soldiers outside a Jewish settlement in Gaza.

But none of these killings captured world headlines like the Hebron massacre on Friday, February 25, 1994.

During the Jewish festival of Purim and the Muslim holy month of Ramadan, an American-born physician named Baruch Goldstein entered Al-Haram Al-Ibrahimi Mosque in Hebron where, according to local tradition, Adam and Eve, Abraham and Sarah, Isaac and Rebekah, and Jacob and Leah are buried. Without warning, Goldstein opened fire, killing twenty-nine Palestinians who had come to pray and wounding well over one hundred before he was beaten to death by an enraged, grief-stricken mob.

We sat and watched through the lens of the television camera as one bloody corpse after another was carried from that holy place. I was in shock. Everything seemed to move in slow motion. One moment my heart pounded with a rage I had never known before, a rage that startled and then soothed me. The next minute I was frozen with grief. Then I was suddenly enraged—then numb again. And I was not alone. It seemed that the emotions of everyone in the occupied territories rose and fell to that surreal rhythm, leaving us exhausted.

Because Goldstein was wearing his Israeli military uniform and the IDF presence was smaller than normal, Palestinians were convinced that he had been sent, or at least covered, by the government in Jerusalem. To us, trigger-happy soldiers and crazy settlers were all one and the same. Hamas now spoke with a voice of terrible resolve. They could only think of revenge for this betrayal, this atrocity.

On April 6, a car bomb destroyed a bus in Afula, killing eight and injuring forty-four. Hamas said it was reprisal for Hebron. That same day, two Israelis were shot and killed and four others were wounded when Hamas attacked a bus stop near Ashdod.

A week later, a historic and awful threshold was crossed as Israel felt the impact of the first official suicide bombing. On Wednesday morning, April 13, 1994—the same day my father was finally released from prison after his deportation to Lebanon—twenty-one-year-old Amar Salah Diab Amarna entered the Hadera bus station between Haifa and Tel Aviv in central Israel. He carried a bag containing hardware and over four pounds of homemade acetone peroxide explosive. At 9:30, he boarded the bus to Tel Aviv. Ten minutes later, as the bus was pulling out of the station, he placed the bag on the floor and detonated it.

The shrapnel ripped through the passengers on the bus, killing six and wounding thirty. A second pipe bomb exploded at the scene just as rescue workers arrived. This was the "second in a series of five attacks" in revenge for Hebron, a Hamas pamphlet later announced.

I was proud of Hamas, and I saw the attacks as a huge victory against the Israeli occupation. At fifteen years of age, I saw everything in stark black and white. There were good guys and bad guys. And the bad guys deserved everything they got. I saw what a two-kilogram bomb packed with nails and ball bearings could do to human flesh, and I hoped it would send a clear message to the Israeli community.

It did.

After every suicide attack, Orthodox Jewish volunteers known as ZAKA (Disaster Victim Identification) arrived at the scene in fluorescent yellow vests. It was their job to collect blood and body parts—including those of non-Jews and the bomber himself—which were then taken to the forensic center in Jaffa. The pathologists there had the job of reassembling what was left of the bodies for identification purposes. Often, DNA testing was the only way for them to connect one piece to another.

Family members who had not been able to find their loved ones among the wounded at the local hospitals were directed to Jaffa, where they often showed up dazed with grief.

Pathologists frequently advised the families not to view the remains, telling them that it was better to remember their loved ones as they were when they were living. But most still wanted to touch the bodies one last time, even if a foot was all that was left.

Because Jewish law required that the entire body be buried the same day a person died, larger body parts were often buried first. Smaller pieces were added later, after identification was confirmed by DNA, reopening the wounds of grieving families.

While Hadera was the first official bombing, it was actually the third attempt, part of a trial-and-error phase during which Hamas bomb maker Yahya Ayyash perfected his craft. Ayyash was an engineering student at Birzeit University. He was not a radical Muslim or a nationalist zealot. He was embittered simply because he had once asked permission to continue his studies in another country, and the government of Israel had denied his request. So he made bombs and became a hero to the Palestinians and one of Israel's most wanted men.

In addition to two failed attempts and the bombings on April 6 and 13, Ayyash would eventually be responsible for the deaths of at least thirty-nine people in five more attacks. He would also teach others, like his friend Hassan Salameh, how to make bombs.

During the Gulf War, Yasser Arafat had supported Saddam Hussein's invasion of Kuwait, which alienated him from both the United States and the Arab states that supported the American-led coalition. Because of that, those states then started shifting their financial support from the PLO to Hamas.

Following the success of the Oslo Accords, however, Arafat was on top again. And the next year, he shared the Nobel Peace Prize with Israeli prime minister Yitzhak Rabin and Israeli minister of foreign affairs Shimon Peres.

The Oslo Accords required Arafat to establish the Palestinian National Authority in the West Bank and Gaza Strip. So on July 1, 1994, he approached Egypt's Rafah border, crossed into Gaza, and settled in.

"National unity," he told the crowds celebrating his return from exile, "is . . . our shield, the shield of our people. Unity. Unity. Unity."[3] But the Palestinian territories were far from unified.

Hamas and its supporters were angry that Arafat had met secretly with Israel and promised that Palestinians would no longer fight for self-determination. Our men were still in Israeli prisons. We had no Palestinian state. The only autonomy we had was over the West Bank city of Jericho—a small town with nothing—and Gaza, a big, overcrowded refugee camp on the coast.

And now Arafat was sitting with the Israelis at the same table and shaking hands. "What about all the Palestinian blood?" our people asked one another. "Did he hold it so cheap?"

On the other hand, some Palestinians conceded that at least the PA had gotten us Gaza and Jericho. What had Hamas gotten us? Had it freed even one little Palestinian village?

Perhaps they had a point. But Hamas didn't trust Arafat—mostly because he was ready to settle for a Palestinian state inside Israel instead of recovering the Palestinian territories that existed before Israel.

"What would you have us do?" Arafat and his spokesmen argued whenever they were pushed. "For decades, we fought Israel and found that there was no way to win. We were thrown out of Jordan and Lebanon and ended up over a thousand miles away in Tunisia. The international community was against us. We had no power. The Soviet Union collapsed, leaving the United States as the only world power. And it backed Israel. We were given an opportunity to get back everything we had before the Six-Day War in 1967 and to govern ourselves. And we took it."

Several months after arriving in Gaza, Arafat visited Ramallah for the first time. My father, along with dozens of religious, political, and business leaders, stood in a reception line for him. When the PLO chief came to Sheikh Hassan Yousef, he kissed my father's hand, recognizing him as a religious as well as a political leader.

Over the next year, my father and other Hamas leaders met frequently with Arafat in Gaza City in an attempt to reconcile and unify the PA and Hamas. But the talks ended in failure when Hamas ultimately refused to participate in the peace process. Our ideologies and goals were still a long way from being reconciled.

The transition of Hamas into a full-blown terrorist organization was complete. Many of its members had climbed the ladder of Islam and reached the top. Moderate political leaders like my father would not tell the militants that what they were doing was wrong. They could not; on what basis could they declare it was wrong? The militants had the full force of the Qur'an to back them up.

So even though he had never personally killed anyone, my father went along with the attacks. And the Israelis, unable to find and arrest the violent young militants, continued to pursue soft targets like my father. I think they figured that since my father was a leader of Hamas, which was carrying out these attacks, his imprisonment would put a stop to them. But they never made an effort to find out who or what Hamas really was. And it would be many painful years before they would begin to understand that Hamas was not an organization as most people understood organizations, with rules and a hierarchy. It was a ghost. An idea. You can't destroy an idea; you can only stimulate it. Hamas was like a flatworm. Cut off its head, and it just grew another.

The trouble was that the central organizing premise and goal of Hamas was an illusion. Syria, Lebanon, Iraq, Jordan, and Egypt had repeatedly tried and failed to drive the Israelis into the sea and transform its lands into a Palestinian state. Even Saddam Hussein and his Scud missiles failed. In order for millions of Palestinian refugees to recover the homes, farms, and property they had lost more than half a century ago, Israel would have to virtually trade places with them. And because that was clearly never going to happen, Hamas was like Sisyphus of Greek mythology—condemned eternally to roll a boulder up a steep hill, only to see it roll back down again, never reaching the goal.

Nevertheless, even those who recognized the impossibility of Hamas's mission clung to the belief that Allah would one day defeat Israel, even if he had to do it supernaturally.

For Israel, the PLO nationalists had been simply a political problem in need of a political solution. Hamas, on the other hand, Islamized the Palestinian problem, making it a religious problem. And this problem could be resolved only with a religious solution, which meant that it could never be resolved because we believed that the land belonged to Allah. Period. End of discussion. Thus for Hamas, the ultimate problem was not Israel's policies. It was the nation-state Israel's very existence.

And what of my father? Had he, too, become a terrorist? One afternoon, I read a newspaper headline about a recent suicide bombing (or "martyrdom operation" as some in Hamas called them) that had killed many civilians, including women and children. It was impossible for me to mentally reconcile the kindness and character of my father and his leadership with an organization that carried out such things. I pointed to the article and asked him how he felt about such acts.

"Once," he answered, "I left the house and there was an insect outside. I thought twice about whether to kill it or not. And I could not kill it." That indirect answer was his way of saying that he could never personally participate in that kind of wanton killing. But the Israeli civilians were not insects.

No, my father did not build the bombs, strap them onto the bombers, or select the targets. But years later I would think of my father's answer when I encountered a story in a Christian Bible that describes the stoning of a young innocent named Stephen. It said, "Saul was there, giving approval to his death" (Acts 8:1).

I loved my father so deeply, and I admired so much about who he was and what he stood for. But for a man who could not bring himself to harm an insect, he had obviously found a way to rationalize the idea that it was fine for somebody else to explode people into scraps of meat, as long as he didn't personally bloody his hands.

At that moment, my view of my father grew much more complicated.

Chapter Nine

GUNS

WINTER 1995–SPRING 1996

AFTER THE OSLO ACCORDS, the international community expected the Palestinian Authority to keep Hamas in check. On Saturday, November 4, 1995, I was watching television when a news bulletin broke into programming. Yitzhak Rabin had been shot during a peace rally in Kings Square in Tel Aviv. It sounded serious. A couple of hours later, officials announced that he was dead.

"Wow!" I said aloud to no one in particular. "Some Palestinian faction still has the power to assassinate Israel's prime minister! That should have happened a long time ago." I was very happy for his death and the damage it would do to the PLO and its watered-down capitulation to Israel.

Then the phone rang. I recognized the caller's voice immediately. It was Yasser Arafat, and he asked to speak to my father.

I listened as my father spoke into the telephone. He didn't say much; he was kind and respectful, and mostly he just agreed with whatever Arafat was saying on the other end of the line.

"I understand," he said. "Good-bye."

Then he turned to me. "Arafat has asked that we try to keep Hamas from celebrating the death of the prime minister," he said. "The assassination was a very big loss for Arafat because Rabin showed such political courage in entering into peace negotiations with the PLO."

We later learned that Rabin had not been killed by a Palestinian after all. Instead, he had been shot in the back by an Israeli law student. Many in Hamas were disappointed by this piece of information; personally, I found it amusing that Jewish fanatics had shared a goal with Hamas.

The assassination put the world on edge, and the world put more pressure on Arafat to get control of the Palestinian territories. So he launched an all-out crackdown on Hamas. PA police came to our house, asked my father to prepare himself, and locked him away in Arafat's compound—all the while treating him with the utmost respect and kindness.

Even so, for the first time, Palestinians were imprisoning other Palestinians. It was ugly, but at least they treated my father respectfully. Unlike many of the others, he was given a comfortable room, and Arafat visited with him from time to time to discuss various issues.

Soon all of the top leaders of Hamas, along with thousands of its members, were locked away in Palestinian prisons. Many were tortured for information. Some died. But others escaped arrest, became fugitives, and continued their attacks against Israel.

Now my hatred had multiple focal points. I hated the Palestinian Authority and Yasser Arafat, I hated Israel, and I hated secular Palestinians. Why should my father, who loved Allah and his people, have to pay such a heavy price while godless men like Arafat and his PLO handed a great victory to the Israelis—whom the Qur'an likened to pigs and monkeys? And the international community applauded Israel because it got the terrorists to recognize its right to exist.

I was seventeen and only months away from my high school graduation. Whenever I visited my father in prison or brought him food from home and other things to make him more comfortable, he encouraged me, saying, "The only thing you have to do is pass your tests. Focus on your school. Don't worry about me. I don't want this to interfere with anything." But life no longer meant anything to me. I could think of nothing else except joining the military wing of Hamas and taking revenge on Israel and the Palestinian Authority. I thought about everything I had seen in my life. Was all the struggle and sacrifice going to end like this, in a cheap peace with Israel? If I died fighting, at least I would die as a martyr and go to heaven.

My father had never taught me to hate, but I didn't know how not to feel this way. Though he passionately fought the occupation, and though I don't believe he would have hesitated to give the order to nuke the nation of Israel if he had had the bomb, he never spoke against Jewish people, like some racist leaders of Hamas did. He was much more interested in the god of the Qur'an than in politics. Allah had given us the responsibility of eradicating the Jews, and my father didn't question that, though he personally had nothing against them.

"How is your relationship to Allah?" he asked me every time I visited him. "Did you pray today? cry? spend time with him?" He never said, "I want you to become a good *mujahid* [guerilla soldier]." His admonition to me as his eldest son was always, "Be very good to your mother, very good to Allah, and very good to your people."

I didn't understand how he could be so compassionate and forgiving, even toward the soldiers who came again and again to arrest him. He treated them like children. When I brought him food at the PA compound, he often invited the guards to join us and share in my mother's specially prepared meat and rice. And after a few months, even the PA guards loved him. While it was easy for me to love him, he was also a very difficult man to understand.

Filled with anger and a desire for revenge, I started hunting for guns. Though weapons were available in the territories by this time, they were very expensive, and I was a student with no money.

Ibrahim Kiswani, a classmate from a village next to Jerusalem, shared my interest and told me he could get the money we needed—not enough for heavy guns, but enough for some cheap rifles and maybe a pistol. I asked my cousin Yousef Dawood if he knew where I could get some weapons.

Yousef and I weren't really that close, but I knew he had connections that I didn't have.

"I have a couple of friends in Nablus who might help," he told me. "What do you want with guns?"

"Every family has its own weapons," I lied. "I want one to protect my family."

Well, it wasn't exactly a lie. Ibrahim lived in a village where every family did indeed have its own weapons for self-defense, and he was like a brother to me.

In addition to wanting to take revenge, I thought it would be cool to be a teenager with a gun. I no longer cared much about school. Why go to school in this crazy country?

Finally one afternoon, I got a call from my cousin Yousef.

"Okay, we're going to Nablus. I know a guy who works for the PA security force. I think he can get us some weapons," he said.

When we arrived in Nablus, a man met us at the door of the small house and led us inside. There he showed us Swedish Carl Gustav M45 submachine guns and a Port Said, which was an Egyptian version of the same weapon. He took us to a remote spot in the mountains and showed us how they operated. When he asked me if I wanted to try one, my heart started to race. I had never fired a machine gun before, and suddenly I was scared.

"No, I trust you," I told him. I purchased a couple of Gustafs and a handgun from the man. I hid them in the door of my car, sprinkling black pepper over them to throw off any Israeli dogs that might be sniffing for weapons at the checkpoints.

As I drove back to Ramallah, I called Ibrahim on the way.

"Hey, I got the stuff!"

"Really?"

"Really."

We knew better than to use words like *guns* or *weapons* because there was a good chance that the Israelis were listening to everything we said. We set up a time for Ibrahim to pick up his "things" and quickly said good night.

It was the spring of 1996. I had just turned eighteen, and I was armed.

One night, Ibrahim called me, and I could tell by the tone of his voice that he was really angry.

"The guns don't work!" he shouted into the phone.

"What are you talking about?" I shot back, hoping no one was listening to our conversation.

"The guns don't work," he repeated. "We were cheated!"

"I can't talk now," I told him.

"Okay, but I want to see you tonight."

When he arrived at my house, I immediately lit into him.

"Are you crazy, talking like that on the phone?" I said.

"I know, but the guns aren't working. The handgun is okay, but the submachine guns won't shoot."

"Okay, they're not working. Are you sure you know how to use them?"

He assured me that he knew what he was doing, so I told him I would deal with it. With my final exams just two weeks away, I didn't really have time for any of this, but I went ahead and made the arrangements to take the malfunctioning guns back to Yousef.

"This is a disaster," I told him when I saw him. "The handgun works, but the machine guns don't. Call your friends in Nablus so we can at least get our money back." He promised to try.

The next day my brother Sohayb gave me some sobering news. "Israeli security forces came to the house last night, looking for you," he told me with a worried strain in his voice.

My first thought was, *We didn't even kill anyone yet!* I was scared, but I also felt a bit important, as though I was becoming dangerous to Israel. The next time I visited my father, he had already heard that the Israelis were looking for me.

"What's going on?" he asked sternly. I told him the truth, and he became very angry. Through his anger, however, it was clear to me that he was mostly disappointed and worried.

"This is very serious," he warned me. "Why did you get yourself into this? You need to be taking care of your mother and brothers and sisters, not running from the Israelis. Don't you understand that they will shoot you?"

I went home, threw together some clothes and my schoolbooks, and asked some Muslim Brotherhood students to hide me until I could take my exams and finish school.

Ibrahim clearly didn't understand the seriousness of my situation. He continued to call me, often on my father's cell phone.

"What's going on? What is happening with you? I gave you all that money. I need it back."

I told him about the security forces that had been to my house, and he started to shout and say careless things on the phone. I quickly hung up before he could implicate himself or me any further. But the next day, the IDF showed up at his place, searched it, and found the handgun. They arrested him immediately.

I felt lost. I had trusted someone I shouldn't have. My father was in prison, and he was disappointed in me. My mother was worried sick about me. I had exams to study for. And I was wanted by the Israelis.

How could things possibly get any worse?

Chapter Ten

THE SLAUGHTERHOUSE
1996

ALTHOUGH I HAD TRIED to take precautions, the Israeli security forces caught up with me. They had listened in on my conversations with Ibrahim, and now here I was, handcuffed and blindfolded, stuffed in the back of a military jeep, trying to dodge rifle butts as best I could.

The jeep rolled to a stop. We had been driving for what seemed like hours. The handcuffs cut deeply into my wrists as the soldiers lifted me by my arms and pulled me up a set of stairs. I could no longer feel my hands. All around me, I heard the sounds of people moving and shouting in Hebrew.

I was taken into a small room where my blindfold and hand-cuffs were removed. Squinting in the light, I tried to get my bearings. With the exception of a small desk in the corner, the room was empty. I wondered what the soldiers had in store for me next. Interrogation? More beatings? Torture? I didn't have to wonder for long. After just a few minutes, a young soldier opened the door. He wore a ring in his nose, and I recognized his Russian accent. He was one of the soldiers who had beaten me in the back of the jeep. Taking me by the arm, he led me down a series of long, wind-ing corridors and into another small room. A blood-pressure cuff and monitor, a computer, and a small TV sat atop an old desk. An overpowering stench filled my nostrils as I entered. I gagged, sure I was about to throw up again.

A man wearing a doctor's jacket entered behind us, looking tired and unhappy. He seemed surprised to see my battered face and eye, which had now swollen to twice its original size. But if he was concerned about my well-being, he certainly didn't show it. I had seen veterinarians who were kinder to their animals than this doctor was as he examined me.

A guard wearing a police uniform came in. He turned me around, put the handcuffs back on, and pulled a dark green hood over my head. I had found the source of the stench. The hood smelled like it had never been washed. It reeked of the unbrushed teeth and foul breath of a hundred prisoners. I retched and tried to hold my breath. But every time I gasped, I sucked the filthy cloth into my mouth. I panicked and felt like I would suffocate if I couldn't get away from the bag.

The guard searched me, taking everything, including my belt and bootlaces. He grabbed me by the hood and dragged me through the corridors. A right turn. A left. Another left. Right. Right again. I didn't know where I was or where he was taking me.

Eventually we stopped, and I heard him fumble for a key. He opened a door that sounded thick and heavy. "Steps," he said. And I felt my way down several treads. Through the hood I could see some sort of flashing light, the kind you see on top of a police car.

The guard pulled off the hood, and I realized I was standing in front of a set of curtains. To my right I saw a basket of hoods. We waited a few minutes until a voice from the other side of the curtain gave us permission to enter. The guard locked manacles onto my ankles and stuffed my head into another bag. Then he grabbed the front of it and pulled me through the curtains.

Cold air poured out of the vents, and music blasted from somewhere in the distance. I must have been walking along a very narrow corridor because I kept bumping into the walls on either side. I felt dizzy and exhausted. Finally, we stopped again. The soldier opened a door and shoved me inside. Then he removed the hood and left, locking the heavy door behind him.

I looked around me, once again surveying my surroundings. The cell was about six feet square—just enough room for a small mattress and two blankets. Whoever had occupied the cell before me had rolled one of them into a pillow. I sat down on the mattress; it felt sticky and the blankets smelled like the hood. I covered my nose with the collar of my shirt, but my clothes reeked of vomit. One weak lightbulb hung from the ceiling, but I couldn't find the switch to turn it on or off. A small opening in the door was the only window in the room. The air was clammy, the floor wet, the concrete covered with mold. Bugs swarmed everywhere. Everything was foul and rotting and ugly.

I just sat there for a long time, not knowing what to do. I had to go to the bathroom and stood to use the rusty toilet in the corner. I pushed the flush handle and immediately wished I hadn't. The waste didn't flush down the hole; instead, it leaked out onto the floor, soaking into the mattress.

I sat down in the only dry corner of the room and tried to think. What a place to have to spend the night! My eye throbbed and burned. I was finding it hard to breathe without choking on the smell of the room. The heat in my cell was unbearable, and my sweat-soaked clothes clung to my frame.

I had had nothing to eat or drink since some goat's milk at my mother's house. And that was now souring all over my shirt and pants. There was a pipe protruding from the wall, and I turned the handle, hoping to get some water from it. The liquid came out thick and brown.

What time was it? Were they going to leave me here all night?

My head pounded. I knew I wouldn't be able to sleep. The only thing I could do was pray to Allah.

Protect me, I asked. *Keep me safe and bring me back to my family quickly.*

Through the thick steel door, I could hear loud music playing in the distance—the same tape, over and over and over. I used the mind-numbing repetitions to help me gauge time.

Again and again, Leonard Cohen sang:

> *They sentenced me to twenty years of boredom*
> *For trying to change the system from within*
> *I'm coming now, I'm coming to reward them*
> *First we take Manhattan, then we take Berlin*[4]

In the distance, doors opened and closed—a lot of them. Slowly, the sounds drew nearer. Then someone opened the door to my cell, shoved a blue tray inside, and slammed the door shut. I looked at the tray as it sat in the sewage that had oozed out after I used the toilet. Its contents included one boiled egg, a single piece of bread, about a spoonful of sour-smelling yogurt, and three olives. A plastic container of water sat to one side, but when I lifted it to my lips, it didn't smell right at all. I drank a little but used the rest to wash my hands. I ate everything on the tray, but I was still hungry. Was this breakfast? What time was it? I guessed afternoon.

While I was still trying to figure out how long I had been there, the door to my cell opened. Someone—or something—was standing there. Was it human? He was short, seemed to be about seventy-five years old, and looked like a hunchbacked ape. He shouted at me in a Russian accent, cursed me, cursed God, and spat in my face. I could not imagine anything uglier.

Apparently, this thing was a guard because he shoved another stinking hood at me and told me to put it over my head. Then he grabbed the front of it and jerked me roughly through the corridors. He opened the door to an office, shoved me inside, and forced me down onto a low plastic chair; it felt like a little child's chair from an elementary school classroom. The chair was secured to the floor.

He handcuffed me, one arm between the chair legs and the other on the outside. Then he shackled my legs. The little seat was slanted, forcing me to lean forward. Unlike my cell, this room was freezing cold. I figured that the air-conditioning must be set around zero.

I sat there for hours, shaking uncontrollably in the cold, bent at an agonizing angle, and unable to shift into a more comfortable position. I tried to breathe through the foul bag without ever taking a full breath. I was hungry, exhausted, and my eye was still swollen with blood.

The door opened, and somebody pulled off my hood. I was surprised to see that it was a civilian, not a soldier or guard. He sat on the edge of the desk. My head was about the level of his knees.

"What is your name?" he asked.

"I am Mosab Hassan Yousef."

"Do you know where you are?"

"No."

He shook his head and said, "Some call it Dark Night. Others call it the Slaughterhouse. You are in big trouble, Mosab."

I tried not to show any emotion at all, keeping my eyes focused on a stain on the wall behind this guy's head.

"How is your father doing in the PA prison?" he asked. "Is it more fun for him than an Israeli prison?"

I shifted slightly in my seat, still refusing to answer.

"Do you realize that you are now in the same place your father was taken after his first arrest?"

So that's where I was: the Maskobiyeh Detention Center in West

Jerusalem. My father had told me about this place. It used to be a Russian Orthodox church, perched on top of six millennia of history. The government of Israel had converted it to a high-security facility that included police headquarters, offices, and an interrogation center for the Shin Bet.

Deep underground was the ancient warren that served as a prison. Black and stained and dark, like the rat-infested medieval dungeons you see in the movies, Maskobiyeh had a nasty reputation.

Now I was suffering the same punishment my father had endured. These were the same men who had beaten him and tortured him all those years ago. They had spent a lot of time working on him, and they knew him well. They also never broke him. He stayed strong and became only stronger.

"Tell me why you are here."

"I have no idea." Of course, I assumed I was here because I had bought those stupid guns that didn't even work. My back felt like it was on fire. My interrogator lifted my chin.

"You want to be tough like your father? You have no idea what is waiting for you outside this room. Tell me what you know about Hamas! What secrets do you know? Tell me about the Islamic student movement! I want to know everything!"

Did he really think I was that dangerous? I couldn't believe that. But then, the more I thought about it, I realized that he probably did. From his point of view, the fact that I was the son of Sheikh Hassan Yousef and was buying automatic weapons was more than enough cause for suspicion.

These men had imprisoned and tortured my father and were about to torture me. Did they really believe this would make me accept their right to exist? My point of view was very different. My people were struggling for our freedom, our land.

When I did not answer his questions, the man slammed the desk with his fist. Again, he lifted my chin.

"I'm going home to spend the night with my family. You have fun here."

I sat in the small chair for hours, still leaning forward awkwardly. Finally, a guard came in, unlocked my handcuffs and shackles, threw another hood over my head, and pulled me back through the corridors. Leonard Cohen's voice grew louder and louder.

We stopped, and the guard barked at me to sit down. The music was deafening now. Once again, I was chained hand and foot to a low chair that was vibrating to the merciless beat of "First we take Manhattan, then we take Berlin!"

My muscles were cramped from the cold, uncomfortable position. I tasted the stench of the hood. This time, however, I was clearly not alone. Even over Leonard Cohen, I could hear other people crying out in great pain.

"Is someone there?" I yelled through the greasy cloth.

"Who are you?" a voice close by yelled over the music.

"I am Mosab."

"How long have you been here?"

"Two days."

He said nothing for a couple of minutes.

"I have been sitting on this chair for three weeks," he said finally. "They let me sleep for four hours every week."

I was stunned. That was the last thing I wanted to hear. Another man told me he had been arrested about the same time I was. I guessed there were about twenty of us in the room.

Our talking was suddenly interrupted when someone struck me in the back of the head—hard. Pain shot through my skull, forcing me to blink back tears inside the hood.

"No talking!" a guard shouted.

Every minute felt like an hour, but I could no longer remember what an hour was anyway. My world had stopped. Outside, I knew that people were getting up, going to their jobs, and returning home to their families. My classmates were studying for their final exams. My mother was cooking and cleaning and hugging and kissing my little brothers and sisters.

But in that room, everyone sat. No one moved.

First we take Manhattan, then we take Berlin! First we take Manhattan, then we take Berlin! First we take Manhattan, then we take Berlin!

Some of the men around me wailed, but I was determined not to cry. I was sure my father had never cried. He was strong. He didn't give in.

"*Shoter! Shoter!* [Guard! Guard!]" one of the men yelled. Nobody answered him because the music was so loud. Finally, after a while, the shoter came.

"What do you want?"

"I want to go to the toilet. I have to go to the toilet!"

"No toilet now. It is not the time for the toilet." And he left.

"Shoter! Shoter!" the man screamed.

Half an hour later, the shoter returned. The man was getting out of control. Cursing him, the shoter opened his chains and dragged him away. A few minutes later, he brought him back, chained him again to the small chair, and left.

"Shoter! Shoter!" screamed another.

I was exhausted and sick to my stomach. My neck ached. I never realized how heavy my head was. I tried to lean against the wall next to me, but just as I was about to drift off to sleep, a guard came and hit me in the head to wake me up. His only job, it seemed, was to keep us awake and quiet. I felt as if I had been buried alive and was being tortured by the angels Munkar and Nakir after giving the wrong answers.

It must have been morning when I heard a guard moving around. One by one, he opened handcuffs and shackles and led people away. After a few minutes, he brought them back, chained them up to the little chairs again, and went on to the next one. Finally, he came to me.

After he unlocked my chains, he grabbed my hood and pulled me through the corridors. He opened a cell door and told me to go in. When he removed the hood, I saw that it was the same hunchbacked, apelike guard with my breakfast. He shoved the blue tray with egg, bread, yogurt, and olives toward me with his foot. Nearly an inch of stinking water covered the floor and splashed into the tray. I would rather have starved than eaten it.

"You have two minutes to eat and use the toilet," he told me.

All I wanted to do was to stretch, lie down, and sleep, just for two minutes. But I just stood there as the seconds slipped away.

"Come on! Come here!"

Before I could grab a bite, the guard pulled the bag over my head again, led me back through the halls, and chained me to the little chair.

First we take Manhattan, then we take Berlin!

Chapter Eleven
THE OFFER
1996

ALL DAY LONG, doors opened and closed, as prisoners were pulled by their foul hoods from one interrogator to another. Uncuffed, cuffed, questioned, beaten. Sometimes an interrogator would shake a prisoner hard. It usually took only ten shakes before he passed out. Uncuffed, cuffed, questioned. Doors opened and doors closed.

Every morning we were taken for our two-minute blue breakfast tray, and then hours later, for our two-minute orange dinner tray. Hour after hour. Day after day. Blue breakfast tray. Orange dinner tray. I quickly learned to long for mealtimes—not because I wanted to eat, but just for the chance to stand erect.

At night after we were all fed, the opening and closing of doors stopped. The interrogators went home. The business day was over. And the endless night began. People cried and moaned and screamed. They no longer sounded like human beings. Some didn't even know what they were saying. Muslims recited verses from the Qur'an, begging Allah for strength. I prayed, too, but I didn't get any strength. I thought about stupid Ibrahim and the stupid guns and the stupid calls to my father's cell phone.

I thought about my father. My heart ached when I realized all that he must have endured while imprisoned. But I knew my father's personality well. Even while being tortured and humiliated, he would have accepted his fate quietly and willingly. He probably even made friends with the guards assigned to carry out the beatings. He would have taken a genuine interest in them as people, asking about their families, their backgrounds, their hobbies.

My father was such an example of humility, love, and devotion; even though he was only five foot seven, he stood head and shoulders above anyone else I had ever known. I very much wanted to be like him, but I knew I still had a long way to go.

One afternoon, my routine was unexpectedly interrupted. A guard came into the cell and unchained me from my chair. I knew it was much too early for dinner, but I didn't ask questions. I was just happy to go anywhere, to hell even, if it meant getting off that chair. I was taken to a small office where I was chained again, but this time to a regular chair. An officer of the Shin Bet entered the room and looked me up and down. Though the pain wasn't as sharp as it once had been, I knew my face still bore the marks from the soldiers' rifle butts.

"How are you?" the officer asked. "What happened to your eye?"

"They beat me."

"Who?"

"The soldiers who brought me here."

"That's not allowed. It's against the law. I'll look into it and find out why this happened."

He seemed very confident and spoke kindly and respectfully to me. I wondered if it was a game to get me to talk.

"You have exams soon. Why are you here?"

"I don't know."

"Of course you know. You are not stupid, and we are not stupid. I am Loai, Shin Bet captain of your area. I know all about your family and your neighborhood. And I know everything about you."

And he really did. Apparently, he was responsible for every person in my neighborhood. He knew who worked where, who was in school, what they studied, whose wife just had a baby, and no doubt what the baby weighed. Everything.

"You have a choice. I came all the way here today to sit down with you and talk. I know that the other interrogators have not been so nice."

I looked closely into his face, trying to read between the lines. Fair skinned and blond, he spoke with a sense of calm I had not heard before. His expression was kind, even a little concerned for me. I wondered if this was part of the Israeli strategy: throwing off the prisoner by beating him one minute, then treating him kindly the next.

"What do you want to know?" I asked.

"Listen, you know why we brought you here. You've got to bring everything out, whatever you have."

"I have no idea what you're talking about."

"Okay, I want to make this easy for you."

On a whiteboard behind the desk he wrote three words: *Hamas, weapons,* and *organization.*

"Go ahead and tell me about Hamas. What do you know about Hamas? What is your involvement in Hamas?"

"I don't know."

"Do you know anything about the weapons they have, where they come from, how they get them?"

"No."

"Do you know anything about the Islamic youth movement?"

"No."

"Okay. It's up to you. I don't know what to tell you, but you are really choosing the wrong path. . . . Can I bring you any food?"

"No. I don't want anything."

Loai left the room and returned minutes later with a steaming plate of chicken and rice and some soup. It smelled wonderful, causing my stomach to grumble involuntarily. No doubt the food had been prepared for the interrogators.

"Please, Mosab, eat. Don't try to be a tough guy. Just eat and relax a little bit. You know, I have known your father for a long time. Your father is a nice guy. He is not a fanatic, and we don't know why you got yourself into trouble. We don't want to torture you, but you need to understand that you are against Israel. Israel is a small country, and we have to protect ourselves. We cannot allow anybody to hurt Israeli citizens. We suffered enough our whole lives, and we will not be easy on those who want to hurt our people."

"I never hurt any Israeli. You hurt us. You arrested my father."

"Yes. He is a good man, but he is also against Israel. He inspires people to fight against Israel. That's why we have to put him in prison."

I could tell that Loai really believed I was dangerous. I knew from talking to others who had been inside Israeli prisons that Palestinians weren't always treated as harshly as I had been. Nor were they all interrogated at such lengths.

What I didn't know at the time was that Hassan Salameh had been arrested about the same time I was.

Salameh had carried out numerous attacks in revenge for master bomb maker Yahya Ayyash's assassination. And when the Shin Bet heard me talking to Ibrahim on my dad's cell phone about getting weapons, they assumed I wasn't working alone. In fact, they were sure I had been recruited by Al-Qassam.

Finally, Loai said, "This is the last time I will make this offer, then I will be gone. I have a lot to do. You and I can resolve this situation right now. We can work something out. You do not have to go through more interrogation. You're just a kid, and you need help."

Yes, I had wanted to be dangerous, and I had dangerous ideas. But clearly, I wasn't very good at being a radical. I was tired of the little plastic chair and smelly hoods. The Israeli intelligence was giving me more credit than I deserved. So I told him the whole story, leaving out the part about my wanting the weapons so I could kill Israelis. I told him I had bought the weapons to help my friend, Ibrahim, protect his family.

"So there are weapons now, I see."

"Yes, there are weapons."

"And where are those weapons?"

I wished they had been at my house because I would gladly have surrendered them to the Israelis. But now I had to involve my cousin.

"Okay, here's the thing. Somebody that has nothing to do with this has the weapons."

"Who is he?"

"My cousin Yousef has them. He is married to an American, and they have a new baby." I hoped they would take his family into account and just go get the weapons, but things are never that easy.

Two days later, I heard scuffling on the other side of the wall in my cell. I leaned down and toward the rusted-out pipe that connected my cell with the one next to it.

"Hello," I called. "Is anybody there?"

Silence.

And then . . .

"Mosab?"

What?! I couldn't believe my ears. It was my cousin!

"Yousef? Is that you?"

I was so excited to hear his voice. My heart started beating wildly. It was Yousef! But then he started cursing me.

"Why did you do this? I have a family. . . ."

I started to cry. I had wanted so much for a human being to talk to while I was in prison. Now a member of my own family sat just on the other side of the wall, and he was yelling at me. And then it hit me: the Israelis were listening; they had put Yousef right next to me so they could listen to our conversation and find out whether I was telling the truth. That was fine by me. I had told Yousef I wanted the guns to protect my family, so I wasn't worried.

Once the Shin Bet realized that my story was true, they moved me to another cell. Alone once again, I thought about how I had screwed up my cousin's life, how I had hurt my family, and how I had thrown away twelve years of school—and all because I trusted a jerk like Ibrahim!

I stayed in that cell for weeks with no human contact. The guards slid food under the door but never said a word to me. I even began to miss Leonard Cohen. I had nothing to read, and my only sense of passing time was the daily rotation of colored food trays. Nothing to do but think and pray.

Finally one day I was again taken to an office, and again, Loai was waiting to talk to me.

"If you decide to cooperate with us, Mosab, I will do my best to see that you don't have to spend more time in prison."

A moment of hope. Maybe I could make him think I was going to cooperate and then he would let me out of here.

We talked a little about general things. Then he said, "What if I offer you a job with us? Israeli leaders are sitting down with Palestinian leaders. They have fought for a long time, and at the end of the day they are shaking hands and having dinner together."

"Islam forbids me to work with you."

"At some point, Mosab, even your father will come and sit down and talk to us and we will talk to him. Let's work together and bring peace to people."

"Is this how we bring peace? We bring peace by ending the occupation."

"No, we bring peace through people with courage who want to make change."

"I don't think so. It's not worth it."

"Are you afraid of being killed as a collaborator?"

"It's not that. After all our suffering, I could never just sit down and talk with you as a friend, much less work with you. I am not allowed to do this. It is against everything I believe."

I still hated everything around me. The occupation. The PA. I had become a radical just because I wanted to destroy something. But it was that impulse that had gotten me into this whole mess. Here I was sitting in an Israeli prison, and now this man was asking me to work for them. If I said yes, I knew I would have to pay a terrible price—both in this life and in the next.

"Okay, I need to think about it," I heard myself saying.

I went back to my cell and thought about Loai's offer. I had heard stories about people who agreed to work for the Israelis but were double agents. They killed their handlers, stashed weapons, and used every opportunity to hurt the Israelis at an even deeper level. If I told him yes, I figured Loai would most likely release me. He would probably even give me the opportunity to have real weapons this time, and with those weapons I was going to kill him.

The fires of hatred burned inside me. I wanted revenge on the soldier who had beaten me so badly. I wanted revenge on Israel. I didn't care about the cost, even if it cost me my life.

But working for the Shin Bet would be a lot riskier than buying weapons. I probably should just forget it, just finish my time in prison, go home and study, be close to my mother, and take care of my brothers and sisters.

The following day, the guard took me back to the office one last time, and a few minutes later Loai came in.

"How are you today? You seem to be feeling much better. Would you like something to drink?"

We sat there drinking coffee like two old friends.

"What if I get killed?" I asked, though I really didn't care about getting killed. I only wanted to make him think I did so he would believe that I was for real.

"Let me tell you something, Mosab," said Loai. "I've been working for the Shin Bet for eighteen years, and during all that time, I know of only one person who was discovered. All those people you have seen getting killed had no relationship with us. People became suspicious of them because they had no families and they did suspicious things, so people killed them. Nobody will know about you. We will cover you so you aren't found out. We will protect you and take care of you."

I stared at him a long time.

"All right," I said. "I will do it. Will you release me now?"

"That's great," Loai said with a big smile. "Unfortunately, we cannot release you right now. Since you and your cousin were arrested right after Salameh was nabbed, the story was on the front page of *Al-Quds* [the main Palestinian newspaper]. Everybody thinks you were arrested because you were involved with a bomb maker. If we release you so soon, people will be suspicious, and you might be exposed as a collaborator. The best way to protect you is to send you to prison—not for long, don't worry. We'll see if there's a prisoner exchange or release agreement we can use to get you out. Once you are there, I'm sure that Hamas will take care of you, especially since you are the son of Hassan Yousef. We'll see you after your release."

They took me back to my cell, where I stayed for another couple of weeks. I couldn't wait to get out of Maskobiyeh. Finally one morning, the guard told me it was time to go. He handcuffed me, but this time my hands were in front of me. No stinking hood. And for the first time in forty-five days, I saw the sun and felt the outside air. I took a deep breath, filling my lungs and relishing the breeze on my face. I climbed into the back of a Ford van and actually sat down on the seat. It was a hot summer day, and the metal bench I was cuffed to was blistering, but I didn't care. I felt free!

Two hours later, we arrived at the prison in Megiddo, but then we had to sit in the van for another hour, waiting for permission to enter. Once we finally got inside, a prison doctor examined me and announced that I was fine. I took a shower with real soap and was provided with clean clothes and other toiletries. At lunchtime, I ate hot food for the first time in weeks.

I was asked what organization I was affiliated with.

"Hamas," I answered.

In Israeli prisons, every organization was allowed to police its own people. The hope was that this would either cut down on some of the social problems or create more conflict among the factions. If prisoners focused their anger on one another, they'd have less energy to fight against the Israelis.

Upon entering a new prison, all prisoners were required to declare an affiliation. We had to choose something: Hamas, Fatah, Islamic Jihad, the Popular Front for the Liberation of Palestine (PFLP), the Democratic Front for the Liberation of Palestine (DFLP), or whatever the case might be. We couldn't simply say we were nothing. Prisoners who really *were* nothing would be given a few days to choose an organization. At Megiddo, Hamas was in total control inside the prison. Hamas was the largest and strongest organization there. Hamas made the rules, and everybody else played their game.

When I entered, the other prisoners welcomed me warmly, patting me on the back and congratulating me for joining the ranks. In the evening, we sat around and shared our stories. After a while, though, I started to feel a little uncomfortable. One of the guys seemed to be kind of a leader for the inmates, and he was asking a lot of questions—too many. Even though he was the emir—the Hamas leader within the prison—I just didn't trust him. I had heard many stories about "birds," another word for prison spies.

If he's a Shin Bet spy, I thought, *why doesn't he trust me? I'm supposed to be one of them now.* I decided to play it safe and say nothing more than I had told the interrogators at the detention center.

I stayed at Megiddo Prison for two weeks, praying and fasting and reading the Qur'an. When new prisoners came through, I warned them about the emir.

"You've got to be careful," I said. "That guy and his friends sound to me like they might be birds." The new arrivals immediately told the emir about my suspicions, and the next day I was sent back to Maskobiyeh. The following morning, I was brought to the office.

"How was your trip to Megiddo?" Loai asked.

"It was nice," I said sarcastically.

"You know, not everybody can spot a bird the first time he meets one. Go and rest now. Soon we will send you back to spend a little more time there. And one day we will do something together."

Yeah, and one day I will shoot you in the head, I thought as I watched him walk away. I was proud of myself for having such radical thoughts.

I spent twenty-five more days at the detention center, but this time I was in a cell with three other prisoners, including my cousin Yousef. We passed the time talking and telling stories. One guy told us how he had killed somebody. Another boasted about sending suicide bombers. Everybody had an interesting story to tell. We sat around, praying, singing, and trying to have fun. Anything to get our minds off our current surroundings. It was not a place for humans.

Finally, all of us except my cousin were sent to Megiddo. But this time we were not going to be on the side with the birds; we were headed to a real prison. And nothing would ever be the same again.

Chapter Twelve

NUMBER 823
1996

THEY COULD SMELL US COMING.

Our hair and beards were long after three months without scissors or razor. Our clothes were filthy. It took about two weeks to get rid of the stink of the detention center. Scrubbing didn't work. It just had to wear off.

Most of the prisoners started their sentence in the *mi'var*, a unit where everyone was processed before being moved to the larger camp population. Some prisoners, however, were considered too dangerous to be in the general population and lived in the mi'var for years. These men, not surprisingly, were all affiliated with Hamas. Some of the guys recognized me and came over to welcome us.

As Sheikh Hassan's son, I was used to being recognized wherever I went. If he was the king, I was the prince—the heir apparent. And I was treated as such.

"We heard you were here a month ago. Your uncle is here. He will come to visit you soon."

Lunch was hot and filling, although not quite as tasty as what I had eaten when I was with the birds. Still, I was happy. Even though I was in prison, I actually felt free. When I had time alone, I wondered about the Shin Bet. I had promised to work with them, but they hadn't told me anything. They never explained how we would communicate or what it would mean to actually work together. They just left me on my own with no tips on how to behave. I was totally lost. I didn't know who I was anymore. I wondered if maybe I had been scammed.

The mi'var was divided into two big dorms—Room Eight and Room Nine—lined with bunks. The dorms formed an L and housed twenty prisoners each. In the angle of the L, there was an exercise yard with a painted concrete floor and a broken-down Ping-Pong table that had been donated by the Red Cross. We were let out for exercise twice a day.

My bed was at the far end of Room Nine, right by the bathroom. We shared two toilets and two showers. Each toilet was just a hole in the floor over which we stood or squatted, and then we doused ourselves with water from a bucket when we were finished. It was hot and humid, and it smelled horrible.

In fact, the entire dorm was that way. Guys were sick and coughing; some never bothered to shower. Everybody had foul breath. Cigarette smoke overwhelmed the weak fan. And there were no windows for ventilation.

We were awakened every morning at four so we could get ready for predawn prayer. We waited in line with our towels, looking the way men look first thing in the morning and smelling the way men smell when there are no fans or ventilation. Then it was time for *wudu*. To begin the Islamic ritual of purification, we washed our hands up to the wrist, rinsed our mouths, and sniffed water into our nostrils. We scrubbed our faces with both hands from forehead to chin and ear to ear, washed our arms up to our elbows, and wiped our heads from the forehead to the back of the neck once with a wet hand. Finally, we wet our fingers and wiped our ears inside and out, wiped around our necks, and washed both feet up to the ankles. Then we repeated the whole process two more times.

At 4:30, when everybody was finished, the imam—a big, tough guy with a huge beard—chanted the adhan. Then he read *Al-Fatihah* (the opening sura, or passage, from the Qur'an), and we went through four *rakats* (repetitions of prayers and standing, kneeling, and bowing postures).

Most of us prisoners were Muslims affiliated with Hamas or Islamic Jihad, so this was our regular routine anyway. But even those who were members of the secular and communist organizations had to get up at the same time, even though they didn't pray. And they were not happy about it.

One guy was about halfway through a fifteen-year sentence. He was sick of the whole Islamic routine, and it took forever to get him up in the morning. Some of the prisoners poked him, punched him, and yelled, "Wake up!" Finally, they had to pour water on his head. I felt sorry for him. All the purifying, praying, and reading took about an hour. Then everybody went back to bed. No talking. Quiet time.

I always had difficulty falling back to sleep, and usually I didn't doze off until it was close to seven. By the time I was finally asleep again, somebody would shout, "*Adad! Adad!* [Number! Number!]" a warning that it was time to prepare for head count.

We sat on our bunks with our backs turned to the Israeli soldier who counted us, because he was unarmed. It took him only five minutes, and then we were allowed to go back to sleep.

"*Jalsa! Jalsa!*" the emir yelled at 8:30. It was time for the twice-daily organizational meetings held by Hamas and Islamic Jihad. Heaven forbid they should let anybody sleep for a couple of hours straight. It got really annoying. Again, the line formed for the toilets so that everybody would be ready for the nine o'clock jalsa.

During the first Hamas jalsa of the day, we studied the rules for reading the Qur'an. I had learned all of this from my father, but most prisoners did not know any of it. The second daily jalsa was more about Hamas, our own discipline inside the prison, announcements of new arrivals, and news about what was going on outside. No secrets, no plans, just general news.

After each jalsa, we often passed the time by watching television on the set at the far end of the room, opposite the toilets. One morning, I was watching a cartoon when a commercial came on.

BANG!

A big wooden board swung down in front of the screen.

I jumped and looked around.

"What just happened?!"

I realized that the board was attached to a heavy rope that hung from the ceiling. At the side of the room, a prisoner held tightly to the end of the rope. His job, apparently, was to watch for anything impure and drop the screen in front of the TV to protect us.

"Why did you drop the board?" I asked.

"Your own protection," the man said gruffly.

"Protection? From what?"

"The girl in the commercial," explained the board banger. "She was not wearing a head scarf."

I turned to the emir. "Is he serious about this?"

"Yes, of course he is," the emir said.

"But we all have TVs in our homes, and we don't do this there. Why do it here?"

"Being in prison presents unusual challenges," he explained. "We don't have women. And things they show on television can cause problems for prisoners and lead to relationships between them that we don't want. So this is the rule, and this is how we see it."

Of course, not everybody saw it the same way. What we were allowed to watch depended a lot on who held the rope. If the guy was from Hebron, he would drop the board to cover even a female cartoon character without a scarf; if he was from liberal Ramallah, we got to see a lot more. We were supposed to take turns holding the rope, but I refused to touch the stupid thing.

After lunch was noontime prayer, followed by another quiet time. Most of the prisoners took a nap during this time. I usually read a book. And in the evening, we were allowed into the exercise area for a little walk or to hang out and talk.

Life in prison was pretty boring for Hamas guys. We were not allowed to play cards. We were supposed to limit our reading to the Qur'an or Islamic books. The other factions were allowed a lot more freedom than we were.

My cousin, Yousef, finally showed up one afternoon, and I was so happy to see him. The Israelis let us have some clippers, and we shaved his head to help get rid of the detention center smell.

Yousef was not Hamas; he was a socialist. He didn't believe in Allah, but he didn't disbelieve in God. That made him a close enough fit to be assigned to the Democratic Front for the Liberation of Palestine. The DFLP fought for a Palestinian state, as opposed to Hamas and Islamic Jihad, which fought for an Islamic state.

A few days after Yousef's arrival, my uncle, Ibrahim Abu Salem, came to visit. He had been under administrative detention for two years, though no official charges had ever been brought against him. And because he was a danger to the security of Israel, he would be there a long time. As a Hamas VIP, my uncle Ibrahim was allowed to travel freely between the mi'var and the actual prison camp and from one camp section to another. So he came to the mi'var to check on his nephew, make sure I was okay, and bring me some clothes—a gesture of concern that seemed out of character for the man who had beaten me and abandoned our family when my father was in prison.

At nearly six feet tall, Ibrahim Abu Salem was larger than life. His ponderous belly—evidence of his passion for food—made him appear to be some sort of jolly gourmet. But I knew better. My uncle Ibrahim was a mean, selfish man, a liar and a hypocrite—the exact opposite of my father.

Yet inside the walls of Megiddo, my uncle Ibrahim was treated like a king. All the prisoners respected him, no matter what faction they were with—for his age, his teaching ability, his work in the universities, and his political and academic accomplishments. Usually, the leaders would take advantage of his visit and ask him to give a lecture.

Everyone liked to listen to Ibrahim when he taught. Rather than lecturing, he was more like an entertainer. He liked to make people laugh, and when he taught about Islam, he presented it using simple language that everyone could understand.

On this day, however, no one was laughing. Instead, all of the prisoners sat in wide-eyed silence as Ibrahim spoke fiercely about collaborators and how they deceived and embarrassed their families and were the enemy of the Palestinian people. From the way he was speaking, I got the feeling he was saying to me, "If you have something that you haven't told me, Mosab, you had better tell me now."

Of course, I didn't. Even if Ibrahim was suspicious about my connection with the Shin Bet, he wouldn't have dared to say so directly to the son of Sheikh Hassan Yousef.

"If you need anything," he said before he left, "just let me know. I will try to get you placed close to me."

It was the summer of 1996. Though I was only eighteen, I felt as if I had lived several lifetimes in just a few months. A couple of weeks after my uncle's visit, a prisoner representative, or *shaweesh*, came into Room Nine and called out, "Eight twenty-three!" I looked up, surprised to hear my number. Then he called out three or four other numbers and told us to gather our belongings.

As we stepped out of the mi'var into the desert, the heat hit me like dragon's breath and made me light-headed for a moment. Stretched ahead of us for as far as I could see was nothing but the tops of big brown tents. We marched past the first section, second section, third section. Hundreds of prisoners ran to the high chain-link fence to see the new arrivals. We arrived at Section Five, and the gates swung open. More than fifty people crowded around us, hugged us, and shook our hands.

We were taken to an administration tent and again asked our organizational affiliations. Then I was led to the Hamas tent, where the emir received me and shook my hand.

"Welcome," he said. "Good to see you. We are very proud of you. We'll prepare a bed for you soon and give you some towels and other things you need." Then he added with typical prison humor, "Just make yourself comfortable and enjoy your stay."

Every section of the prison had twelve tents. Each tent housed twenty beds and footlockers. Maximum section capacity: 240 prisoners. Picture a rectangular picture frame, bordered with razor wire. Section Five was divided into quarters. A wall, topped with razor wire, bisected the section from north to south, and a low fence bisected it from east to west.

Quadrants One and Two (upper right and left) housed three Hamas tents each. Quadrant Three (lower right) had four tents— one each for Hamas, Fatah, the combined DFLP/PFLP, and Islamic Jihad. And Quadrant Four (lower left) had two tents, one for Fatah and one for the DFLP/PFLP.

Quadrant Four also had the kitchen, toilets, showers, an area for the shaweesh and kitchen workers, and basins for wudu. We lined up in rows for prayer in an open area in Quadrant Two. And, of course, there were guard towers at every corner. The main gate to Section Five was in the fence between Quadrants Three and Four.

One more detail: The fence running east and west had gates between Quadrants One and Three and between Two and Four. They were left open during most of the day, except during head counts. Then they were closed so officials could isolate half a section at a time.

I was assigned to the Hamas tent in the upper corner of Quadrant

One, third bunk on the right. After the first head count, we were all sitting around talking when a distant voice shouted, "*Bareed ya mujahideen! Bareed!* [Mail from the freedom fighters! Mail!]."

It was the *sawa'ed* in the next section, giving everyone a heads up. The sawa'ed were agents for the Hamas security wing inside the prison, who distributed messages from one section to another. The name came from the Arabic words meaning "throwing arms."

At the call, a couple of guys ran out of their tents, held out their hands, and looked toward the sky. As if on cue, a ball seemed to fall out of nowhere into their waiting hands. This was how Hamas leaders in our section received encoded orders or information from leaders in other sections. Every Palestinian organization in the prison used this method of communication. Each had its own code name, so that when the warning was shouted, the appropriate "catchers" knew to run into the drop zone.

The balls were made of bread that had been softened with water. The message was inserted and then the dough was rolled into a ball about the size of a softball, dried, and hardened. Naturally, only the best pitchers and catchers were selected as "postmen."

As quickly as the excitement started, it was over. Then it was time for lunch.

Chapter Thirteen

TRUST NO ONE

1996

AFTER BEING HELD UNDERGROUND for so long, it was wonderful to see the sky. It seemed as though I hadn't seen the stars for years. They were beautiful, despite the huge camp lights that dimmed their brightness. But stars meant it was time to head to our tents to prepare for head count and bed. And that was when things got really confusing for me.

My number was 823, and prisoners were billeted in numerical order. That meant I should have been placed in the Hamas tent in Quadrant Three. But that tent was full, so I had been assigned to the corner tent in Quadrant One.

When it came time for head count, however, I still had to stand in the appropriate place in Quadrant Three. That way, when the guard went down his list, he wouldn't have to remember all the housekeeping adjustments that had been made to keep things tidy.

Every movement of the head count was choreographed.

Twenty-five soldiers, M16s at the ready, entered Quadrant One and then moved from tent to tent. We all stood facing the canvas, our backs to the troops. Nobody dared move for fear of being shot.

When they had finished there, the soldiers moved into Quadrant Two. After that, they closed both gates in the fence, so that no one from One or Two could slip into Three or Four to cover for a missing prisoner.

On my first night in Section Five, I noticed that a mysterious kind of shell game was taking place. When I first took my place in Three, a very sickly looking prisoner stood next to me. He looked horrible, almost as if he was about to die. His head was shaved; he was clearly exhausted. He never made eye contact. *Who is this guy, and what happened to him?* I wondered.

When the soldiers finished the head count in One and moved on to Two, somebody grabbed the guy, dragged him out of the tent, and another prisoner took his place next to me. I learned later that a small opening had been cut in the fence between One and Three so they could swap the prisoner with someone else.

Obviously, nobody wanted the soldiers to see the bald guy. But why?

That night, lying in my bed, I heard somebody moaning in the distance, somebody who was clearly in a lot of pain. It didn't last long, however, and I quickly drifted off to sleep.

Morning always came too quickly, and before I knew it, we were being awakened for predawn prayer. Of the 240 prisoners in Section Five, 140 guys got up and stood in line to use the six toilets—actually six holes with privacy barriers over a common pit. Eight basins for wudu. Thirty minutes.

Then we lined up in rows for prayer. The daily routine was pretty much the same as it had been in the mi'var. But now there were twelve times as many prisoners. And yet I was struck by how smoothly everything went, even with that many people. No one ever seemed to make a mistake. It was almost eerie.

Everybody seemed to be terrified. No one dared break a rule. No one dared stay a little too long at the toilet. No one dared make eye contact with a prisoner under investigation or with an Israeli soldier. No one ever stood too close to the fence.

It didn't take long, though, before I began to understand. Flying under the radar of the prison authorities, Hamas was running its own show, and they were keeping score. Break a rule, and you got a red point. Collect enough red points, and you answered to the *maj'd*, the Hamas security wing—tough guys who didn't smile and didn't make jokes.

Most of the time, we didn't even see the maj'd because they were busy collecting intelligence. The message balls thrown from one section to another were from them and for them.

One day, I was sitting on my bed when the maj'd came in and shouted, "Everybody evacuate this tent!" Nobody said a word. The tent was empty in seconds. They took a man inside the now-empty tent, closed the flap, and posted two guards. Somebody turned on the TV. Loud. Other guys started to sing and make noises.

I didn't know what was going on inside the tent, but I had never heard a human being scream like that guy did. *What could he have done to deserve that?* I wondered. The torture went on for about thirty minutes. Then two maj'd brought him out and took him to another tent, where the interrogation began again.

I had been talking to a friend named Akel Sorour, who was from a village close to Ramallah, when we were evacuated.

"What's going on in that tent?" I asked.

"Oh, he is a bad guy," he said simply.

"I know he is a bad guy, but what are they doing to him? And what has he done?"

"He didn't do anything in prison," Akel explained. "But they say when he was in Hebron he gave the Israelis information about a Hamas member, and it sounded like he was talking a lot. So they torture him from time to time."

"How?"

"They usually put needles under his fingernails and melt plastic food trays onto his bare skin. Or they burn off his body hair.

Sometimes they put a big stick behind his knees, force him to sit on his ankles for hours, and don't let him sleep."

Now I understood why everyone was so careful to toe the line and what had happened to the bald man I saw when I first arrived. The maj'd hated collaborators, and until we could prove otherwise, we were all suspected of being collaborators, spies for the Israelis.

Because Israel had been so successful in identifying Hamas cells and imprisoning its members, the maj'd assumed that the organization must be riddled with spies, and they were determined to expose them. They watched every move we made. They watched our manners and listened to everything we said. And they tallied up the points. We knew who they were, but we didn't know who their spies were. Somebody I thought was a friend could work with the maj'd, and I could find myself being investigated tomorrow.

I decided my best bet was to keep to myself as much as I could and be very careful whom I trusted. Once I understood the atmosphere of suspicion and treachery in the camp, my life changed dramatically. I felt as though I was in an entirely different prison—one in which I could not move freely, talk freely, trust or relate or befriend. I was afraid to make a mistake, be late, sleep through wake-up calls, or nod off during jalsa.

If someone was "convicted" by the maj'd of being a collaborator, his life was over. His family's life was over. His kids, his wife, everyone abandoned him. Being known as a collaborator was the worst reputation anyone could have. Between 1993 and 1996, more than 150 suspected collaborators were investigated by Hamas inside Israeli prisons. About sixteen were murdered.

Because I could write very fast and neatly, the maj'd asked if I would be their clerk. The information I would handle was top secret, they said. And they warned me to keep it to myself.

I spent my days copying dossiers on prisoners. We were very careful to keep this information out of reach of the prison officials.

We never used names, just code numbers. Written on the thinnest paper available, the files read like the worst kind of pornography. Guys confessed to having had sex with their mothers. One said he had had sex with a cow. Another had had sex with his daughter. Yet another had had sex with his neighbor, filmed it with a spy camera, and given the photographs to the Israelis. The Israelis, the report said, showed the pictures to the neighbor and threatened to send them to her family if she refused to work with their spy. So they kept having sex together and collecting information and having sex with others and filming it, until the entire village seemed to be working for the Israelis. And this was just the first file I was asked to copy.

It seemed crazy to me. As I continued to copy the files, I realized that suspects under torture were being asked things they couldn't possibly know about and giving answers they thought their torturers wanted to hear. It seemed obvious that they would say anything just to make the torture stop. I also suspected that some of these bizarre interrogations served no purpose other than to feed the sexual fantasies of the imprisoned maj'd.

Then one day, my friend Akel Sorour became one of their victims. He was a member of a Hamas cell and had been arrested many times, but for some reason he was never accepted by the urban Hamas prisoners. Akel was a simple farmer. The way he spoke and ate seemed funny to the others, and they took advantage of him. He tried his best to gain their trust and respect by cooking and cleaning for them, but they treated him like trash because they knew he served them out of fear.

And Akel had reason to be afraid. His parents were dead. His sister was the only family he had left. This made him extremely vulnerable because there was no one to take revenge for his torture. In addition, a friend from his cell had been interrogated by the maj'd and mentioned Akel's name under torture. I felt very sorry for him.

But how could I help him? I was just a confused kid with no authority. I knew that the only reason I was immune from the same treatment was because of my father.

Once a month, our families were permitted to visit us. The Israeli prison cuisine left a lot to be desired, so they usually brought us homemade food and personal items. Because Akel and I were from the same area, our families came on the same day.

After a long application process, the Red Cross gathered family members from a particular area and loaded them onto buses. It was only a two-hour drive to Megiddo. But because the buses had to stop at every checkpoint and all the passengers had to be searched at every stop, our families had to leave the house at four in the morning in order to reach the prison by noon.

One day, after a pleasant visit with his sister, Akel returned to Section Five with the bags of food she had brought him. He was happy and had no idea what awaited him. My uncle Ibrahim had come to lecture, which was always a bad sign. I had learned that Ibrahim often gathered everyone together and preached to provide cover for the maj'd when they took someone to interrogation. This time, the "someone" was Akel. The maj'd took away his gifts and led him into a tent. He disappeared behind a curtain, where his worst nightmare began.

I looked at my uncle. Why didn't he stop them? He had been in prison with Akel many times. They had suffered together. Akel had cooked for him and taken care of him. My uncle knew this man. Was it because Akel was a poor, quiet farmer from the village and my uncle was from the city?

Whatever the reasons, Ibrahim Abu Salem sat with the maj'd, laughing and eating the food Akel's sister had brought for her imprisoned brother. Nearby, fellow Hamas members—fellow Arabs, fellow Palestinians, fellow Muslims—shoved needles under Akel's fingernails.

I saw Akel only a few times over the next few weeks. His head and beard had been shaved, his eyes were glued to the ground. He was skinny and looked like an old man at death's door.

Later, I was given his file to copy. He had confessed to having sex with every woman in his village as well as with donkeys and other animals. I knew that every word was a lie, but I copied the file, and the maj'd sent it to his village. His sister disowned him. His neighbors shunned him.

To me, the maj'd were far worse than any collaborator. But they were also powerful and influential within the inner workings of the prison system. I thought I might be able to use them to reach my own objectives.

Anas Rasras was a maj'd leader. His father was a college professor in the West Bank and a close friend of my uncle Ibrahim. After I arrived at Megiddo, my uncle had asked Anas to help me get adjusted and learn the ropes. Anas was from Hebron, about forty years old, very secretive, very intelligent, and very dangerous. He was under the eyes of the Shin Bet every moment he was out of prison. He had few friends, but he never participated in torture. Because of this, I grew to respect and even trust him.

I told him about how I had agreed to collaborate with the Israelis so that I could become a double agent, obtain high-level weaponry, and kill them from the inside. I asked if he could help me.

"I have to check this out," he said. "I won't tell anybody, but I will see."

"What do you mean you will see? Can you help me or not?"

I should have known better than to trust this man. Instead of trying to help me, he immediately told my uncle Ibrahim and some of the other members of the maj'd about my plan.

The next morning, my uncle came to see me.

"What do you think you are doing?"

"Don't freak out. Nothing happened. I have a plan. You don't have to be part of it."

"This is very dangerous, Mosab, for your reputation and your father's, for your entire family's. Other people do things like this, not you."

He began to question me. Did the Shin Bet give me a contact inside the prison? Did I meet this particular Israeli guy or that security guy? What was I told? What did I tell others? The more he interrogated me, the angrier I became. Finally, I just blew up in his face.

"Why don't you stick to your religious stuff and leave security alone! All these guys are torturing people for nothing. They have no idea what they're doing. Look, I have nothing else to say. I am going to do what I want, and you do what you want."

I knew that things didn't look good for me. I was pretty sure they wouldn't torture or interrogate me because of my father, but I could tell that my uncle Ibrahim didn't know if I was telling the truth or not.

At that point, I wasn't sure either.

I recognized that I had been foolish to trust the maj'd. Had I been just as foolish to trust the Israelis? They still hadn't told me anything. They had given me no contacts. Were they playing a game with me?

I went to my tent and felt myself beginning to shut down mentally and emotionally. I no longer trusted anyone. Other prisoners saw that something was wrong with me, but they didn't know what it was. Though the maj'd kept what I told them to themselves, they never took their eyes off of me. Everyone was suspicious of me. Likewise, I suspected everyone. And we all lived together in an open-air cage with no place else to go. No place to get away or hide.

Time dragged on. Suspicion grew. Every day, there was screaming; every night, torture. Hamas was torturing its own people! As much as I wanted to, I simply could not find a way to justify that.

Soon it got even worse. Instead of one person, three would be under investigation at the same time. One morning at four o'clock, a guy ran through the section, scrambled up and over the perimeter fence, and in twenty seconds was outside the camp, his clothes and his flesh shredded by the razor wire. An Israeli tower guard swung his machine gun around and took aim.

"Don't shoot!" the guy screamed. "Don't shoot! I'm not trying to escape. I'm trying to get away from them!" And he pointed to the panting maj'd who glared out at him through the fence. Soldiers ran out the gate, threw the inmate to the ground, searched him, and took him away.

Was this Hamas? Was this Islam?

Chapter Fourteen

RIOT

1996–1997

MY FATHER WAS ISLAM TO ME.

If I were to put him on the scale of Allah, he would weigh more than any other Muslim I had ever met. He never missed a prayer time. Even when he came home late and tired, I often heard him praying and crying out to the god of the Qur'an in the middle of the night. He was humble, loving, and forgiving—to my mother, to his children, even to people he didn't know.

More than an apologist for Islam, my father lived his life as an example of what a Muslim should be. He reflected the beautiful side of Islam, not the cruel side that required its followers to conquer and enslave the earth.

However, over the ten-year period that followed my imprisonment, I would watch him struggle with an inner, irrational conflict. On the one hand, he didn't see those Muslims who killed settlers and soldiers and innocent women and children as wrong. He believed that Allah gave them the authority to do that. On the other hand, he personally could not do what they did. Something in his soul rejected it. What he could not justify as right for himself he rationalized as right for others.

But as a child, I saw only his virtues and assumed they were the fruit of his beliefs. Because I wanted to be just like him, I believed what he believed without question. What I didn't know at the time was that no matter how much we weighed on Allah's scale, all of our righteousness and good works were like filthy rags to God.

Even so, the Muslims I saw in Megiddo bore no resemblance to my father. They judged people as if they thought they were greater than Allah himself. They were mean and petty, blocking a television screen to prevent us from seeing a bareheaded actress. They were bigots and hypocrites, torturing those who got too many red points—though only the weakest, most vulnerable people seemed to accumulate these points. Prisoners who were well connected walked with immunity—even a confessed Israeli collaborator, if he was the son of Sheikh Hassan Yousef.

For the first time, I began to question things I had always believed in.

"Eight twenty-three!"

It was time for my trial. I had been in prison for six months. The IDF drove me to Jerusalem, where the prosecutors asked the judge to sentence me to sixteen months.

Sixteen months! The Shin Bet captain had promised me I would have to stay in prison for only a short time! What did I do to deserve such a harsh sentence? Sure, I had a crazy idea and bought a few guns. But they were worthless guns that didn't even work!

"Sixteen months."

The courts gave me credit for the time I already had served, and I was sent back to Megiddo for my final ten months.

"Okay," I told Allah. "I could serve another ten months, but please not there! Not in hell!" But there was no one I could complain to—certainly not the Israeli security guys who had recruited and then abandoned me.

At least I was able to see my family once a month. My mother made the grueling trip to Megiddo every four weeks. She was permitted to bring only three of my brothers and sisters, so they took turns. And every time, she brought me a fresh batch of delicious spinach patties and baklava. My family never missed a visit.

Seeing them was a great relief for me, even though I couldn't share what was happening inside the fence and behind the curtains. And seeing me seemed to ease their suffering a little as well. I had been like a father to my little brothers and sisters—cooking for them, cleaning up after them, bathing and dressing them, taking them to and from school—and in prison I had also become a hero of the resistance. They were very proud of me.

During one visit, my mother told me that the Palestinian Authority had released my dad. I knew that he had always wanted to make hajj—a pilgrimage to Mecca—and my mother said he had set out for Saudi Arabia shortly after returning home. Hajj is the fifth pillar of the Islamic religion, and every Muslim who is physically and financially able is required to make the trip at least once during his or her lifetime. More than two million go every year.

But my father never made it. Crossing the Allenby Bridge between Israel and Jordan, he was arrested again, this time by the Israelis.

One afternoon, the Hamas faction at Megiddo presented prison officials with a list of petty demands, gave them twenty-four hours to meet them, and threatened to riot if they didn't.

Obviously, prison officials didn't want an uprising. A riot might end up with prisoners being shot, and the government bureaucrats in Jerusalem didn't want to have to deal with the big fuss that would be made by the Red Cross and the human rights organizations if that happened. Riots were a lose-lose scenario for everybody concerned. So the Israelis met with the main shaweesh, who was billeted in our section.

"We cannot work like this," the prison officials told him. "Give us more time, and we'll work something out."

"No," he insisted. "You have twenty-four hours."

Of course, the Israelis could not show weakness by giving in. And, frankly, I didn't know what all the fuss was about. Even though I was miserable here, compared to other facilities I had heard about, Megiddo was a five-star prison. The demands seemed silly and pointless to me—more phone time, longer visiting hours, that sort of thing.

Throughout the day, we waited as the sun moved across the sky. And as the deadline passed, Hamas told us to prepare to riot.

"What are we supposed to do?" we asked.

"Just be destructive and violent! Break up the blacktop and throw the pieces at the soldiers. Throw soap. Throw hot water. Throw anything you can lift!"

Some guys filled containers with water so that if the soldiers threw gas canisters, we could grab them and drop them into the buckets. We started chopping up the exercise area. All at once, the sirens went off and things became very dangerous. Hundreds of soldiers in riot gear deployed throughout the camp and aimed their weapons at us through the perimeter fence.

The only thing that kept running through my mind was how insane this all seemed to be. *Why are we doing this?* I wondered. *This is crazy! Just because of that lunatic shaweesh?* I wasn't a coward, but this was pointless. The Israelis were heavily armed and protected, and we were going to throw chunks of tar.

Hamas gave the signal, and prisoners in every section started throwing wood, blacktop, and soap. Within seconds, a hundred black gas canisters flew into the sections and exploded, filling the camp with thick white fog. I couldn't see anything. The stink was indescribable. Guys all around me dropped to the ground and gasped for fresh air.

All of this occurred in only three minutes. And the Israelis had just started.

Soldiers aimed big pipes at us that spewed billows of yellow gas. But that stuff didn't blow around in the air like the tear gas; being heavier than air, it hugged the ground and pushed all the oxygen away. Prisoners began to pass out.

I was trying to catch my breath when I saw the fire.

The Islamic Jihad tent in Quadrant Three was burning. Within seconds, the flames shot twenty feet into the air. The tents were treated with some kind of petroleum-based waterproofing and burned as if they were soaked with petrol. The wooden poles and frames, mattresses, footlockers—all went up in flames. The wind spread the fire to the DFLP/PFLP and Fatah tents, and ten seconds later, they, too, were swallowed by the inferno.

The raging fire was moving our way very quickly. A huge piece of crackling tent flew into the air and over the razor wire. Soldiers surrounded us. There was no way to escape except through the flames.

So we ran.

I covered my face with a towel and raced for the kitchen area. There was only ten feet between the burning tents and the wall. More than two hundred of us tried to pass through at once as the soldiers continued to saturate the section with the yellow gas.

Within minutes, half of Section Five was gone—everything we owned, what little there had been. Nothing left but ashes.

Many prisoners were hurt. Miraculously, no one had been killed. Ambulances came to collect the injured, and after the riots, those of us whose tents had burned were relocated. I was moved to the middle Hamas tent in Quadrant Two.

The only good that came out of the Megiddo riots was that the torture by Hamas leaders stopped. Surveillance continued, but we felt a little more at ease and allowed ourselves to become a little more careless. I made a couple of friends whom I thought I might be able to trust. But mostly, I walked around for hours by myself doing nothing, day after day.

"Eight twenty-three!"

On September 1, 1997, a prison guard returned my belongings and the little bit of money I had when I was arrested, handcuffed me, and put me in a van. The soldiers drove to the first checkpoint they came to in Palestinian territory, which was Jenin in the West Bank. They opened the door of the van and removed the handcuffs.

"You're free to go," one of the men said. And then they drove off in the direction we had come from, leaving me standing alone on the side of the road.

I couldn't believe it. It was wonderful just to walk outside. I was eager to see my mother and my brothers and sisters. I was still a two-hour drive away from home, but I didn't want to walk quickly. I wanted to savor my freedom.

I strolled a couple of miles, filling my lungs with free air and my ears with sweet silence. Beginning to feel human again, I found a taxi that took me to the center of a town. Another taxi took me to Nablus, then to Ramallah and home.

Driving down the streets of Ramallah, seeing familiar shops and people, I longed to jump out of the taxi and lose myself in it all. Before I stepped out of the taxi in front of my house, I caught a glimpse of my mother standing in the doorway. Tears rolled down her cheeks as she called out to me. She ran toward the car and threw her arms around me. As she clung to me and patted my back, my shoulders, my face, and my head, all the pain she had held in for nearly a year and a half poured out of her.

"We've been counting the days until your return," she said. "We were so worried we might never see you again. We are so very proud of you, Mosab. You are a true hero."

Like my father, I knew I could not tell her or my brothers and sisters what I had gone through. It would have been too painful for them. To them I was a hero who had been in an Israeli prison with all the other heroes, and now I was home. They even saw it as a good experience for me, almost a rite of passage. Did my mother find out about the guns? Yes. Did she think it was stupid? Probably, but it all came under the heading of the resistance and was rationalized away.

We celebrated the entire day of my return and ate wonderful food and joked and had fun, as we always did when we were together. It was almost as though I had never been away. And over the next few days, many of my friends and my father's friends came to rejoice with us.

I stayed around the house for a few weeks, soaking up the love and stuffing myself with my mother's cooking. Then I went out and enjoyed all the other sights, sounds, and smells I had missed so much. In the evenings I spent time hanging out downtown with my friends—eating falafel at Mays Al Reem and drinking coffee at the Kit Kat with Basam Huri, the shop's owner. As I walked the busy streets and talked with my friends, I inhaled the peace and simplicity of freedom.

Between my father's release from the PA prison and his rearrest by the Israelis, my mother had become pregnant again. That was a big surprise for my parents, because they had planned to stop having children after my sister Anhar was born seven years earlier. By the time I got home, my mother was about six months along and the baby was getting big. Then she broke her ankle, and the healing process was very slow because our developing baby brother was consuming all her calcium. We didn't have a wheelchair, so I had to carry her wherever she needed to go. She was in a lot of pain, and it broke my heart to see her that way. I got a driver's license so we could do errands and buy groceries. And when Naser was born, I took on the duties of feeding and bathing him and changing his diapers. He began his life thinking I was his dad.

Needless to say, I had missed my exams and did not graduate from high school. They had offered the exam to all of us in prison, but I was the only one who failed. I could never understand why, because representatives from the Education Ministry came to the prison and gave everybody an answer sheet before the test. It was crazy. One guy who was sixty years old and illiterate had to have someone write down the answers for him. And even he passed! I had the answers, too, plus I had gone to school for twelve years and was familiar with the material. But when the results came, everybody passed except me. The only thing I could figure was that Allah didn't want me to pass by cheating.

So when I got home, I began taking night classes at Al-Ahlia, a Catholic school in Ramallah. Most of the students were traditional Muslims who went because it was the best school in town. And going to school at night enabled me to work during the day at the local Checkers hamburger shop to help take care of my family.

I only got a 64 percent on my exams, but it was enough to pass. I hadn't tried hard because I wasn't very interested in the subject matter. I didn't care. I was just grateful to have that behind me.

Chapter Fifteen

DAMASCUS ROAD

1997–1999

TWO MONTHS AFTER MY RELEASE, my cell phone rang.

"Congratulations," said a voice in Arabic.

I recognized the accent. It was my "faithful" Shin Bet captain, Loai.

"We would love to see you," Loai said, "but we cannot talk long on the phone. Can we meet?"

"Of course."

He gave me a phone number, a password, and some directions. I felt like a real spy. He told me to go to a specific location, and then to another, and then to call him from there.

I followed his instructions, and when I made the call, I was given more directions. I walked for about twenty minutes until a car pulled up beside me and stopped. A man inside the car told me to get in, which I did. I was searched, told to lie down on the floor, and covered with a blanket.

We drove for about an hour, during which time no one spoke. When we finally stopped, we were inside a garage at somebody's house. I was glad it wasn't another military base or a detention center. Actually, I learned later that it was a government-owned house in an Israeli settlement. As soon as I arrived, I was searched again, this time much more thoroughly, and led into a nicely furnished living room. I sat there for a while, and then Loai came in. He shook my hand—and then he hugged me.

"How are you doing? How was your experience in prison?"

I told him I was doing fine and that my prison experience had not been very good, especially since he had told me that I would spend only a short time there.

"I am sorry; we had to do that to protect you."

I thought about my comments to the maj'd about being a double agent and wondered whether Loai knew about them. I figured I had better try to protect myself.

"Look," I said, "they were torturing people in there, and I had no choice but to tell them that I had agreed to work for you. I was afraid. You never warned me about what was going on in there. You never told me I would have to watch out for my own people. You didn't train me, and I was freaking out. So I told them that I promised to be a collaborator so I could become a double agent and kill you guys."

Loai looked surprised, but he wasn't angry. Though the Shin Bet could not condone torture within the prison, they certainly knew about it—and understood why I might have felt afraid.

He called his supervisor and told him everything I had said. And maybe because it was so hard for Israel to recruit members of Hamas or maybe because, as the son of Sheikh Hassan Yousef, I was a particularly valuable prize, they let it go at that.

These Israelis were nothing like I had expected them to be.

Loai gave me a few hundred dollars and told me to go buy myself some clothes, take care of myself, and enjoy my life.

"We'll be in touch later," he said.

What? No secret assignment? No codebook? No gun? Just a wad of cash and a hug? This made no sense at all.

We met again a couple of weeks later, this time at a Shin Bet house in the heart of Jerusalem. Every house was completely furnished, loaded with alarms and guards, and so secret that not even the next-door neighbors had a clue what was going on inside. Most of the rooms were set up for meetings. And I was never allowed to move from one room to another without an escort, not because they didn't trust me, but because they didn't want me to be seen by other Shin Bet guys. Just another layer of security.

During this second meeting, the members of Shin Bet were extremely friendly. They spoke Arabic well, and it was clear they understood me, my family, and my culture. I had no information, and they asked for none. We simply talked about life in general.

This was not at all what I had expected. I really wanted to know what they wanted me to do, though because of the files I had read in prison, I was also a bit afraid they might tell me to do something like have sex with my sister or my neighbor and bring them the video. But there was never anything like that.

After the second meeting, Loai gave me twice as much money as the first time. In a month's time, I had gotten about eight hundred dollars from him, an awful lot of money for a twenty-year-old to earn at the time. And still I had given the Shin Bet nothing in return. In fact, during my first few months as a Shin Bet agent, I learned much more than I shared.

My training started with some basic rules. I was not to commit adultery because this could expose—or burn—me. In fact, I was told not to have any out-of-wedlock relationship with a woman at all—Palestinian or Israeli—while I was working for them. If I did, I would be gone. And I wasn't to tell anyone my double-agent story anymore.

Every time we met, I learned more about life and justice and security. The Shin Bet was not trying to break me down to make me do bad things. They actually seemed to be doing their best to build me up, to make me stronger and wiser.

As time went on, I began to question my plan to kill the Israelis.

These people were being so kind. They clearly cared about me. *Why would I want to kill them?* I was surprised to realize that I no longer did.

The occupation had not gone away. The cemetery in Al-Bireh was still being filled with the bodies of Palestinian men, women, and children killed by Israeli soldiers. And I had not forgotten the beating I suffered on the way to prison or the days I was chained to that little chair.

But I also remembered the screams from the torture tents at Megiddo and the man who nearly impaled himself on the razor-wire fence trying to escape his Hamas tormentors. Now I was gaining understanding and wisdom. And who were my mentors? My enemies! But were they really? Or were they only nice to me so they could use me? I was even more confused than before.

During one meeting, Loai said, "Since you are working with us, we are thinking about releasing your father so you can be close to him and see what is going on in the territories." I didn't know that had even been a possibility, but I was happy to be getting my dad back.

In later years, my father and I would compare notes about our experiences. He did not like to go into detail about the things he suffered, but he wanted me to know that he had set some things right during his time at Megiddo. He told me about a time when he had been watching television in the mi'var when somebody dropped a board over the screen.

"I am not going to watch TV if you keep covering the screen with that board," he told the emir. They hauled up the board, and that was the end of that. And when he was moved to the prison camp, he was even able to put an end to the torture. He ordered the maj'd to give him all their files, studied them, and found that at least 60 percent of the suspected collaborators were innocent. So he made sure their families and their communities were told about the false accusations. One of the innocent men was Akel Sorour.

The certificate of innocence my father sent to Akel's village could not erase what he had suffered, but at least he was able to live in peace and honor.

After my father was released from prison, my uncle Ibrahim came to visit. My dad also wanted him to know that he had ended the torture at Megiddo and found that most of the men whose lives and families had been ruined by the maj'd were innocent. Ibrahim pretended to be shocked. And when my father mentioned Akel, my uncle said he had tried to defend him and told the maj'd there was no way Akel was a collaborator.

"Allah be praised," Ibrahim said, "that you helped him out!"

I couldn't stand his hypocrisy, and I left the room.

My father also let me know that during his time at Megiddo, he had heard about the double-agent story I had told the maj'd. But he wasn't angry with me. He simply told me that I had been foolish to even talk with them in the first place.

"I know, Father," I said. "I promise you don't have to worry about me. I can take care of myself."

"That's good to hear," he said. "Please just be more careful from now on. There is no one I trust more than you."

When we met later that month, Loai told me, "It's time you get started. Here is what we want you to do."

Finally, I thought.

"Your assignment is to go to college and get your bachelor's degree."

He handed me an envelope filled with money.

"That should cover your schooling and your expenses," he said. "If you need more, please let me know."

I couldn't believe it. But for the Israelis, it made perfect sense. My education, inside and outside the classroom, was a good investment for them. It wouldn't be very prudent for national security to work with someone who was uneducated and had no prospects. It was also dangerous for me to be perceived as a loser because the wisdom on the streets of the territories was that only losers worked with the Israelis. Obviously, this wisdom had not been very well thought out because losers had nothing to offer the Shin Bet.

So I applied to Birzeit University, but they would not accept me because my high school grades were too low. I explained that there had been exceptional circumstances and that I had been in prison. I was an intelligent young man, I argued, and would be a good student. But they didn't make exceptions. My only option was to enroll at Al-Quds Open University and study at home.

This time, I did well in school. I was a little bit wiser and a lot more motivated. And who did I have to thank? My enemy.

Whenever I met with my Shin Bet handlers, they told me, "If you need anything, just let us know. You can go purify yourself. You can pray. You don't need to be afraid." The food and drink they offered me did not violate Islamic law. My handlers were very careful to avoid doing anything they knew to be offensive to me: They didn't wear shorts. They didn't sit with their legs on the desk and their feet in my face. They were always very respectful. And because of this, I wanted to learn more from them. They didn't behave like military machines. They were human beings, and they treated me like a human being. Nearly every time we met, another stone in the foundation of my worldview crumbled.

My culture—not my father—had taught me that the IDF and the Israeli people were my enemies. My father didn't see soldiers; he saw individual men doing what they believed to be their duty as soldiers. His problem was not with people but with the ideas that motivated and drove the people.

Loai was more like my father than any Palestinian I had ever met. He did not believe in Allah, but he respected me anyway.

So who was my enemy now?

I talked with the Shin Bet about the torture at Megiddo. They told me they knew all about it. Every move of the prisoners, everything anyone said, was recorded. They knew about the secret messages in dough balls and the torture tents and the hole cut in the fence.

"Why didn't you stop it?"

"First of all, we cannot change that kind of mentality. It is not our job to teach Hamas to love one another. We cannot come in and say, 'Hey, don't torture one another; don't kill each other,' and make everything okay. Second, Hamas destroys itself more from the inside than anything Israel can do to it from the outside."

The world I knew was relentlessly eroding, revealing another world that I was just beginning to understand. Every time I met with the Shin Bet, I learned something new, something about my life, about others. It wasn't brainwashing through mind-numbing repetition, starvation, and sleep deprivation. What the Israelis were teaching me was more logical and more real than anything I had ever heard from my own people.

My father had never taught me any of this because he had always been in prison. And honestly, I suspected he could not have taught me these things anyway because my father did not know much of it himself.

Among the seven ancient gates that offer access through the walls of the Old City of Jerusalem, one is more ornate than all the others. The Damascus Gate, constructed by Suleiman the Magnificent nearly five hundred years ago, is situated near the middle of the northern wall. Significantly, it brings people into the Old City at the border where the historic Muslim Quarter meets the Christian Quarter.

In the first century, a man named Saul of Tarsus passed through an earlier version of this gate on his way to Damascus, where he planned to lead a brutal suppression of a new Jewish sect he considered heretical. The targets of this persecution would come to be called Christians. A surprising encounter not only kept Saul from reaching his destination, it also forever changed his life.

With all the history that permeates the atmosphere in this ancient spot, maybe I shouldn't have been surprised to have a life-changing encounter there myself. Indeed, one day my best friend Jamal and I were walking past the Damascus Gate. Suddenly I heard a voice directed toward me.

"What's your name?" a guy who looked to be about thirty asked in Arabic, though clearly he was not an Arab.

"My name is Mosab."

"Where are you going, Mosab?"

"We're going home. We're from Ramallah."

"I'm from the United Kingdom," he said, switching to English. Though he continued speaking, his accent was so thick that I had trouble understanding him. After a little back-and-forth, I figured out he was talking about something to do with Christianity and a study group that met at the YMCA by the King David Hotel in West Jerusalem.

I knew where it was. I was a little bored at the time and thought it might actually be interesting to learn about Christianity. If I could learn so much from the Israelis, maybe other "infidels" might have something valuable to teach me as well. Besides, after hanging out with nominal Muslims, zealots, and atheists, the educated and the ignorant, right-wingers and left-wingers, Jews and Gentiles, I wasn't picky anymore. And this guy seemed like a simple man who was inviting me just to come and talk, not to vote for Jesus in the next election.

"What do you think?" I asked Jamal. "Should we go?"

Jamal and I had known each other since we were very young. We went to school together, threw stones together, and attended mosque together. Six foot three and handsome, Jamal never spoke much. He rarely started a conversation, but he was an outstanding listener. And we never argued, not even once.

In addition to growing up together, we had been together in Megiddo Prison. After Section Five burned during the riots, Jamal was transferred with my cousin Yousef to Section Six and released from there.

Prison, however, had changed him. He stopped praying and going to mosque, and he started smoking. He was depressed and spent most of his time just sitting at home watching TV. At least I had beliefs to hold on to while I was in prison. But Jamal was from a secular family that didn't practice Islam, so his faith was too thin to hold him together.

Now Jamal looked at me, and I could tell he wanted to go to the Bible study. He was clearly just as curious—and bored—as I was. But something inside him resisted.

"You go on without me," he said. "Call me when you get home."

There were about fifty of us who met inside an old storefront that night, mostly students about my age of various ethnic and religious backgrounds. A couple of people translated the English presentation into Arabic and Hebrew.

I called Jamal when I got home.

"How was it?" he asked.

"It was great," I said. "They gave me a New Testament written in both Arabic and English. New people, new culture; it was fun."

"I don't know about this, Mosab," Jamal said. "It could be danger- ous for you if people discovered you were hanging out with a bunch of Christians."

I knew Jamal meant well, but I wasn't really very worried. My father had always taught us to be open-minded and loving toward everyone, even those who didn't believe as we did. I looked down at the Bible in my lap. My father had a huge library of five thousand books, including a Bible. When I was a kid, I had read the sexual passages in the Song of Solomon, but never went any further. This New Testament, however, was a gift. Because gifts are honored and respected in Arab culture, I decided the least I could do was to read it.

I began at the beginning, and when I got to the Sermon on the Mount, I thought, *Wow, this guy Jesus is really impressive! Everything he says is beautiful.* I couldn't put the book down. Every verse seemed to touch a deep wound in my life. It was a very simple message, but somehow it had the power to heal my soul and give me hope.

Then I read this: "You have heard that it was said, 'Love your neighbor and hate your enemy.' But I tell you: Love your enemies and pray for those who persecute you, that you may be sons of your Father in heaven" (Matthew 5:43-45).

That's it! I was thunderstruck by these words. Never before had I heard anything like this, but I knew that this was the message I had been searching for all my life.

For years I had struggled to know who my enemy was, and I had looked for enemies outside of Islam and Palestine. But I suddenly realized that the Israelis were not my enemies. Neither was Hamas nor my uncle Ibrahim nor the kid who beat me with the butt of his M16 nor the apelike guard in the detention center. I saw that enemies were not defined by nationality, religion, or color. I understood that we all share the same common enemies: greed, pride, and all the bad ideas and the darkness of the devil that live inside us.

That meant I could love anyone. The only real enemy was the enemy inside me.

Five years earlier, I would have read the words of Jesus and thought, *What an idiot!* and thrown away the Bible. But my experiences with my crazy butcher neighbor, the family members and religious leaders who beat me when my father was in prison, and my own time at Megiddo had all combined to prepare me for the power and beauty of this truth. All I could think in response was, *Wow! What wisdom this man had!*

Jesus said, "Do not judge, or you too will be judged" (Matthew 7:1). What a difference between him and Allah! Islam's god was very judgmental, and Arab society followed Allah's lead.

Jesus rebuked the hypocrisy of the scribes and Pharisees, and I thought of my uncle. I remembered a time when he received an invitation to attend a special event and how angry he had been that he was not given the best seat. It was as though Jesus was talking to Ibrahim and every sheikh and imam in Islam.

Everything Jesus said on the pages of this book made perfect sense to me. Overwhelmed, I started to cry.

God used the Shin Bet to show me that Israel was not my enemy, and now he put the answers to the rest of my questions right in my hands in that little New Testament. But I had a long way to go in my understanding of the Bible. Muslims are taught to believe in all of God's books, both the Torah and the Bible. But we are also taught that men have changed the Bible, making it unreliable. The Qur'an, Mohammad said, was God's final and inerrant word to man. So I would first have to abandon my belief that the Bible had been altered. Then I would have to figure out how to make both books work in my life, to somehow put Islam and Christianity together. No small challenge—reconciling the irreconcilable.

At the same time, while I believed in the teachings of Jesus, I still did not connect him with being God. Even so, my standards had changed suddenly and dramatically, because they were being influenced by the Bible instead of the Qur'an.

I continued to read my New Testament and go to the Bible study. I attended church services and thought, *This is not the religious Christianity I see in Ramallah. This is real.* The Christians I had known before had been no different from traditional Muslims. They claimed a religion, but they didn't live it.

I began spending more time with people from the Bible study and found myself really enjoying their fellowship. We had such a good time talking about our lives, our backgrounds, our beliefs. They were always very respectful of my culture and my Muslim heritage. And I found that I could really be myself when I was with them.

I ached to bring what I was learning into my own culture, because I realized that the occupation was not to blame for our suffering. Our problem was much bigger than armies and politics.

I asked myself what Palestinians would do if Israel disappeared— if everything not only went back to the way it was before 1948 but if all the Jewish people abandoned the Holy Land and were scattered again. And for the first time, I knew the answer.

We would still fight. Over nothing. Over a girl without a head scarf. Over who was toughest and most important. Over who would make the rules and who would get the best seat.

It was the end of 1999. I was twenty-one years old. My life had begun to change, and the more I learned, the more confused I became.

"God, the Creator, show me the truth," I prayed day after day. "I'm confused. I'm lost. And I don't know which way to go."

Chapter Sixteen

SECOND INTIFADA
SUMMER-FALL 2000

HAMAS—once the ascendant power among Palestinians—was in shambles. The shattered organization's bitter rival for hearts and minds was now in complete control.

Through intrigue and deal making, the Palestinian Authority had accomplished what Israel had been unable to do through sheer might. It had destroyed the military wing of Hamas and thrown its leadership and fighters into prison. Even after they were released, the Hamas members went home and did nothing more against the PA or the occupation. The young feda'iyeen were exhausted. Their leaders were divided and deeply suspicious of one another.

My father was on his own again, so he went back to working in the mosque and the refugee camps. Now when he spoke, he did so in the name of Allah, not as the leader of Hamas. After years of separation through our respective imprisonments, I relished the opportunity to travel and spend time with him once again. I had missed our long talks about life and Islam.

As I continued to read my Bible and spend time learning about Christianity, I found that I was really drawn to the grace, love, and humility that Jesus talked about. Surprisingly, it was those same character traits that drew people to my father—one of the most devoted Muslims I had ever known.

As for my relationship with the Shin Bet, now that Hamas was virtually out of the picture and the PA was keeping things calm, there seemed to be nothing for me to do. We were just friends now. They could let me go whenever they wanted to, or I could say good-bye to them at any time.

The Camp David Summit between Yasser Arafat, American president Bill Clinton, and Israeli prime minister Ehud Barak ended on July 25, 2000. Barak had offered Arafat about 90 percent of the West Bank, the entire Gaza Strip, and East Jerusalem as the capital of a new Palestinian state. In addition, a new international fund would be established to compensate Palestinians for the property that had been taken from them. This "land for peace" offer represented a historic opportunity for the long-suffering Palestinian people, something few Palestinians would have dared imagine possible. But even so, it was not enough for Arafat.

Yasser Arafat had grown extraordinarily wealthy as the international symbol of victimhood. He wasn't about to surrender that status and take on the responsibility of actually building a functioning society. So he insisted that all the refugees be permitted to return to the lands they had owned prior to 1967—a condition he was confident Israel would not accept.

Though Arafat's rejection of Barak's offer constituted a historic catastrophe for his people, the Palestinian leader returned to his hard-line supporters as a hero who had thumbed his nose at the president of the United States, as someone who had not backed down and settled for less, and as a leader who stood tough against the entire world.

Arafat went on television, and the world watched as he talked about his love for the Palestinian people and his grief over millions of families living in the squalor of the refugee camps. Now that I was traveling with my father and attending meetings with Arafat, I began to see for myself how much the man loved the media attention. He seemed to relish being portrayed as some kind of Palestinian Che Guevara and a peer of kings, presidents, and prime ministers.

Yasser Arafat made it clear that he wanted to be a hero who was written about in the history books. But as I watched him, I often thought, *Yes, let him be remembered in our history books, not as a hero, but as a traitor who sold out his people for a ride on their shoulders. As a reverse Robin Hood, who plundered the poor and made himself rich. As a cheap ham, who bought his place in the limelight with Palestinian blood.*

It was also interesting to see Arafat through the eyes of my contacts in Israeli intelligence. "What is this guy doing?" my Shin Bet handler asked me one day. "We never thought our leaders would give up what they offered Arafat. Never! And he said no?"

Indeed, Arafat had been handed the keys to peace in the Middle East along with real nationhood for the Palestinian people—and he had thrown them away. As a result, the status quo of quiet corruption continued. But things would not remain quiet for long. For Arafat, there always seemed to be more to gain if Palestinians were bleeding. Another intifada would surely get the blood flowing and the Western news cameras rolling once again.

Conventional wisdom among the world's governments and news organizations tells us that the bloody uprising known as the Second Intifada was a spontaneous eruption of Palestinian rage triggered by General Ariel Sharon's visit to what Israel calls the Temple Mount complex. As usual, the conventional wisdom is wrong.

—

The evening of September 27, my father knocked at my door and asked if I would drive him to Marwan Barghouti's house the next morning after dawn prayer.

Marwan Barghouti was secretary-general of Fatah, the largest political faction of the PLO. He was a charismatic young Palestinian leader, a strong advocate of a Palestinian state, and a foe of the corruption and human rights abuses of the PA and Arafat's security forces. A short, casual man who wore blue jeans most of the time, Marwan was favored to be the next Palestinian president.

"What's going on?" I asked my dad.

"Sharon is scheduled to visit the Al-Aqsa Mosque tomorrow, and the PA believes this is a good opportunity to launch an uprising."

Ariel Sharon was the leader of the conservative Likud Party and the political nemesis of Prime Minister Ehud Barak's left-leaning Labor Party. Sharon was in the middle of a close political race in which he was challenging Barak for leadership of the Israeli government.

An uprising? Were they serious? The PA leaders who put my father into prison were now asking him to help start another intifada. It was galling, though it wasn't difficult to deduce why they approached my father about this plan. They knew the people loved and trusted him as much as—if not more than—they hated and distrusted the PA. They would follow my father anywhere, and the leadership knew it.

They also knew that Hamas, like a worn-out boxer, was down for the count. They wanted my father to pick it up, splash water in its face, and send it in for another round so the PA could knock it cold again before a cheering crowd. Even the Hamas leaders—weary from years of conflict—warned my father to watch out.

"Arafat only wants to use us as fuel for his political furnace," they told him. "Don't go too far with this new intifada of his."

But my father understood the importance of making this gesture. If he didn't at least appear to be working with the PA, they would simply point the finger at Hamas, blaming us for disrupting the peace process.

Regardless of what we did, we seemed to be in a lose-lose situation, and I was deeply concerned about the plan. But I knew my father needed to do this, so the next morning I drove him to Marwan Barghouti's house. We knocked on the door, got no immediate response, and eventually learned that Marwan was still in bed.

Typical, I said to myself. *Fatah involves my father in their stupid plans and then can't even be bothered to get out of bed to help carry them out.*

"Never mind," I told my father. "Don't bother. Get into the car, and I'll take you to Jerusalem."

Of course, driving my father to the site of Sharon's visit was risky, given that most Palestinian cars were not allowed to enter Jerusalem. Ordinarily, if a Palestinian driver was caught by the Israeli police, he would be fined, but given who we were, my father and I would probably be arrested on the spot. I had to be very careful, keeping to the side roads and trusting that my Shin Bet connections would protect me if necessary.

The Al-Aqsa Mosque and the Dome of the Rock are built on the rubble and remains of two ancient Jewish Temples—the Temple of Solomon from the tenth century BC and Herod the Great's Temple from the time of Christ. Thus it is with good reason that some have described this rocky hill as the most volatile thirty-five acres on earth. The place is holy to all three of the world's great monotheistic religions. But from a scientific and historical standpoint, it is also a site of enormous archaeological significance—even to the most hardened of atheists.

In the weeks prior to Sharon's visit to the site, the Muslim Waqf—governing Islamic authority there—had closed off the Temple Mount entirely to any archaeological oversight by the Israel Antiquities Authority. Then in carrying out construction work on new underground mosques at the site, they brought in heavy earthmoving equipment. The evening news in Israel carried images of bulldozers, backhoes, and dump trucks working in and upon the site. Over the course of several weeks, dump trucks moved some thirteen thousand tons of rubble from the Temple Mount complex to city garbage dumps. News reports from the dumps showed archaeologists shaking their heads in disbelief as they held up remnants of artifacts retrieved from the rubble, some of them dating back to the First and Second Temple periods.

To many Israelis, it seemed clear that the intention was to turn the entire thirty-five-acre compound into an exclusively Muslim site by erasing every sign, remnant, and memory of its Jewish past. This included the destruction of any archaeological findings that represented evidence of that history.

Sharon's visit was designed to deliver a silent but clear message to Israeli voters: "I'll put a stop to this unnecessary destruction." In planning the trip, Sharon's people had received assurances from Palestinian security chief Jibril Rajoub that his visit would not be a problem as long as he did not set foot in a mosque.

My father and I got to the site a few minutes before Sharon's arrival. It was a quiet morning. A hundred or so Palestinians had come to pray. Sharon arrived during normal tourist hours with a Likud delegation and about a thousand riot police. He came, he looked around, and he left. He said nothing. He never entered the mosque.

It all seemed like a big nonevent to me. On the way back to Ramallah, I asked my father what the big deal had been.

"What happened?" I said. "You didn't start an intifada."

"Not yet," he answered. "But I have called some activists in the Islamic student movement and asked them to meet me here for a protest."

"Nothing happened in Jerusalem, so now you want to demonstrate in Ramallah? That's crazy," I told him.

"We have to do what we have to do. Al-Aqsa is our mosque, and Sharon had no business being there. We cannot allow this."

I wondered if he was trying to convince me or himself.

The demonstration in Ramallah was anything but a dramatic spectacle of spontaneous combustion. It was still early in the day, and people were walking around town as usual, wondering what was up with these students and guys from Hamas who didn't even seem to know what they were protesting.

A number of men stood up with bullhorns and made speeches, and the small group of Palestinians who had gathered around them occasionally broke out into chanting and shouting. But for the most part, nobody really seemed to care too deeply. Things had calmed down quite a bit within the Palestinian territories. Every day was simply occupation as usual. Israeli soldiers had become a fixture. Palestinians were allowed to work and go to school inside Israel. Ramallah enjoyed a thriving nightlife, so it was difficult to figure out what these guys were all worked up about.

As far as I was concerned, this demonstration seemed like another nonevent. So I called some of my friends from Bible study, and we headed up to Galilee to camp out at the lake.

Cut off from any source of news, I didn't know that on the following morning a large number of rock-throwing Palestinian demonstrators clashed with Israeli riot police near the site of Sharon's visit. The rock throwing escalated to lobbing Molotov cocktails, and then gunfire with Kalashnikovs. Police used rubber-coated metal bullets and, by some reports, live ammunition to disperse the demonstrators. Four protesters were killed, and about two hundred more were injured. Fourteen police personnel were injured as well. And all of this was precisely what the Palestinian Authority had counted on happening.

The next day, I received a telephone call from the Shin Bet.

"Where are you?"

"I'm in Galilee camping with some friends."

"Galilee! What? You're crazy!" Loai started to laugh. "You are really unbelievable," he said. "The whole West Bank is upside down and you're out having fun with your Christian friends."

When he told me what had been happening, I jumped in the car and immediately headed home.

Yasser Arafat and the other PA leaders had been determined to spark another intifada. They had been planning it for months, even as Arafat and Barak had been meeting with President Clinton at Camp David. They had simply been waiting for a suitable triggering pretext. Sharon's visit provided just such an excuse. So after a couple of false starts, the Al-Aqsa Intifada began in earnest and the tinderbox of passions in the West Bank and Gaza were inflamed once again. Especially in Gaza.

There, Fatah launched demonstrations that resulted in the globally televised death of a twelve-year-old boy named Mohammed al-Dura. The boy and his father, Jamal, had gotten caught in the cross fire and taken cover behind a concrete cylinder. The boy was hit by a stray bullet and died in his father's arms. The entire heartrending scene was captured by a Palestinian cameraman working for French public television. Within hours, the video clip had circled the globe and enraged millions against the Israeli occupation.

In the ensuing months, however, there would be a heated international controversy over this event. Some cited evidence that Palestinian gunfire was actually responsible for the boy's death. Others continued to blame the Israelis. There were even some who argued that the film was a carefully staged hoax. Since the footage did not actually show the boy being shot or even his body, many suspected a propaganda ploy by the PLO. If the latter was the case, it was brilliant and effective.

Whatever the truth, I suddenly found myself caught awkwardly in the middle of a war in which my father was a key leader—albeit a leader who had no idea what he was leading or where it would lead him. He was simply being used and manipulated by Arafat and Fatah to start trouble, thereby providing the PA with fresh bargaining chips and fund-raising fodder.

Meanwhile, people were once again dying at the checkpoints. All sides were shooting indiscriminately. Children were being killed. Day after bloody day, a tearful Yasser Arafat stood before the Western news cameras wringing his hands and denying that he had anything to do with the violence. Instead, he pointed his finger at my father, at Marwan Barghouti, and at the people in the refugee camps. He assured the world that he was doing everything he could to put down the uprising. But all the time, his other finger was resting firmly on the trigger.

Soon, however, Arafat discovered he had released a terrible genie. He had shaken the Palestinian people awake and stirred them up because doing so suited his purposes. But it wasn't long before they were completely out of control. As they saw IDF soldiers shoot down their fathers and mothers and children, the people became so enraged they wouldn't listen to the PA or anybody else.

Arafat also discovered that the battered boxer he had set back on its feet was made of sterner stuff than he had imagined. The streets were the natural environment for Hamas. The boxer had gotten its start there, and it was there that it was at its strongest.

Peace with Israel? Camp David? Oslo? Half of Jerusalem? Forget all of it! Any mood for compromise had evaporated in the white-hot furnace of conflict. Palestinians were back to the all-or-nothing mentality of the past. And now it was Hamas rather than Arafat that was fanning the flames.

Tit for tat, the violence escalated. With each passing day, each side's list of grievances grew even as their respective reservoirs of grief overflowed.

- October 8, 2000, Jewish mobs attacked Palestinians in Nazareth. Two Arabs were killed, and dozens were injured. In Tiberias, Jews destroyed a two-hundred-year-old mosque.

- October 12, a Palestinian mob killed two IDF soldiers in Ramallah. Israel retaliated by bombing Gaza, Ramallah, Jericho, and Nablus.
- November 2, a car bomb killed two Israelis near the Mahane Yehuda market in Jerusalem. Ten others were injured.
- November 5, the thirty-eighth day of the Al-Aqsa Intifada is marked, with more than 150 Palestinians among the dead so far.
- November 11, an Israeli helicopter detonated an explosive device that had been planted in the car of a Hamas activist.
- November 20, a roadside bomb exploded alongside a bus carrying children to school. Two Israelis were killed. Nine others, including five children, were injured.[5]

I couldn't believe what I was seeing. Something had to be done to stop this rolling madness. I knew the time had come for me to begin working with Shin Bet. And I went at it with all my heart.

Chapter Seventeen

UNDERCOVER

2000–2001

WHAT I AM ABOUT TO REVEAL has, until now, been unknown to all except a handful in Israeli intelligence. I am disclosing this information in the hope that it will shed light on a number of significant events that have long been shrouded in mystery.

On the day of decision—the day I decided to do all I could to stop the madness—I began by learning everything I could about the activities and plans of Marwan Barghouti and the Hamas leaders. I told everything I learned to the Shin Bet, which was doing all it could to find these leaders.

Within the Shin Bet, I had been assigned the code name the Green Prince. *Green* reflected the color of the Hamas flag, and *prince* was an obvious reference to the position of my father—a king within Hamas. Thus, at the age of twenty-two, I became the Shin Bet's only Hamas insider who could infiltrate Hamas's military and political wings, as well as other Palestinian factions.

But this responsibility was not all on my shoulders. It was clear to me by now that God had specifically placed me at the core of both Hamas and Palestinian leadership, in Yasser Arafat's meetings, and with the Israeli security service for a reason. I was in a unique position to do the job. And I could feel that God was with me.

I wanted to go deep, to know everything that was going on. I had been in the center of the First Intifada, surrounded by violence. The dead had filled to capacity a cemetery in which I had played soccer as a child. I threw stones. I violated curfew. But I didn't understand why our people pursued violence. Now I wanted to know why we were doing it all over again. I needed to understand.

From Yasser Arafat's perspective, the uprising seemed to be all about politics, money, and holding on to power. He was a grand manipulator, the Palestinian puppet master. On camera, he condemned Hamas for its attacks against civilians inside Israel. Hamas did not represent the PA or the Palestinian people, he insisted. But he did little to interfere, content to let Hamas do his dirty work and take the heat from the international community. He had become a sly old politician who knew that Israel could not stop the attacks without partnering with the PA. And the more attacks there were, the sooner Israel would come to the bargaining table.

During that time, a new group appeared on the scene. It called itself the Al-Aqsa Martyrs Brigades. IDF soldiers and settlers were its targets of choice. But nobody knew who these guys were or where they came from. They seemed religious, though nobody in Hamas or Islamic Jihad knew them. They didn't appear to be nationalist offshoots of the PA or Fatah.

The Shin Bet was as puzzled as everyone else. Once or twice a week, another settler's car or bus was attacked with deadly accuracy. Even heavily armed Israeli soldiers were no match for this group.

One day, Loai called me.

"We have reports of some unidentified men visiting Maher Odeh, and we need you to find out who they are and what their connection to him is. You're the only one we can trust not to screw it up."

Maher Odeh was a top Hamas leader who was wanted badly by the Shin Bet. He was a head of Hamas's security wing within the prison system, and I knew he had been responsible for much of the torture that went on there. I suspected that he was the mover and shaker behind the suicide attacks. Odeh was also a very secretive person, which made it almost impossible for the Shin Bet to gather the evidence necessary to authorize his arrest.

That evening, I drove through central Ramallah. It was Ramadan, and the streets were empty. The sun had set, so everybody was home breaking their daily fast as I pulled into a parking lot down the road from Maher Odeh's apartment building. Though I hadn't been trained for this kind of operation, I knew the basics. In the movies, guys sit in a car across the street from the suspect's home and maintain surveillance with fancy cameras and other spy gear. Though the Shin Bet had extremely sophisticated equipment at their disposal, the only things I had for this mission were my car and my eyes. I simply needed to watch the building and keep track of who came and who went.

After about half an hour, several armed men left the two-story building and entered a new green Chevy with Israeli tags. The whole scene was wrong. First of all, Hamas members, especially those from the military wing, never carried their weapons in public. Second, guys like Maher Odeh didn't hang out with armed men.

I started my car and waited for a couple of cars to pass between us before I pulled out. I followed the green Chevy for a short distance down the main street toward Betunia, where my parents lived, and then I lost them.

I was angry at myself and at the Shin Bet. This was not like the movies. This was real life, and in real life, spying could get you killed. If they wanted me to follow armed men like that, especially at night, they needed to send me some help. This was a job for several people, not just one. I had always assumed that an operation like this would also involve air and satellite surveillance—cool high-tech stuff. But there was just me. I might have gotten lucky, or I might have gotten shot. In this case, I got nothing. I drove home feeling like a man who had just lost a million-dollar business deal.

The next morning I got up, determined to find that car. But after driving around for hours, I came up empty. Frustrated once again, I gave up and decided to wash my car. And there it was—just sitting inside the car wash. Same green Chevy. Same guys. Same guns.

Was this luck or God's intervention or what?

I got a much better look at them now that it was daylight, and I was much closer to them than I had been the night before. With their classy suits, AK-47s, and M16s, I recognized them immediately as Force 17, an elite commando unit that had been around since the early 1970s. These were the guys who watched Arafat's back and protected him from a growing list of wannabes and usurpers.

Something didn't seem right. They couldn't have been the same men I saw at Maher Odeh's place, could they? What would Maher Odeh be doing with gunmen? He didn't have anything to do with Arafat, did he? None of it made any sense.

After they left, I asked the owner of the car wash who they were. He knew I was the son of Hassan Yousef, so he wasn't at all surprised by my questions. He confirmed that they were Force 17 and told me they lived in Betunia. Now I was even more confused. Why did these guys live a couple of minutes from my parents' house instead of in Arafat's compound?

I drove to the address I had gotten from the car-wash owner and found the Chevy parked outside. I hurried back to Shin Bet headquarters and told Loai everything I had discovered. He listened carefully, but his boss kept arguing with me.

"That doesn't make any sense," he said. "Why would Arafat's guards be living outside the compound? You got something wrong."

"I got nothing wrong!" I snapped. I knew this wasn't adding up, and I was frustrated by the fact that although I knew what I had seen, I couldn't explain it. Now this guy was telling me that I hadn't seen it.

"The whole situation is wrong," I told him. "I don't care if this makes sense to you or not. I saw what I saw."

He was indignant that I talked to him like that and stormed out of the meeting. Loai encouraged me to calm down and to go back over all the details one more time. Apparently, the Chevy didn't fit the information they had about the Brigades. It was a stolen Israeli car, which was what PA guys tended to drive, but we couldn't figure out how it connected them with the new faction.

"Are you sure it was a green Chevy?" he asked. "You didn't see a BMW?"

I was sure it was a green Chevy, but I went back to the apartment anyway. There was the Chevy, parked in the same spot. Beside the apartment, however, I saw another car covered by a white sheet. I carefully crept to the side of the building and lifted the back corner of the sheet. Underneath was a 1982 silver BMW.

"Okay, we got 'em!" Loai yelled back into my cell phone when I called to tell him what I had found.

"What are you talking about?"

"Arafat's guards!"

"What do you mean? I thought my information was all wrong," I said with some sarcasm.

"No, you were absolutely right. That BMW has been used in every shooting in the West Bank for the past couple of months."

He went on to explain that this information was a real breakthrough because it was the first proof that the Al-Aqsa Martyrs Brigades was none other than Yasser Arafat's own guards—funded directly by him with taxpayer money from America and international donors. Discovering this link was a huge step toward being able to put a stop to the horrific string of bombings that was killing innocent civilians. The evidence I gave to the Shin Bet would later be used against Arafat before the UN Security Council.[6] Now, all we had to do was catch the members of this new cell—cut off the head of the snake, as the Israelis liked to say.

We learned that the most dangerous members were Ahmad

Ghandour, a leader of the Brigades, and Muhaned Abu Halawa, one of his lieutenants. They had already killed a dozen people. Putting these guys out of business didn't appear to be too difficult a task. We knew who they were and where they lived. And, crucially, they didn't know that we knew.

The IDF launched an unmanned drone to circle the apartment complex and gather intelligence. Two days later, the Brigades made another attack inside Israel, and the Israelis wanted to hit back. The 120 mm cannon of a sixty-five-ton Israeli Merkava battle tank fired twenty shells into the Brigades' building. Unfortunately, no one had bothered to check the surveillance drone to see if the guys were there. They weren't.

Even worse, now they knew that we were on to them. Not surprisingly, they took refuge in Yasser Arafat's compound. We knew they were there, but at that time it was politically impossible to go in and get them. Now their attacks became more frequent and aggressive.

Because he was a leader, Ahmad Ghandour was at the top of the wanted list. After he moved inside the compound, we figured we would never get him. And as it turned out, we didn't. He got himself.

Walking down the street one day, close to the old cemetery in Al-Bireh, I encountered a military funeral.

"Who died?" I asked out of curiosity.

"Somebody from the north," a man said. "I doubt you know him."

"What's his name?"

"His name is Ahmad Ghandour."

I tried to control my excitement and asked casually, "What happened to him? I think I've heard that name before."

"He didn't know his gun was loaded, and he shot himself in the head. They say his brain stuck to the ceiling."

I called Loai.

"Say good-bye to Ahmad Ghandour, because Ahmad Ghandour is dead."

"Did you kill him?"

"Did you give me a gun? No, I didn't kill him. He shot himself. The guy is gone."

Loai couldn't believe it.

"The man is dead. I'm at his funeral."

Throughout the first years of the Al-Aqsa Intifada, I accompanied my father everywhere he went. As his eldest son, I was his protégé, his bodyguard, his confidant, his student, and his friend. And he was my everything—my example of what it meant to be a man. Though our ideologies were clearly no longer the same, I knew that his heart was right and his motives were pure. His love for Muslim people and his devotion to Allah never waned. He ached for peace among his people, and he had spent his entire life working toward that goal.

This second uprising was mostly a West Bank event. Gaza had a few demonstrations, and the death of the young Mohammed al-Dura had touched the flame to the tinder. But it was Hamas that fanned that fire into an inferno in the West Bank.

In every village, town, and city, angry crowds clashed with Israeli soldiers. Every checkpoint became a bloody battlefield. You could scarcely find an individual who had not buried dear friends or family members in recent days.

Meanwhile, the leaders of all the Palestinian factions—top-level, high-profile men—met daily with Yasser Arafat to coordinate their strategies. My father represented Hamas, which had again become the largest and most important organization. He, Marwan Barghouti, and Arafat also met weekly, apart from the others. On several occasions, I was able to accompany my father to those private meetings.

I despised Arafat and what he was doing to the people I loved.

But given my role as a mole for the Shin Bet, it clearly wasn't prudent for me to show my feelings. Still, on one occasion, after Arafat kissed me, I instinctively wiped my cheek. He noticed and was clearly humiliated. My father was embarrassed. And that was the last time my father took me along.

The intifada leaders invariably arrived for those daily meetings in their seventy-thousand-dollar foreign cars, accompanied by other cars filled with bodyguards. But my father always drove in his dark blue 1987 Audi. No bodyguard, just me.

These meetings were the engine that made the intifada run. Although I now had to sit outside the meeting room, I still knew every detail that went on inside because my father took notes. I had access to those notes and made copies. There was never any super-sensitive information in the notes—like the who, where, and when of a military operation. Rather, the leaders always spoke in general terms that revealed patterns and direction, such as focusing an attack inside Israel or targeting settlers or checkpoints.

The meeting notes did, however, include dates for demonstrations. If my father said Hamas would have a demonstration tomorrow at one o'clock in the center of Ramallah, runners would quickly be sent to the mosques, refugee camps, and schools to inform all the Hamas members to be there at one o'clock. Israeli soldiers showed up too. As a result, Muslims, refugees, and, all too often, schoolchildren were killed.

The fact is, Hamas had been all but dead before the Second Intifada. My father should have left it alone. Every day, the people of the Arab nations saw his face and heard his voice on Al-Jazeera TV. He was now the visible leader of the intifada. That made him amazingly popular and important throughout the Muslim world, but it also made him the consummate bad guy as far as Israel was concerned.

At the end of the day, however, Hassan Yousef was not puffed up. He just felt humbly content that he had done the will of Allah.

Reading my father's meeting notes one morning, I saw that a demonstration had been scheduled. The next day, I walked behind him at the head of the deafening mob to an Israeli checkpoint. Two hundred yards before we reached the checkpoint, the leaders peeled off and moved to the safety of a hilltop. Everybody else—the young men and children from the schools—surged forward and began throwing stones at the heavily armed soldiers, who responded by firing into the crowd.

In these situations, even rubber-coated bullets could be deadly. Children were particularly vulnerable. This ammunition was easily lethal when fired at a range closer than the minimum forty meters prescribed by IDF regulations.

As we watched from our perch on the hill, we saw dead and wounded lying everywhere. Soldiers even fired at the arriving ambulances, shooting at drivers and killing those emergency workers trying to get to the wounded. It was brutal.

Soon everybody was shooting. Stones hailed down on the checkpoint. Thousands lunged against the barriers, trying to force their way past the soldiers, straining with one obsession, one thought—to reach the settlement at Beit El and destroy everything and everyone in their path. They were insane with rage triggered by the sight of fallen loved ones and the smell of blood.

Just when it seemed things could not possibly become more chaotic, the 1200 hp diesel engine of a Merkava thundered into the fray. Suddenly, its cannon shattered the air like a sonic boom.

The tank was responding to the PA forces, who had begun shooting toward the IDF soldiers. As the tank advanced, bodyguards grabbed their charges and whisked them to safety. Chunks of bodies littered the hill under our feet as I tried to get my father to the car. When we finally reached it, we quickly raced toward Ramallah, headed for the hospital that was gorged with wounded, dying, and dead. There were not enough rooms. The Red Crescent set up outside in a desperate attempt to stop people from bleeding to death before they could get in. But it was simply not enough.

The hospital walls and floors were smeared with blood. People slipped on it as they made their way down the halls. Husbands and fathers, wives and mothers and children sobbed with grief and shrieked with rage.

Amazingly, in the midst of their sorrow and anger, the people seemed extremely grateful for the Palestinian leaders like my father who had come to share it with them. Yet these were the very Palestinian leaders who had led them and their children like goats to a slaughter and then ducked out of range to watch the carnage from a comfortable distance. That sickened me more than the gore.

And that was only one demonstration. Night after night, we sat in front of the television and listened to the open-ended litany of the dead. Ten in this city. Five there. Twenty more here.

I saw one report of a guy named Shada who was at work drilling a hole in the wall of a building across from a demonstration. An Israeli tank gunner saw him and thought the drill was a gun. He launched a cannon shell that hit Shada's head.

My father and I went to the slain man's house. He had a beautiful new bride. But that was not the worst of it. The Palestinian leaders who had come to comfort the widow began to fight with one another over who would preach at Shada's funeral. Who would be in charge of receiving mourners for three days? Who would be in charge of food for the family? They were all calling Shada "our son," trying to claim that he had been a member of their faction, and trying to prove that their faction was participating in the intifada more than the others.

The competing factions had been reduced to ridiculous bickering over the dead. And most of the time, the dead were people who had nothing at all to do with the movement. They were just people who had been swept up in the tide of emotion. Many others, like Shada, were just in the wrong place at the wrong time.

All the while, Arabs throughout the world burned American and Israeli flags, demonstrated, and poured billions of dollars into the Palestinian territories to crush the occupation. In the first two and a half years of the Second Intifada, Saddam Hussein paid thirty-five million dollars to the families of Palestinian martyrs—ten thousand dollars to the family of anyone killed fighting Israel and twenty-five thousand to the family of every suicide bomber. You could say a lot of things about this mindless battle over real estate. But you could never say that life was cheap.

Chapter Eighteen

MOST WANTED
2001

PALESTINIANS NO LONGER BLAMED Yasser Arafat or Hamas for their troubles. Now they blamed Israel for killing their children. But I still couldn't escape a fundamental question: Why were those children out there in the first place? Where were the parents? Why didn't their mothers and fathers keep them inside? Those children should have been sitting at their desks in school, not running in the streets, throwing stones at armed soldiers.

"Why do you have to send children to die?" I asked my father after one particularly horrific day.

"We don't send children," he said. "They want to go. Look at your brothers."

A chill went down my spine.

"If I hear that one of my brothers goes out there and throws stones, I'm going to break his arm," I said. "I would rather that he suffer a broken arm than get killed."

"Really? You might be interested to know that they were throwing stones yesterday." He said it so casually; I couldn't believe this was simply a way of life for us now.

Four of my brothers were no longer little children. Sohayb was twenty-one and Seif was eighteen, both old enough to go to prison.

At sixteen and fourteen, Oways and Mohammad were old enough to get themselves shot. And all of them should have known better. But when I questioned them, they denied throwing rocks.

"Listen, I am very serious about this," I told them. "I haven't spanked you for a long time, because you're grown-up now. But that will change if I hear you're going out there."

"You and Dad were there at the demonstrations too," Mohammad protested.

"Yes, we were there. But we didn't throw stones."

In the midst of all this—especially with the big checks flowing from Iraq's ruthless dictator, Saddam Hussein—Hamas found it had lost its monopoly on suicide bombing. Now the bombers also came from Islamic Jihad and the Al-Aqsa Martyrs Brigades, the secularists, the communists, and the atheists. And they all competed with one another to see who could kill the most Israeli civilians.

There was too much blood. I couldn't sleep. I couldn't eat. I didn't see it just through the eyes of a Muslim or a Palestinian or even as the son of Hassan Yousef anymore. Now I saw it through Israeli eyes too. And even more importantly, I watched the mindless killing through the eyes of Jesus, who agonized for those who were lost. The more I read the Bible, the more clearly I saw this single truth: Loving and forgiving one's enemies is the only real way to stop the bloodshed.

But as much as I admired Jesus, I didn't believe my Christian friends when they tried to convince me that he was God. Allah was my god. But whether I realized it fully or not, I was gradually adopting the standards of Jesus and rejecting those of Allah. Accelerating my departure from Islam was the hypocrisy I saw all around me. Islam taught that a devoted servant of Allah who became a martyr went straight to heaven. No questioning by weird angels or torture in the grave. But suddenly it seemed that *anyone* killed by the Israelis—whether a nominal Muslim, a communist, even an atheist—was being treated as a holy martyr. The imams and the sheikhs told the families of the dead, "Your loved one is in heaven."

Of course, the Qur'an didn't support their rhetoric. The Qur'an is clear about who goes to heaven and who goes to hell. But these leaders didn't seem to care. This wasn't even about truth or theology; it was about lying to people for strategic advantage and political expediency. It was about Islamic leaders drugging their people with lies to make them forget the pain those leaders were causing them.

As the Shin Bet passed on more and more information to me, I was consistently amazed at what they knew about the people in my life—often old friends who had become very dangerous individuals. Some had even become part of the hard core of the Hamas military wing. One of those people was Daya Muhammad Hussein Al-Tawil. He was a handsome young man whose uncle was a Hamas leader.

In all the years I knew him, Daya had never been religiously motivated. In fact, his dad was a communist, so he really had had nothing to do with Islam. His mom was a Muslim in the cultural sense, but she was definitely not a radical. And his sister was an American-educated journalist, a U.S. citizen, and a modern woman who did not wear a head scarf. They lived in a nice home and were all well educated. Daya had studied engineering at Birzeit University, where he was first in his class. To my knowledge, he had never even participated in a Hamas demonstration.

Given all of that, I was shocked when on March 27, 2001, we heard that Daya had blown himself up at the French Hill junction in Jerusalem. Though no one else was killed, twenty-nine Israelis were injured.

Daya wasn't a stupid kid who could easily be talked into doing something like this. He wasn't a dirt-poor refugee who had nothing to lose. He didn't need money. So what made him do it? Nobody understood. His parents were stunned, and so was I. Even Israeli intelligence couldn't figure it out.

The Shin Bet called me in for an emergency meeting. They handed me a photograph of a decapitated head and asked me to identify it. I assured them that it was Daya. And I went home asking myself over and over, *Why?* I don't think anyone will ever know. No one saw it coming. Not even his Hamas uncle.

Daya was the first suicide bomber of the Al-Aqsa Intifada. His attack suggested the existence of a military cell that seemed to be operating independently somewhere. And the Shin Bet was determined to find that cell before it launched another attack.

Loai showed me a list of suspects. At the top were five familiar names. They were Hamas guys whom the PA had released from prison before the beginning of the intifada. Arafat knew they were dangerous, but with Hamas all but in its grave, he couldn't see any reason to hold them any longer.

He was wrong.

The main suspect was Muhammad Jamal al-Natsheh, who had helped found Hamas with my dad and ultimately became the head of its military wing in the West Bank. Al-Natsheh was from the largest family in the territories, so he feared nothing. About six feet tall, he was every inch a warrior—tough, strong, and intelligent. Paradoxically, though he was filled with hatred for the Jews, I knew him to be a very caring man.

Saleh Talahme—another name on the list—was an electrical engineer, very smart and well educated. I didn't know it at the time, but the two of us would eventually become very close friends.

Another, Ibrahim Hamed, led the security wing in the West Bank. These three men were assisted by Sayyed al-Sheikh Qassem and Hasaneen Rummanah.

Sayyed was a good follower—athletic, uneducated, and obedient. Hasaneen, on the other hand, was a handsome young artist who had been very active in the Islamic student movement, especially during the First Intifada when Hamas was trying to prove itself on the streets as a force to be reckoned with. As a Hamas leader, my father had worked hard to obtain their release and return them to their families. And on the day Arafat let them go, my dad and I picked them up from prison, stuffed everybody into our car, and got them settled in an apartment at the Al Hajal in Ramallah.

When Loai showed me the list, I said, "Guess what? I know all those guys. And I know where they live. I was the one who drove them to their safe house."

"Are you serious?" he said with a big grin. "Let's go to work."

When my father and I had picked them up from prison, I had no idea how dangerous they had become or how many Israelis they had killed. And now I was one of only a few people in Hamas who knew where they were.

I paid them a visit, carrying with me the Shin Bet's most sophisticated spy toys so we could monitor every move they made, every word they said. But once I started talking with them, it was clear they weren't going to give us any solid information.

I wondered if maybe they weren't the guys we were looking for.

"Something is wrong," I said to Loai. "These guys didn't give me anything. Could it be another cell?"

"It could," he admitted. "But those guys have the history. We need to keep watching them until we get what we need."

They indeed had the history, but history wasn't enough to arrest them. We needed hard evidence. So we patiently continued to collect information. We didn't want to make a costly mistake and grab the wrong guys, leaving the real terrorists free to launch the next bomb.

Maybe my life wasn't complicated enough, or maybe it just seemed like a good idea at the time, but that same month I started a job in the Capacity-Building Office of the United States Agency for International Development (USAID) Village Water and Sanitation

Program, headquartered in Al-Bireh. Long title, I know, but then again, it was a very important project. Because I didn't have a college degree, I began as a receptionist.

Some of the Christians I attended Bible study with had introduced me to one of the American managers, who immediately took a liking to me and offered me a job. Loai thought it would make a great cover since my new ID card, stamped by the U.S. Embassy, would allow me to travel freely between Israel and the Palestinian territories. It would also keep people from getting too suspicious about why I always had plenty of spending money.

My father saw it as a great opportunity and was grateful to the United States for providing safe drinking water and sanitation to his people. At the same time, however, he could not forget that the Americans also provided Israel with the weapons used to kill Palestinians. This typifies the ambivalence most Arabs feel about the United States.

I jumped at the chance to be part of the biggest U.S.-funded project in the region. The media always seemed focused on the sexy bargaining chips—land, independence, and reparations. But water really was a much bigger issue than land in the Middle East. People have battled over it since Abram's herdsmen fought with those of his nephew, Lot. The chief water source for Israel and the occupied territories is the Sea of Galilee, also known as Gennesaret or Tiberias. It is the lowest freshwater lake on earth.

Water has always been a complicated issue in the land of the Bible. For modern Israel, the dynamic has changed with the nation's boundaries. For example, one of the outcomes of the Six-Day War in 1967 was that Israel took control of the Golan Heights from Syria. This gave Israel control of the entire Sea of Galilee, and with that came control of the Jordan River and every other spring and rivulet that flowed into and out of it. Violating international law, Israel diverted water from the Jordan away from the West Bank and Gaza Strip by means of its National Water Carrier, providing Israeli citizens and settlers with well over three-quarters of the water from West Bank aquifers. The United States has spent hundreds of millions of dollars digging wells and establishing independent sources of water for my people.

USAID was actually more than just a cover for me. The men and women who worked there became my friends. I knew that God had given me this job. It was USAID's policy not to employ anyone who was politically active, much less someone whose father led a major terrorist organization. But for some reason my boss decided to keep me. His kindness would soon pay off in ways he would never know.

Because of the intifada, the U.S. government allowed its employees to enter the West Bank only for the day and only to work. But that meant they had to pass through dangerous checkpoints. They actually would have been safer living in the West Bank than running the gauntlet of checkpoints every day and driving the streets in 4 x 4 American jeeps with yellow Israeli tags on them. The average Palestinian didn't distinguish between those who had come to help and those who had come to kill.

The IDF always warned USAID to evacuate if it was planning an operation that would put them in danger, but the Shin Bet didn't issue such warnings. After all, we were all about secrecy. If we heard that a fugitive was headed to Ramallah from Jenin, for example, we launched an operation without forewarning.

Ramallah was a small city. During these operations, security troops rushed in from every direction. People barricaded the streets with cars and trucks and set fire to tires. Black smoke choked the air. Crouched gunmen ran from cover to cover, shooting whatever was in their paths. Young men threw rocks. Children cried in the streets. Ambulance sirens mingled with screams of women and the crack of small-arms fire.

Not long after I started working for USAID, Loai told me the security forces would be coming into Ramallah the following day. I called my American manager and warned him not to come to town and to tell everyone else to stay home. I said I couldn't tell him how I had gotten this information, but I encouraged him to trust me. He did. He probably figured I had inside information because I was the son of Hassan Yousef.

The next day, Ramallah was ablaze. People were running through the streets, shooting everything in sight. Cars burned along the side of the road and shop windows were broken, leaving the stores vulnerable to bandits and looters. After my boss saw the news, he told me, "Please, Mosab, whenever something like that is going to happen again, let me know."

"Okay," I said, "on one condition: You don't ask any questions. If I say don't come, just don't come."

Chapter Nineteen

SHOES

2001

THE SECOND INTIFADA seemed to roll on and on without even pausing to catch its breath. On March 28, 2001, a suicide bomber killed two teenagers at a gas station. On April 22, a bomber killed one person and himself and wounded about fifty at a bus stop. On May 18, five civilians were killed and more than one hundred wounded by a suicide bomber outside a shopping mall in Netanya.

And then on June 1, at 11:26 p.m., a group of teenagers were standing in line, talking and laughing and horsing around, eager to enter a popular Tel Aviv disco known as the Dolphi. Most of the kids were from the former Soviet Union, their parents recent émigrés. Saeed Hotari stood in line, too, but he was Palestinian and a little older. He was wrapped in explosives and metal fragments.

The newspapers didn't call the Dolphinarium attack a suicide bombing. They called it a massacre. Scores of kids were ripped apart by ball bearings and the sheer force of the blast. Casualties were high: 21 died; 120 were wounded.

No suicide bomber had ever killed so many people in a single attack. Hotari's neighbors in the West Bank congratulated his father. "I hope that my other three sons will do the same," Mr. Hotari told an interviewer. "I would like all members of my family, all the relatives, to die for my nation and my homeland."[7]

Israel was more determined than ever to cut off the head of the snake. It should have learned by then, however, that if imprisoning faction leaders did nothing to stop the bloodshed, assassinating them was unlikely to work either.

Jamal Mansour was a journalist, and like my father, was one of the seven founders of Hamas. He was one of my father's closest friends. They had been exiled together in south Lebanon. They talked and laughed on the phone nearly every day. He was also the chief advocate of suicide bombings. In a January interview with *Newsweek*, he defended the killing of unarmed civilians and praised the bombers.

On Tuesday, July 31, after a tip from a collaborator, a pair of Apache helicopter gunships approached Mansour's media offices in Nablus. They fired three laser-guided missiles through the window of his second-floor office. Mansour, Hamas leader Jamal Salim, and six other Palestinians were incinerated by the blasts. Two of the victims were children, aged eight and ten, who had been waiting to see the doctor on the floor below. Both were crushed beneath the rubble.

This seemed crazy. I called Loai.

"What in the world is going on? Are you sure those guys were involved in suicide bombings? I know they supported the attacks, but they were in the political wing of Hamas with my father, not the military wing."

"Yes. We have intelligence that Mansour and Salim were directly involved in the Dolphinarium massacre. They have blood on their hands. We had to do this."

What could I do? Argue with him? Tell him he didn't have the right information? It suddenly dawned on me that the Israeli government must also be determined to assassinate my father. Even if he hadn't organized the suicide bombings, he was still guilty by association. Besides, he had information that could have saved lives, and he withheld it. He had influence, but he didn't use it. He could have tried to stop the killing, but he didn't. He supported the movement and encouraged its members to continue their opposition until the Israelis were forced to withdraw. In the eyes of the Israeli government, he, too, was a terrorist.

With all my Bible reading, I was now comparing my father's actions with the teachings of Jesus, not those found in the Qur'an. He was looking less and less like a hero to me, and it broke my heart. I wanted to tell him what I was learning, but I knew he would not listen. And if those in Jerusalem had their way, my father would never get the opportunity to see how Islam had led him down the wrong path.

I consoled myself with the knowledge that my father would be safe at least for a while because of my connection with the Shin Bet. They wanted him alive as much as I did—for very different reasons, of course. He was their main source of inside information regarding Hamas activities. Of course, I couldn't explain that to him, and even the Shin Bet's protection could end up being dangerous to him. After all, it would seem pretty suspicious if all the other Hamas leaders were forced into hiding while my father was allowed to walk freely down the street. I needed to at least go through the motions of protecting him. I immediately went to his office and pointed out that what had just happened to Mansour could just as easily have happened to him.

"Get rid of everybody. Get rid of your bodyguards. Close the office. Don't come here again."

His response was as I expected.

"I'll be okay, Mosab. We'll put steel over the windows."

"Are you crazy? Get out of here now! Their missiles go through tanks and buildings, and you think you're going to be protected by a sheet of metal? If you could seal the windows, they would come through the ceiling. Come on; let's go!"

I couldn't really blame him for resisting. He was a religious leader and a politician, not a soldier. He had no clue about the army or about assassinations. He didn't know all that I knew. He finally agreed to leave with me, though I knew he wasn't happy about it.

But I was not the only one who came to the conclusion that Mansour's old friend, Hassan Yousef, would logically be the next target. When we walked down the street, it seemed that everyone around us looked worried. They quickened their pace and glanced anxiously at the sky as they tried to move away from us as quickly as possible. I knew that, like me, they were listening closely for the chug of incoming helicopters. Nobody wanted to end up as collateral damage.

I drove my father to the City Inn Hotel and told him to stay there.

"Okay, this guy here at the desk is going to change your room every five hours. Just listen to him. Don't bring anybody to your room. Don't call anyone but me, and don't leave this place. Here's a safe phone."

As soon as I left, I told the Shin Bet where he was.

"Okay, good. Keep him there, out of trouble."

To do that, I had to know where he was every moment. I had to know every breath he took. I got rid of all his bodyguards. I couldn't trust them. I needed my father to rely on me totally. If he didn't, he would almost certainly make a mistake that would cost him his life. I became his aide, bodyguard, and gatekeeper. I arranged for all of his needs. I kept an eye on everything that happened anywhere near the hotel. I was his contact with the outside world, and I was the outside world's contact with him. This new role carried the added benefit of keeping me entirely free from suspicion of being a spy.

I started acting the part of a Hamas leader. I carried an M16, which identified me as a man with means, connections, and authority. In those days, such weapons were in big demand and short supply (my assault rifle went for ten thousand dollars). And I traded heavily on my relationship to Sheikh Hassan Yousef.

Hamas military guys began to hang around me just to show off. And because they thought I knew all the secrets of the organization, they felt comfortable sharing their problems and frustrations with me, believing I could help them with their issues.

I listened carefully. They had no idea they were giving me little bits of information that I was piecing together to create much bigger pictures. These snapshots led to more Shin Bet operations than I could describe to you in a single book. What I will tell you is that many innocent lives were saved as a result of those conversations. There were many fewer grieving widows and shattered orphans at gravesides because of the suicide bombings we were able to prevent.

At the same time, I gained trust and respect within the military wing and became the go-to Hamas guy for other Palestinian factions as well. I was the person they expected to provide them with explosives and to coordinate operations with Hamas.

One day, Ahmad al-Faransi, an aide to Marwan Barghouti, asked me to get him some explosives for several suicide bombers from Jenin. I told him I would, and I began to play the game—stalling until I could uncover the bombers' cells in the West Bank. Games like that were very dangerous. But I knew I was covered from several directions. Just as being the eldest son of Sheikh Hassan Yousef kept me safe from Hamas-on-Hamas torture in prison, it also protected me when I worked among terrorists. My job with USAID gave me a certain amount of protection and freedom as well. And the Shin Bet always had my back.

Any mistake, however, could have cost me my life, and the Palestinian Authority was always a threat. The PA had some fairly sophisticated electronic eavesdropping gear that had been provided by the CIA. Sometimes they used it to ferret out terrorists. Other times it was deployed to root out collaborators. So I had to be very careful, especially of falling into the hands of the PA, since I knew more about how the Shin Bet operated than any other agent.

Because I had become the only point of access to my father, I was in direct contact with every Hamas leader in the West Bank, Gaza Strip, and Syria. The only other guy with that level of access was Khalid Meshaal in Damascus. Meshaal was born in the West Bank, but he lived most of his life in other Arab countries. He joined the Muslim Brotherhood in Kuwait and studied physics at Kuwait University. After Hamas was founded, Meshaal headed up the Kuwaiti chapter. And following the Iraqi invasion, he moved to Jordan, then to Qatar, and finally to Syria.

Living in Damascus, he was not subject to the travel restrictions of Hamas leaders in the territories. So he turned into a kind of diplomat, representing Hamas in Cairo, Moscow, and the Arab League. As he traveled, he raised money. In April 2006 alone, he collected one hundred million dollars from Iran and Qatar.

Meshaal didn't make many public appearances; he lived in secret places, and he could not return to the occupied territories for fear of assassination. He had good reason to be careful.

In 1997, when Meshaal had still been in Jordan, a couple of Israeli intelligence agents broke into his room and injected a rare poison into his ear while he slept. His bodyguards spotted the agents leaving the building, and one of them went to check on Meshaal. He saw no blood, but his leader was down on the ground and unable to speak. The bodyguards ran after the Israeli agents, one of whom fell into an open drain. The agents were captured by Jordanian police.

Israel had recently signed a peace agreement with Jordan and exchanged ambassadors, and now the botched attack jeopardized that new diplomatic arrangement. And Hamas was embarrassed that one of their key leaders could be reached so easily. The story had been humiliating to all the parties involved, and thus everybody tried to cover it up. But somehow the international media found out.

Demonstrations broke out in the streets of Jordan, and King Hussein demanded that Israel release Sheikh Ahmed Yassin, Hamas's spiritual leader, and other Palestinian prisoners in exchange for the red-faced Mossad agents. In addition, Mossad was to send a medical team immediately to inject Meshaal with an antidote to the poison. Reluctantly, Israel agreed.

Khalid Meshaal called me at least once a week. Other times, he left very important meetings to take my phone calls. One day, Mossad called the Shin Bet.

"We have a very dangerous person from Ramallah who talks to Khalid Meshaal every week, and we can't find out who he is!"

They were referring to me, of course. We all had a good laugh, and the Shin Bet chose to keep the Mossad guessing about me. It seems there is competition and rivalry between security agencies in every country—as with the Federal Bureau of Investigation, Central Intelligence Agency, and National Security Agency in the United States.

One day, I decided to take advantage of my relationship with Meshaal. I told him I had very important information that I could not give him over the phone.

"Do you have a secure way to deliver it?" he asked.

"Of course. I will call you in a week and give you the details."

The normal means of communication between the territories and Damascus was to send a letter with someone who had no police record and no known relationship with Hamas. Such letters were written on very thin paper, rolled down to a tiny size, and then slipped into an empty medicine capsule or simply wrapped with nylon thread. Just before crossing the border, the courier swallowed the capsule, then regurgitated it in a restroom on the other side. Sometimes, a courier would have to carry as many as fifty letters at once. Naturally, these "mules" had no idea what the letters contained.

I decided to do something different and open a new secret channel to outside leadership, thus extending my access from the personal level to the operational and security levels.

The Shin Bet loved the idea.

I chose a local Hamas member and told him to meet me at my old cemetery in the middle of the night. To impress him, I showed up carrying my M16.

"I want you to carry out a very important mission," I told him.

Clearly terrified yet excited, he hung on to every word from the son of Hassan Yousef.

"You can tell no one—not your family, not even your local Hamas leader. By the way, who is your leader?"

I asked him to write out his entire history in Hamas, everything he knew, before I would tell him more about his mission. He couldn't get everything down on paper fast enough. And I couldn't believe the amount of information he gave me, including updates on every movement in his area.

We met a second time, and I told him he was being sent out of Palestine.

"Do exactly what I tell you," I warned, "and don't ask questions."

I told Loai that the guy was involved in Hamas up to his neck, so if the organization decided to check him out, they would find a very active and loyal member. The Shin Bet did its own vetting, approved him, and opened the border for him.

I wrote a letter, telling Khalid Meshaal that I had all the keys to the West Bank and he could totally rely on me for special and complicated missions that he could not entrust to normal Hamas channels. I told him I was ready for his orders, and I guaranteed success.

My timing was perfect, since Israel had assassinated or arrested most of the Hamas leaders and activists by that time. Al-Qassam Brigades was exhausted, and Meshaal was desperately low on human resources.

I did not, however, instruct the courier to swallow the letter. I had designed a more complicated mission, mostly because it was more fun. I was discovering that I loved this spy stuff, especially with Israeli intelligence paving the way.

We bought the courier some very nice clothes—a complete outfit, so that his attention would not be drawn to the shoes in which, unknown to him, we had hidden the letter.

He put on the clothes, and I gave him enough money for the trip and a little extra to have some fun in Syria. I told him his contacts would recognize him only by his shoes, so he had to keep them on. Otherwise, they would think he was someone else and he would be in serious danger.

After the courier arrived in Syria, I called Meshaal and told him to expect to be contacted soon. If anyone else had told him that, Khalid would have immediately become suspicious and refused a meeting. But this man had been sent by his young friend, the son of Hassan Yousef. So he believed he had nothing to worry about.

When they met, Khalid requested the letter.

"What letter?" our courier asked. He didn't know he was supposed to have a letter.

I had given Khalid a hint about where to look, and they found the compartment in one of the shoes. In this way, a new communications channel was established with Damascus, even though Meshaal had no idea that he was actually on a party line with the Shin Bet listening in.

Chapter Twenty

TORN
SUMMER 2001

A LITTLE BEFORE 2 P.M. on August 9, 2001, twenty-two-year-old Izz al-Din Shuheil al-Masri blew himself up at the crowded Sbarro pizza parlor at King George Street and Jaffa Road. Al-Masri was from an affluent family in the West Bank.

Between five and ten kilograms of explosives sprayed nails, nuts, and bolts into the summer crowd, killing 15 people and maiming another 130. Between this horror and the Dolphinarium bombing a few months earlier, the citizenry of Israel was almost blind with grief and rage. Whatever group or faction was behind these attacks had to be identified and stopped before more innocents were killed. Otherwise, events would very likely spiral out of control and unleash unprecedented death and heartache across the region.

Again and again, the Shin Bet pored over every detail of the bombing, trying to connect it to the five guys at the safe house—Muhammad Jamal al-Natsheh, Saleh Talahme, Ibrahim Hamed, Sayyed al-Sheikh Qassem, and Hasaneen Rummanah—but not a shred of evidence tied them to the Dolphinarium or Sbarro attacks.

Who could have made such bombs? Certainly not some chemistry or engineering student. We knew every one of them, the grades they got, and what they ate for breakfast.

Whoever was building these bombs was an expert, didn't seem to be affiliated with any of the Palestinian factions, and was flying way below our radar. Somehow, we had to find him before he made more bombs. This guy was superdangerous.

What we didn't realize at the time was that Arafat's people had received a call from the CIA shortly after the Sbarro attack. "We know who made the bombs," the Americans told them. "His name is Abdullah Barghouti; he lives with a relative named Bilal Barghouti. Here is their address. Go arrest them."

Within hours, Abdullah and Bilal Barghouti were in PA custody—not that the Palestinian Authority wanted to arrest them, but to keep the money and logistical support flowing from Washington, Arafat knew it had to at least *appear* that the PA was doing its part to keep the peace. I believe Arafat would have preferred to give Abdullah Barghouti a medal rather than a prison sentence.

No sooner was Abdullah comfortably secured at Preventive Security Headquarters than another Barghouti—Marwan—showed up to get him out. The PA could not release Abdullah—the CIA had dropped him into their laps, and America expected them to deal with him. Israel expected the same and would definitely take more decisive action if the PA neglected its duty. So Marwan gave Abdullah food, clothes, and money, keeping him under a type of house arrest—working in a nice office, smoking, drinking coffee, and chatting with top security officers.

Though not related, Marwan Barghouti and Abdullah Barghouti shared an interesting common history. They both had connections to the twenty-three-year-old certifiable lunatic named Muhaned Abu Halawa, who had been a lieutenant to Ahmad Ghandour.

Halawa was a Fatah field commander and a member of Force 17. When you think of elite troops like Force 17 and Saddam Hussein's Republican Guards, discipline, skill, and sharp training come to mind. But Halawa didn't fit the model. He was an uneducated loose cannon who often carried around one of the huge machine guns usually mounted on jeeps. Halawa routinely distributed guns to other extremists and unsavory characters who then used them when driving by checkpoints, strafing soldiers and civilians indiscriminately.

Back in May, for example, he had given someone a couple of loaded AK-47s and a sack of bullets. Not long after, this man and a friend waited in ambush along a road coming out of Jerusalem and put thirteen of those bullets into a Greek Orthodox monk named Tsibouktsakis Germanus. Halawa rewarded the killers with more guns for an attack he was planning at Hebrew University on Mount Scopus.

Understandably, it wasn't long before Israel pressured the Shin Bet to put Halawa permanently out of business. Because of my Hamas connections, I was the only one in the Shin Bet who could identify him. But for the first time in my life, I was facing a real moral dilemma. Something inside me was completely opposed to killing this man, regardless of how bad he was.

I went home and pulled out my now-worn Bible. I searched and searched and could find nothing in the Bible that would sanction murder. But I also couldn't deal with the blood that would be on my hands if we let him go on living and shooting people. I felt caught.

I kept thinking and praying to God Almighty, until finally I prayed, *Forgive me, Lord, for what I am about to do. Forgive me. This man cannot live.*

"That's good," Loai said, when I told him my decision. "We'll get him. You just make sure that Marwan Barghouti is not in the car with him."

Marwan was not only a big-shot Palestinian, he was also a terrorist in his own right with a lot of Israeli blood on his hands. And as much as the Shin Bet hated him, they did not want him assassinated because he would make a formidable martyr.

On August 4, 2001, I was sitting in my car outside of Barghouti's office when I saw Halawa walk in. A couple of hours later, he came out, got into his gold VW Golf, and drove off. I called the security forces and assured them that Halawa was alone.

From inside a tank at the top of a nearby hill, IDF soldiers watched Halawa's car, waiting for a clear shot with no civilians close by. The first armor-piercing missile headed for the windshield, but Halawa must have seen it coming, because he opened his door and tried to jump out. He wasn't fast enough. The missile exploded and threw him out of the car. My car—which was sitting several hundred yards away—shook with the force of the blast. A second missile missed and hit the street. The Golf was in flames, and so was Halawa—but he wasn't dead. As I watched him run through the streets, screaming in pain as the flames engulfed his body, my heart nearly pounded out of my chest.

What had we done?

"What are you doing!" the Shin Bet yelled at me through my cell phone when they caught sight of my car so close to the scene. "Do you want to get killed? Get out of there!"

Though I was not supposed to be anywhere near the attack site, I had driven down to see what would happen. I felt responsible and obligated to see what I was a part of. It was indeed stupid. If I had been spotted, it would have been too much of a coincidence for anybody to believe that I wasn't involved in the assassination attempt, and I would have been exposed for sure.

That evening, I went with my father and Marwan Barghouti to the hospital to visit Halawa. His face was so horribly burned I couldn't even look at him. But it seemed he was too fanatical to die.

He went into hiding for several months, and I heard that he had shot himself accidentally and almost bled to death. But even that wasn't enough to slow him down. He just kept killing people. Then one day, Loai called me.

"Where are you?"

"I'm at home."

"Okay, stay there."

I didn't ask what was going on. I had learned to trust Loai's instructions. A couple of hours later, Loai called again. Apparently, Halawa had been eating with some friends at a fried chicken restaurant close to my house. An Israeli spy spotted him and verified his identity. When Halawa and his friends left the restaurant, two helicopters dropped out of the sky, launched their missiles, and that was it.

After Halawa's assassination, some members of the Al-Aqsa Martyrs Brigades visited that restaurant and found a seventeen-year-old kid who had been one of the last people to see Halawa before he got into his car. He was an orphan with no family to protect him. So they tortured him, and he confessed to collaborating with the Israelis. They shot him, tied his body to the back of a car, dragged it through the streets of Ramallah, and hung him from the tower in the square.

At the same time, the media started screaming that Israel had tried to kill Marwan Barghouti, which of course, it hadn't. I knew the organization had taken care to avoid killing him. But everybody believed the newspapers and Al-Jazeera, so Marwan Barghouti decided to make some political capital out of the rumor. He began boasting, "Yes, they tried to assassinate me, but I was too smart for them."

When Abdullah Barghouti heard the news in prison, he believed it, too, and sent a few of his special bombs to Marwan's assistant to be used to unleash a terrible revenge on the Israelis. Marwan very much appreciated the gesture and felt indebted to Abdullah.

Abdullah's arrival had marked a dramatic change in the conflict between Israel and Palestine. First, his bombs were dramatically more sophisticated and devastating than anything we had seen before, making Israel a lot more vulnerable and increasing pressure on the administration to stop the bombers.

Second, the Al-Aqsa Intifada was no longer confined to Palestine. Barghouti was an outsider, born in Kuwait. Who could tell what other threats to Israel might lie in wait beyond its borders?

Third, Barghouti was not somebody who was easy to keep track of. He wasn't Hamas. He wasn't PA. He was just Barghouti, an anonymous independent death machine.

Soon after Abdullah's arrest, the PA asked Marwan to talk to him about any future attacks he may have planned.

"Okay," Marwan said. "I'll have Hassan Yousef talk to him."

Marwan knew my father felt strongly about political corruption and had heard about his efforts to make peace between Hamas and the PA. He called my dad, who agreed to go talk with Abdullah.

My father had never heard of Abdullah Barghouti, who certainly wasn't a member of Hamas. But he warned Abdullah, "If you have anything planned, you need to tell the PA so we can stop it for now and take off some of the pressure we're getting from Israel, at least for the next few weeks. If there is another explosion like the ones at the Dolphinarium or Sbarro, Israel will come into the West Bank in force. They'll get tough with the PA leaders, and they'll take you."

Abdullah admitted that he had sent several bombs to Nablus, where some fighters were planning to load the explosives into four cars, surround Israeli foreign minister Shimon Peres while he was traveling, and assassinate him. He also revealed that Hamas operatives in the north were going to blow up a number of Israeli lawmakers. Unfortunately, he didn't know who the bombers were, who they had targeted, or who was planning to assassinate Peres. He had only a telephone number.

My father came home and shared what he had learned with me. We were now privy to information about a plot to assassinate one of Israel's highest-ranking officials—the foreign minister. The ramifications were chilling.

Obviously, there was nothing to do but place a call to Abdullah's contact. Marwan Barghouti didn't want Abdullah to use his phone, and my father didn't want him to use his either. We all knew that the Israelis would be listening, and neither man wanted to be connected with the terrorist operations.

So my father sent me out to buy a disposable cell phone on which we could make the call before throwing the phone into the trash. I bought the phone, wrote down the number, and called it in to the Shin Bet so they could trace the call.

Abdullah called his contact in Nablus and told him to stop whatever he was doing until he heard otherwise. As soon as Israeli intelligence learned what had been planned, they put extra security on every member of the Knesset and the cabinet. Finally, after a couple of months, things began to calm down a little.

In the meantime, Marwan continued to work toward Abdullah's release, not only because Abdullah had provided him with bombs, but also because he wanted him free to kill more Israelis. In addition to being one of the leaders of the Second Intifada, Marwan Barghouti was also a terrorist who was personally shooting soldiers and settlers.

Eventually, the PA did release Abdullah Barghouti. The Shin Bet was furious.

Then everything got really crazy.

Chapter Twenty-One

THE GAME

SUMMER 2001–SPRING 2002

On August 27, 2001, an Israeli helicopter fired two rockets into the office of Abu Ali Mustafa, secretary-general of the PFLP. One of the rockets struck him as he sat at his desk.

The following day, more than fifty thousand outraged Palestinians, along with Mustafa's family, attended his funeral. Mustafa had opposed the peace process and the Oslo Accords. Nevertheless, he was a moderate like my father, and we had gone together to hear him lecture many times.

Israel credited him with nine car-bomb attacks, but it wasn't true. Like my dad, he was a political leader, not a military leader. Israel had absolutely no evidence against him. I knew that for a fact. But it didn't matter. They assassinated Mustafa anyway—perhaps in retaliation for the carnage at the Sbarro restaurant, or perhaps because of the Dolphinarium massacre. More likely, they simply wanted to send a message to Yasser Arafat. In addition to his role in the PFLP, Mustafa was also a member of the PLO's Executive Committee.

Two weeks later, on September 11, nineteen Al-Qaeda terrorists hijacked four jetliners in the United States. Two crashed into the World Trade Center in New York City. Another crashed into the Pentagon in Washington. And the fourth went down in a field in

Somerset County, Pennsylvania. All told, 2,973 people died in addition to the terrorists themselves.

As the news media struggled to keep up with the unbelievable events continuing to unfold, I sat with the rest of the world watching again and again the reports of the Twin Towers collapsing, white ash covering Church Street like a February blizzard. I felt a rush of shame when I saw the footage of Palestinian children celebrating in the streets of Gaza.

The attack reduced the Palestinian cause to ashes, too, as the world shouted with one voice against terrorism—any terrorism, for any cause. In the weeks to follow, the Shin Bet began searching for lessons to be found in the rubble of what would come to be known simply as 9/11.

Why had the U.S. intelligence services not been able to prevent the disaster? For one thing, they operated independently and competitively. For another, they relied mostly on technology and rarely collaborated with terrorists. Those tactics may have been fine in the Cold War, but it's pretty tough to combat fanatical ideals with technology.

Israeli intelligence, on the other hand, relied mostly on human resources; had countless spies in mosques, Islamic organizations, and leadership roles; and had no problem recruiting even the most dangerous terrorists. They knew they had to have eyes and ears on the inside, along with minds that understood motives and emotions and that could connect the dots.

America understood neither Islamic culture nor its ideology. That, combined with open borders and lax security, made it a much softer target than Israel. Even so, although my role as a spy enabled Israel to take hundreds of terrorists off the streets, our work couldn't begin to put an end to terrorism—even in a tiny country like Israel.

About a month later, on October 17, four PFLP gunmen walked into the Jerusalem Hyatt Hotel and assassinated Israeli tourism minister Rehavam Ze'evi. They said it was revenge for the Mustafa assassination. Despite his seemingly apolitical portfolio, Ze'evi was an obvious target. He publicly advocated a policy of making life so miserable for the three million people in the West Bank and Gaza that they would voluntarily move to other Arab countries. Mixing his metaphors, Ze'evi reportedly once told an Associated Press reporter that some Palestinians were like "lice" who should be stopped like a "cancer spreading within us."[8]

Tit for tat, the reciprocal killing continued. An eye for an eye—and there was no shortage of eyes.

For several years now, I had worked hard to gather every scrap of information I could to help the Shin Bet stop the bloodbath. We continued to keep an eye on Muhammad Jamal al-Natsheh, Saleh Talahme, and the other three guys I had stashed away after their release from the PA prison compound. They changed locations several times, and only Saleh kept in touch with me. But we tracked the others through their families and by monitoring calls on public telephones.

Saleh trusted me, always told me where he was living, and frequently invited me to visit. As I got to know him, I found that I really liked Saleh. He was an amazing man—a brilliant scholar, graduating at the top of his electrical engineering class and one of the best students in the history of Birzeit University. To him, I was the son of Hassan Yousef, a good friend and a good listener.

I spent a lot of time with Saleh; his wife, Majeda; and their five children (two boys and three girls). Their older son was named Mosab, like me. Majeda and the kids had come to Ramallah from Hebron to spend a little time with Saleh in his apartment hideout. I was still working on my degree at the time, and one evening, Saleh asked me how school was going.

"Any problems with anything?"

"Yeah, Economical Statistics."

"Okay, tomorrow you bring the book and we'll sit down together and study. It will be our own little class."

When I told Loai and others in the Shin Bet about it, they were pleased. They thought that these tutoring sessions would make a good cover for intelligence gathering.

But it wasn't entirely a cover. Saleh and I were becoming friends. He taught me, and I actually did very well on the exam a couple of weeks later. I loved him, and I loved his children. I often ate with the family, and over time, a strong bond began to form among all of us. It was a strange relationship because I knew that by now Saleh had become a very dangerous guy. But then again, so had I.

One night in March 2002, I was sitting at home when two men came to the door.

Suspicious, I asked, "How can I help you?"

"We're looking for Sheikh Hassan Yousef. It's important."

"Tell me why it's important."

They explained that they were two of the five suicide bombers who had just arrived from Jordan. Their contact had been arrested, and they needed a safe place to stay.

"Okay," I said. "You came to the right place."

I asked what they needed.

"We have a car full of explosives and bombs, and we need someplace safe to leave it."

Great, I thought, *what am I going to do with a car stuffed with explosives?* I had to think quickly. I decided to keep their car in the garage beside our house. It was obviously not one of my brighter ideas, but I was forced to think on my feet.

"Okay, here's some money," I said, emptying my wallet. "Go find a place to stay, get back to me here tonight, and we'll figure out what to do."

After they left, I called Loai, and to my relief, the Shin Bet came and took the car away.

All five suicide bombers returned a short time later. "Okay," I told them, "from now on, I am your connection to Hamas. I will provide your targets, locations, transportation, everything you need. Do not talk to anyone else, or you might be dead before you have a chance to kill any Israelis."

This situation constituted an extraordinary windfall in terms of intelligence. Up to now, no one ever knew about suicide bombers before they detonated their explosives. Suddenly, five of them had shown up at my door with a carload of bombs. Thirty minutes after I told the Shin Bet their location, Prime Minister Sharon authorized their assassinations.

"You can't do that," I told Loai.

"What!"

"I know they are terrorists, and they are about to blow themselves up. But those five men are ignorant. They don't know what they're doing. You can't kill them. If you kill them, this is my last operation."

"Are you threatening us?"

"No, but you know how I work. I made an exception once with Halawa, and you remember how that ended. I will not be part of killing people."

"What option is there?"

"Arrest them," I said, though even as I spoke the words, I knew it was a crazy idea. We had the car and the bombs, but these guys still had their belts. If a soldier got within a hundred yards of their one-room flat, they would detonate the belts and take everybody with them.

Even if we managed to get them out alive without anybody else getting killed, they would be sure to mention my name to their interrogators, and I would be burned for sure. Self-preservation told me the safest thing for all concerned was just to let a helicopter fire a couple of missiles into their apartment and be done with it.

But my conscience was being rewired. Though not yet a Christian, I was really trying to follow the ethical teachings of Jesus. Allah had no problem with murder; in fact, he insisted on it. But Jesus held me to a much higher standard. Now I found I couldn't kill even a terrorist.

At the same time, I had become far too valuable to the Shin Bet for them to risk losing me. They weren't happy about it, but they finally agreed to call off the assassination.

"We have to know what is going on inside that room," they told me. I headed over to the apartment under the pretext of taking the bombers a few pieces of simple furniture. What they didn't know was that we had placed bugs inside the furniture that allowed us to hear every word they said. Together, we listened in as they discussed who would go first, second, third, etc. Everyone wanted to be first, so they didn't have to watch their friends die. It was eerie. We were listening to dead men talking.

On March 16, security forces troops moved into position. The bombers were in the center of Ramallah, so the IDF couldn't bring in tanks. Because the troops had to go in on foot, the operation was very dangerous. I followed the events from my place, as Loai talked to me on the phone and kept me informed of everything that was going on.

"They are going to sleep."

We all waited until sounds of snoring came across the monitors.

The greatest risk was waking them too soon. The troops had to get through the door and reach the beds before any bomber could move a muscle.

A soldier fixed an explosive charge to the door as we listened to the monitors for the slightest noise, the slightest interruption in the snoring. Then they gave the signal.

The door exploded. Special forces troops rushed into the small apartment, catching all but one of the men. He grabbed a gun and jumped through the window—he was dead before he hit the ground.

Everyone breathed a sigh of relief. Everyone except me. As soon as they got the guys into the jeep, one of them mentioned my name, exposing me as a collaborator.

My worst fears had been realized. I was burned. Now what?

Loai had the solution. The Shin Bet simply deported the guy back to Jordan, sending his friends to prison. So while he was home free, having fun with his family, the other three would assume that he had been the traitor, not me. It was brilliant.

I had gotten away with it one more time, though just barely. But it was clear I was pushing my luck a little too hard.

One day, I received a message from Shin Bet chief Avi Dichter, thanking me for the work I was doing for them. He said he had opened all the files in Israel's war on terrorism and found the Green Prince in every one. While this was flattering, it was also a warning. I recognized it, and Loai recognized it. If I continued the way I was going, I would end up dead. The trail out there was too long. Somebody was sure to stumble across it. Somehow I needed to be sanitized.

My stubborn refusal to allow the five suicide bombers to be killed had compromised my situation in a big way. Even though everybody believed that the bomber who had been sent back to Jordan was responsible for the arrests, they also knew that Israel doesn't hesitate to pick up anyone suspected of providing suicide bombers with help. And I had helped them a lot. So why hadn't I been arrested?

A week after the bomber arrests, the Israeli security team came up with two ideas that could save me from being burned. First, they could arrest me and put me back into prison. But I was afraid that would be the same thing as a death sentence for my father, who would no longer have me to protect him from Israeli assassination attempts.

"The other option is for us to play the game."

"Game? What game?"

Loai explained that we needed to trigger a high-profile event, something big enough to convince all of Palestine that Israel wanted me arrested or dead. In order to be persuasive, it couldn't be staged. It had to be real. The Israeli Defense Forces had to really attempt to capture me. And this meant the Shin Bet had to manipulate and deceive the IDF—their own people.

The Shin Bet gave the IDF only a few hours to prepare for this major operation. As the son of Hassan Yousef, I was a very dangerous young man, they warned, because I had a tight relationship to suicide bombers and might be armed with explosives. They said they had good intelligence that I would come to my father's house that night to visit my mother. I would stay only a short time, and I would be armed with an M16.

What a buildup they gave me. It was indeed an elaborate *game*.

The IDF was made to believe that I was a very high-profile terrorist who might disappear for good if they screwed up. So they did everything they could to make sure that didn't happen. Undercover special forces dressed as Arabs, along with highly trained snipers, entered the area in Palestinian vehicles, stopped two minutes from the house, and waited for a signal. Heavy tanks were stationed fifteen minutes away on the territorial border. Helicopter gunships were ready to provide air cover, in case there was trouble with Palestinian street fighters.

Outside my father's house, I sat in my car waiting for a call from the Shin Bet. When it came, I would have exactly sixty seconds to get away before the special forces surrounded the house. There was no margin for error on my end either.

I felt a stab of regret when I imagined how terrified my mother and little brothers and sisters would be within moments. As usual, they would have to pay the price for everything my father and I did.

I looked at my mother's beautiful garden. She had gathered flowers from all over, taking cuttings from friends and family whenever she could. She cared for her flowers like they were her children.

"How many flowers do we need?" I sometimes teased her.

"Just a few more" was always the reply.

I recalled the time she pointed to one and said, "This plant is older than you. When you were a child, you broke its pot, but I saved it and it's still alive."

Would it still be alive a few minutes from now after arriving troops crushed it under their feet?

My cell phone rang.

Blood rushed to my head. My heart pounded. I started my engine and sped toward the center of town where I had established a new secret location. I was no longer pretending to be a fugitive. Soldiers who would rather kill me than arrest me were searching for me at that very moment. One minute after my departure, ten civilian cars with Palestinian plates slammed on their brakes. Israeli special forces surrounded the house, automatic weapons covering every door and window. The neighborhood was full of children, including my brother Naser. They stopped their soccer game and scattered, terrified.

As soon as the troops were in position, more than twenty tanks thundered in. Now the whole city knew something was going on. I could hear the massive diesel engines from my hideout. Hundreds of armed Palestinian militants rushed to my father's house and surrounded the IDF. But they couldn't shoot because children were still running for cover and because my family was inside.

With the arrival of the feda'iyeen, the helicopters were called in.

I suddenly wondered if I had been wrong to spare the suicide bombers. If I had just let the IDF drop a bomb on them, my family and our neighborhood would not be at risk now. If one of my siblings died in this chaos, I would never forgive myself.

To make certain our elaborate production became a global news event, I had tipped off Al-Jazeera that there was going to be an attack on the home of Sheikh Hassan Yousef. They all thought the Israelis had finally gotten my father, and they wanted to broadcast his arrest live. I imagined what their reaction would be when the loudspeakers started to crackle and the soldiers demanded that his oldest son, Mosab, come out with his hands up. As soon as I got to my apartment, I flipped on the TV and watched the drama along with the rest of the Arab world.

The army evacuated my family and questioned them. My mother told them that I had left one minute before they arrived. Of course, they didn't believe her. They believed the Shin Bet, the ones who had staged the entire production and the only people besides myself who knew that the game had begun. When I didn't surrender, they threatened to start shooting.

For a tense ten minutes, everyone waited to see whether I would come out and, if I did, whether I would emerge shooting or with my hands in the air. Then time was up. They opened fire, and more than two hundred bullets riddled my second-floor bedroom (and are still in the walls today). There was no more talking. They had obviously decided to kill me.

Suddenly, the shooting stopped. Moments later, a missile whistled through the air and blew up half our house. Soldiers rushed inside. I knew they were searching every room. No corpse and no hiding fugitive.

The IDF was embarrassed and enraged that I had slipped from their grasp. If they caught me now, Loai warned over the phone, they would shoot me on sight. For us, however, the operation was a success. No one had been hurt, and I had advanced to the most-wanted list. The whole city was talking about me. Overnight, I had become a dangerous terrorist.

For the next few months, I had three priorities: stay out of the army's way, protect my dad, and continue to gather intelligence. In that order.

Chapter Twenty-Two

DEFENSIVE SHIELD
SPRING 2002

THE ESCALATION IN VIOLENCE WAS DIZZYING.

Israelis were shot and stabbed and blown up. Palestinians were assassinated. Round and round it went, faster and faster. The international community tried in vain to pressure Israel.

"End the illegal occupation. . . . Stop the bombing of civilian areas, the assassinations, the unnecessary use of lethal force, the demolitions and the daily humiliation of ordinary Palestinians," demanded UN secretary-general Kofi Annan in March 2002.[9]

On the same day that we had arrested the four suicide bombers I had protected from assassination, European Union leaders called on both Israel and the Palestinians to rein in the violence. "There is no military solution to this conflict," they said.[10]

In 2002, Passover fell on March 27. In a dining room on the ground floor of the Park Hotel in Netanya, 250 guests had gathered for the traditional Seder meal.

A twenty-five-year-old Hamas operative named Abdel-Basset Odeh walked past the front security guard, past the registration desk in the lobby, and into the packed hall. Then he reached into his jacket.

The explosion killed 30 people and wounded about 140 others. Some were Holocaust survivors. Hamas claimed responsibility, saying that the purpose of the attack was to derail the Arab Summit being held in Beirut. Nevertheless, the next day, the Saudi-led Arab League announced that it had voted unanimously to recognize the State of Israel and normalize relations, as long as Israel agreed to withdraw to the 1967 boundaries, resolve the refugee problem, and establish an independent Palestinian state with East Jerusalem as its capital. Receiving these concessions from Israel would have been a huge victory for our people if Hamas wasn't still committed to its all-or-nothing idealism.

Recognizing this, Israel was planning its own extreme solution.

Two weeks earlier, officials had decided to test the waters for a major incursion into the Palestinian territories by invading the twin cities of Ramallah and Al-Bireh. Military analysts warned of high Israeli casualties. They needn't have worried.

The IDF killed five Palestinians, imposed curfews, and occupied a few buildings. Huge D9 armored bulldozers also demolished several homes in Al-Amari refugee camp, including that of Wafa Idris, the first female suicide bomber, who had killed an eighty-one-year-old Israeli man and injured a hundred others outside a shoe store in Jerusalem back on January 27.

After the Park Hotel outrage, however, the test incursion became irrelevant. The Israeli cabinet gave the green light to launch an unprecedented operation, code-named Defensive Shield.

My phone rang. It was Loai.

"What's up?" I asked.

"The whole IDF is gathering," Loai said. "Tonight, we will have Saleh and every other fugitive in custody."

"What do you mean?"

"We are going to reoccupy the entire West Bank and search every house and office building, however long it takes. Stay put. I'll keep in touch."

Wow, I thought. *This is great! Maybe it will finally put an end to this mindless war.*

Rumors flew throughout the West Bank. The Palestinian leadership knew something was up but had no idea what. People left work, clinics, and classrooms and went home to sit by their television sets, waiting for news. I had moved my father to a house owned by a couple of American citizens, and the Shin Bet assured me he would be safe there.

On March 29, I checked into the City Inn Hotel on Nablus Road in Al-Bireh, where the BBC, CNN, and the rest of the international media were housed. My father and I kept in touch with two-way radios.

The Shin Bet expected me to be at my hotel, eating chips and watching TV. But I didn't want to miss anything so important. I wanted to be on top of everything, so I slung my M16 over my shoulder and headed out. Looking every bit the fugitive, I went to the top of the hill next to the Ramallah Library, from which I could see the southeast side of town where my father was. I figured I would be safe there, and I could run to the hotel as soon as I heard the tanks.

Around midnight, hundreds of Merkavas roared into the city. I hadn't expected them to invade from every direction at once—or to be moving so quickly. Some of the streets were so narrow that the tank drivers had no choice but to climb over the tops of the cars. Other streets were wide enough, but the soldiers seemed to enjoy the screech of grating metal under their treads. Streets in the refugee camps were little more than paths between cinder-block houses that the tanks ground into gravel.

"Turn off your radio!" I told my father. "Stay down! Keep your head down!"

I had parked my father's Audi at the curb. And I watched in horror as a tank tread crushed it to pulp. It wasn't supposed to be there. I didn't know what to do. I certainly couldn't call Loai and ask him to stop the operation just because I had decided to play Rambo.

I ran toward the center of the city and ducked into an underground parking garage, just a few yards from an oncoming tank. No troops were on the ground yet; they were waiting for the Merkavas to secure the area. Suddenly, I had a terrifying realization. A number of Palestinian resistance factions had offices in the building directly above my head. I had taken refuge in a key target.

Tanks have no discernment. They can't tell the difference between Shin Bet collaborators and terrorists, Christians and Muslims, armed fighters and unarmed civilians. And the kids inside those machines were just as scared as I was. All around me, guys who looked just like me fired AK-47s at the tanks. *Ping. Ping. Ping.* The bullets ricocheted like toys. *BOOM!* The tank shouted back, nearly bursting my eardrums.

Huge pieces of the buildings around us began to collapse into smoking heaps. Every cannon thump was a punch in the gut. Automatic weapons chattered and echoed off every wall. Another explosion. Blinding dust clouds. Flying chips and chunks of stone and metal.

I had to get out of there. But how?

Suddenly, a group of Fatah fighters ran into the garage and crouched around me. This wasn't good. What if the soldiers came now? The feda'iyeen would open up on them. Would I shoot too? If so, at whom? If I didn't shoot, they would kill me anyway. But I couldn't kill anyone. At one time I might have been able to, but not anymore.

More fighters came, calling to others as they ran. Suddenly, everything seemed to stop. Nobody breathed.

IDF soldiers made their way cautiously into the garage. Closer. Whatever was going to happen would cut loose in seconds. Their torches searched for the whites of eyes or a reflection from a weapon. They listened. And we watched. Sweaty index fingers on both sides were poised on triggers.

Then the Red Sea parted.

Maybe they were afraid to go any deeper into the black, humid parking garage, or maybe they simply yearned for the familiar companionship of a tank. For whatever reason, the soldiers stopped, turned, and just walked out.

Once they were clear, I made my way upstairs and found a room where I could call Loai.

"Could you ask the IDF to back off a couple of blocks so I can get back to my hotel?"

"What! Where are you? Why aren't you in the hotel?"

"I'm doing my job."

"You're nuts!"

There was an uncomfortable silence.

"Okay, we'll see what we can do."

It took a couple of hours to move the tanks and troops, who must have wondered why they had been pulled back. Once they moved, I nearly broke my leg jumping from one rooftop to another to return to my room. I shut the door, stripped, and stuffed my terrorist outfit and weapon into the air-conditioning duct.

Meanwhile, the house where my father was hiding was right in the center of the storm. The IDF searched inside every house around him, behind every building, and under every rock. But they had orders not to enter that particular house.

Inside, my father read his Qur'an and prayed. The owner of the house read the Qur'an and prayed. His wife read the Qur'an and prayed. Then, for no apparent reason, the troops left and began searching another area.

"You will not believe the miracle, Mosab!" my father said into my handset later. "It was unbelievable! They came. They searched every house around us, the entire neighborhood—except where we were. Allah be praised!"

You're welcome, I thought.

There had been nothing like Operation Defensive Shield since the Six-Day War. And this was only the beginning. Ramallah was the spearhead of the operation. Bethlehem, Jenin, and Nablus followed. While I had been running around dodging Israeli troops, the IDF had surrounded Yasser Arafat's compound. Everything was locked down. Strict curfews were imposed.

On April 2, tanks and armored personnel carriers surrounded the Preventive Security Compound near our house in Betunia. Helicopter gunships chugged overhead. We knew the PA was hiding at least fifty wanted men at the compound, and the Shin Bet was frustrated because it was coming up empty-handed everywhere else.

The compound included four buildings, in addition to the four-story office building that housed Colonel Jibril Rajoub[11] and other security officials. The entire facility had been designed, built, and equipped by the CIA. The police were trained and armed by the CIA. The CIA even had offices there. Hundreds of heavily armed police were inside, along with a large number of prisoners, including Bilal Barghouti and others on Israel's hit list. The Shin Bet and IDF were in a no-nonsense mood. Loudspeakers announced that the army would blow up Building One in five minutes and ordered everybody out.

Exactly five minutes later, *boom!* Building Two. "Everybody out!" *Boom!* Building Three. *Boom!* Building Four. *Boom!*

"Take off your clothes!" came the demand over the loudspeakers. The Israelis took no chances that someone might still be armed or packed with explosives. Hundreds of men stripped naked. They were given jumpsuits, loaded onto buses, and taken to nearby Ofer Military Base—where the Shin Bet discovered its mistake.

Of course there were too many people to lock up, but the Israelis wanted only the fugitives anyway. They had planned to sift through the detainees and release all but those on its list of suspects. The problem was that everybody had left their clothes—with their ID cards—back at the compound. How would the security forces distinguish between wanted men and police?

Ofer Dekel, Loai's boss's boss, was in charge. He called Jibril Rajoub, who had been away from the compound at the time of the attack. Dekel gave Rajoub a special permit so he could pass safely through hundreds of tanks and thousands of soldiers. When he arrived, Dekel asked Rajoub if he would mind pointing out which men worked for him and which were fugitives. Rajoub said he would be happy to. Quickly, Rajoub identified police as fugitives and fugitives as police, and the Shin Bet released all the wanted men.

"Why did you do that to me?" Dekel asked, after he figured out what had happened.

"You just blew up my offices and my compound," Rajoub calmly explained in what amounted to a Palestinian version of "Duh." Dekel also seemed to have forgotten that his PA pal had been wounded a year earlier when IDF tanks and helicopters leveled his home, making him even less inclined to do favors for the Israelis.

The Shin Bet was deeply embarrassed. The only thing they could do in retaliation was release an official account that branded Rajoub as a traitor for turning over the wanted men to Israel in a deal brokered by the CIA. As a result, Rajoub lost his power and ended up as head of the Palestinian Soccer Association.

This was clearly a debacle.

Over the next three weeks, the Israelis did lift the curfew from time to time, and during a break on April 15, I was able to bring some food and other necessities to my father. He told me he didn't feel safe in that house and wanted to move. I called one of the Hamas leaders and asked if he knew of any place where Hassan Yousef could be protected. He told me to take my father to the location where Sheikh Jamal al-Taweel, another high-profile Hamas fugitive, was hiding.

Wow, I thought. The arrest of Jamal al-Taweel would certainly make the Shin Bet feel much better about Operation Defensive Shield. I thanked him but said, "Let's not put my father in the same place. It might be too dangerous for both of them to be there together." We agreed on another spot, and I quickly got my father settled in his new safe house. Then I called Loai.

"I know where Jamal al-Taweel is hiding."

Loai couldn't believe the news; al-Taweel was arrested that very night.

That same day, we also nabbed another of the IDF's most wanted men—Marwan Barghouti.

Though Marwan was one of Hamas's most elusive leaders, his capture actually turned out to be quite simple. I called one of his guards and talked with him briefly on his cell phone while the Shin Bet traced the call. Barghouti was later tried in a civilian court and sentenced to five consecutive life sentences.

Meanwhile, not a day passed when Operation Defensive Shield did not make international headlines. Few were flattering. Out of Jenin came rumors of a large-scale massacre, which no one could verify because the IDF had sealed the city. Palestinian cabinet minister Saeb Erekat said 500 were dead. The figure was later revised to about 50.

In Bethlehem, more than 200 Palestinians were under siege in the Church of the Nativity for about five weeks. After the dust had settled and most of the civilians had been allowed to leave, 8 Palestinians had been killed, 26 were sent to Gaza, 85 were checked by the IDF and released, and the 13 most wanted were exiled to Europe.

All told during Defensive Shield, nearly 500 Palestinians were killed, 1,500 were wounded, and nearly 4,300 were detained by the IDF. On the other side, 29 Israelis were dead, and 127 were wounded. The World Bank estimated the damage at more than $360 million.

Chapter Twenty-Three
SUPERNATURAL PROTECTION
SUMMER 2002

WEDNESDAY, JULY 31, 2002, was a scorcher. One hundred and two degrees Fahrenheit. On the Mount Scopus campus of Hebrew University, no classes were in session, though some students were still taking exams. Others lined up to register for fall classes. At 1:30 p.m., the university's Frank Sinatra Cafeteria was packed with people cooling off, enjoying iced drinks, and chatting. Nobody noticed the bag that had been left there by a contract painter.

The massive explosion gutted the cafeteria and left nine people dead, including five Americans. Eighty-five others were injured, fourteen seriously.

That same day, my good friend Saleh disappeared. When we checked the locations of the other four on our most-wanted list, we found that they, too, had disappeared without a trace, even severing all connection with their families. We were able to identify the Hamas cell that planted the bomb and found that its members were from inside Israel, not the occupied territories. They carried blue Israeli ID cards that allowed them to go anywhere they wanted. Five were from East Jerusalem: married, nice families, good jobs.

During the course of the investigation, one name came to the surface: Mohammed Arman, a man who lived in one of the Ramallah villages. Under torture, Arman was asked to identify the man behind the Hebrew University attack. He said he knew him only by the name "Sheikh."

The interrogators brought in photographs of suspected terrorists, like a book of mug shots in an American police station, and told him to point to "Sheikh." Arman identified a picture of Ibrahim Hamed, providing us with the first hard evidence of his involvement with suicide bombings.

We would learn later that, once identified, Hamed used his exposure to protect Saleh and the other members of his cell. All the cells under his command had been told that if they were captured, they were to blame everything on Hamed, since he no longer had anything to lose. So for the time being, the trail ended with Ibrahim Hamed. And he was nowhere to be found.

During the months following Operation Defensive Shield, Ramallah was under curfew. Arafat's operations were pretty much shut down. USAID had suspended its projects and was not allowing its employees to enter the West Bank. Israeli checkpoints strangled the city, letting nothing but ambulances in or out. And I was officially a fugitive. All of this made it very difficult for me to get around. Nevertheless, I still had to meet with the Shin Bet every other week or so to discuss ongoing operations that could not be discussed on the telephone.

Equally important, I needed emotional support. The loneliness was terrible. I had become a stranger in my own city. I couldn't share my life with anybody, not even my own family. And I couldn't trust anyone else. Ordinarily, Loai and I met at one of the Shin Bet safe houses in Jerusalem. But I could no longer get out of Ramallah. It wasn't even safe for me to be seen on the streets in the daytime. None of the usual options were possible.

If special forces came in Palestinian cars to pick me up, they risked being stopped by feda'iyeen and exposed by their accents. If security agents in IDF uniforms pretended to kidnap me, somebody might spot me jumping into the jeep. And even if it worked, how many times could we get away with that ruse?

Finally the Shin Bet came up with a more creative way for us to meet.

Ofer Military Base, a couple of miles south of Ramallah, was one of Israel's highest-security facilities. The place was crammed with secrets and wrapped in security. The Shin Bet local offices were there.

"Okay," Loai told me. "From now on, we're going to meet at Ofer. All you have to do is break in."

We both laughed. And then I realized he was serious.

"If you're caught," he explained, "it will look to everyone like you were trying to infiltrate a major military installation to plan an attack."

"*If* I'm caught?"

The plan was troubling. And late one night when the time came to put it into action, I felt like an actor on opening night—about to step onto a set he had never seen before, dressed in a costume he had never worn before, with no script and no rehearsal.

I didn't know that the Shin Bet had positioned their own agents in the two guard towers flanking the spot in the outer perimeter that I was supposed to breach. Nor did I know that more armed security agents equipped with night-vision gear were stationed along my route to protect me in the unlikely event that somebody might be following.

I just kept thinking, *What if I make a mistake?*

I parked my car out of sight. Loai had instructed me to wear dark clothes, not to carry a flashlight, and to bring a pair of bolt cutters. I took a deep breath.

Heading into the hills, I could see the twinkle of the base lights in the distance. For a while, a pack of stray dogs barked at my heels as I followed the rise and fall of the rugged terrain. That was okay, as long as they didn't draw any unwelcome attention.

Finally I came to the outer fence and called Loai.

"From the corner, count seven stanchions," he said. "Then wait for my sign and start cutting."

I cut through what had become the old fence after a new one had been built about twenty feet inside at the start of the Second Intifada.

I had been warned about the guard pigs (yes, I said guard pigs), but I didn't encounter them, so it didn't matter. The area between the outer and inner perimeters formed a run that, at any other military base in the world, would be patrolled by German shepherds or other highly trained attack dogs. Ironically, the kosher-conscious Israelis used pigs. It's true.

It was thought that the presence of pigs and the threat of possible contact with them would serve as a psychological deterrent to any prospective terrorist who was a devout Muslim. Islam forbids contact with pigs as vehemently as does Orthodox Judaism. Perhaps even more so.

I never saw pigs guarding a settlement, but Loai told me later that they did sentry duty at Ofer Military Base.

I found a small door in the inner fence that had been left unlocked. I went through, and there I was, with guard towers rising up on either side like the devil's horns, inside one of the most secure military installations in Israel.

"Keep your head down," Loai said into my ear, "and wait for a sign."

There were bushes all around me. After a few moments, several of them started moving. Turns out, some of them were actually the agents who were usually present in our meetings, but now they were carrying heavy machine guns and wearing IDF camouflage uniforms with branches sticking out all over. I could tell they were having fun playing commando—just one more dress-up role in a repertoire that ranged from terrorists and feda'iyeen to old men and the occasional woman.

"How are you doing?" they asked me, as if we had just sat down together in a coffeehouse. "Is everything okay?"

"Everything is okay."

"Have you got anything?"

Sometimes I brought them recording devices or other evidence or intelligence, but I was empty-handed this time.

It started to rain, and we ran up and over a hill to an area where two jeeps waited. Three of the men jumped into the first jeep, and I jumped in the back. The others stayed with the second jeep to secure my return. I felt sorry for the guys we left behind because it was raining pretty hard. But they still seemed to be enjoying themselves.

After meeting with Loai, his boss, and the guards for a few hours, I left the same way I had come—pleased with myself, even though the trek back was long, wet, and cold.

This became our standard way of meeting. It was perfectly choreographed and executed flawlessly every time. I didn't have to cut the fence again, but I always carried the cutters, just in case.

After my "escape" from the highly visible IDF raid, I continued to keep tabs on my father to make sure he was okay and see if there was anything he needed. Every once in a while, I stopped by the USAID office, but since we had suspended most of our work, what little I needed to do I was able to finish from my computer at home. At night, I hung out with wanted people and gathered intelligence. And late at night, once or twice a month, I infiltrated a top secret military installation to attend a meeting.

In my spare time, I continued to hang out with my Christian friends to talk about the love of Jesus. Actually, it was a lot more than talk. Even though I was still just a follower of the Teacher, I felt as if I was experiencing God's love and protection every day, and it seemed to be extending to the members of my family as well.

One afternoon, special forces troops were searching the City Inn for fugitives and came up empty, so they decided to take a break at a nearby house. This was common practice. The IDF didn't need orders or authorization. When things were relatively quiet, their special forces soldiers simply commandeered somebody's house in order to grab a few hours of rest and maybe get something to eat. Sometimes during heavy fighting, they even broke into local homes and used the occupants as human shields—much like the feda'iyeen often did.

On this particular day, they chose the house in which my father was hiding. The Shin Bet didn't know this was happening. None of us did. The fact that soldiers picked that particular house on that particular day was something no one could have predicted or prevented. And when they arrived, my father "happened" to be in the basement.

"Could you please not bring the dogs in here?" the woman who lived there asked the soldiers. "I have little children."

Her husband was terrified that the troops would find Hassan Yousef and arrest them for harboring a fugitive. So he tried to act normal and unafraid. He told his seven-year-old daughter to go and shake hands with the commander. The commander was charmed by the little girl and figured she and her parents were just a regular family who had nothing to do with terrorists. He asked the woman politely if his men could rest for a little while upstairs, and she said that would be fine. About twenty-five Israeli soldiers stayed in that house for more than eight hours, unaware that my father was literally right beneath them.

I could not explain away the sense of supernatural protection and intervention. It was real to me. When Ahmad al-Faransi (who had once asked me for explosives to give to his suicide bombers) called me from the middle of Ramallah and asked if I could pick him up and drive him home, I told him I was in the area and would be there in a few minutes. When I arrived, he climbed into the car, and we started driving.

We had not gone far when al-Faransi's cell phone rang. Al-Faransi was on Jerusalem's assassination list, and Arafat's headquarters was calling to warn him that Israeli helicopters had been following him. I opened the window and heard two Apaches closing in. Though it may seem strange to those who have not sensed God speaking to them in an internal voice, on this day I heard God speak to my heart, instructing me to turn left between two buildings. I later learned that had I continued to go straight, the Israelis would have had a clean shot at my car. I turned the car and instantly heard that divine voice say, *Get out of the car and leave it.* We jumped out and ran. By the time the helicopter reacquired its target, the only thing its pilot could see was a parked car and two open doors. It hovered for about sixty seconds and then turned and flew away.

I learned later that intelligence had received a message that al-Faransi had been spotted getting into a dark blue Audi A4. There were many just like it in town. Loai wasn't in the operations room at the time to check my location, and no one knew to ask whether this Audi might belong to the Green Prince. Few members of the Shin Bet even knew of my existence.

Somehow, I seemed to always benefit from divine protection. I wasn't even a Christian yet, and al-Faransi certainly didn't know the Lord. My Christian friends were praying for me every day, however. And God, Jesus said in Matthew 5:45, "causes his sun to rise on the evil and the good, and sends rain on the righteous and the unrighteous." This was certainly a far cry from the cruel and vengeful god of the Qur'an.

Chapter Twenty-Four

PROTECTIVE CUSTODY
FALL 2002–SPRING 2003

I WAS EXHAUSTED. I was tired of playing so many dangerous roles at once, tired of having to change my personality and appearance to fit the current company I was keeping. When I was with my father and other Hamas leaders, I had to play the part of a dedicated member of Hamas. When I was with the Shin Bet, I had to play the part of an Israeli collaborator. When I was at home, I often played the part of father and protector of my siblings, and when I was at work, I had to play the part of a regular working guy. I was in my last semester of college, and I had exams to study for. But I couldn't concentrate.

It was the end of September 2002, and I decided that it was time for act 2 of the play that had opened with the Shin Bet's phony attempt to arrest me.

"I can't keep up like this," I told Loai. "What will it take? A few months in prison? We go through the motions of interrogation. You release me. Then I can go back and finish school. I can go back to my job at USAID and live a normal life."

"What about your father?"

"I'm not going to leave him behind to be assassinated. Go ahead and arrest him too."

"If that's what you want. The government will certainly be happy that we finally caught Hassan Yousef."

I told my mother where my father was hiding, and I let her visit him. Five minutes after she arrived at the safe house, special forces poured into the area. Soldiers ran through the neighborhood, shouting at all the civilians to get inside.

One of those "civilians," smoking a narghile (Turkish water pipe) in front of his house, was none other than master bomb maker Abdullah Barghouti, who had no idea that he had been living across the street from Hassan Yousef. And the poor IDF soldier who told him to get inside had no idea that he had been shouting at Israel's most wanted mass murderer.

Everybody was clueless. My father had no idea that his son had given him up in order to protect him from being assassinated. And the IDF had no idea that the Shin Bet had known the whereabouts of Hassan Yousef all along and that some of their soldiers had even eaten lunch and enjoyed a nap in the house where he was hiding.

As usual, my father surrendered peacefully. And he and the other Hamas leaders assumed the Shin Bet had followed my mother to his hideout. Naturally, my mother was sad, but she was also relieved that her husband was somewhere safe and no longer on Israel's assassination list.

"We'll see *you* tonight," Loai told me after the dust settled.

As the sun began to set on the horizon, I sat inside my house, looking out the window, watching as about twenty special forces troops moved in fast and took their positions. I knew I needed to get my head down now and prepare for a little rough treatment. A couple of minutes later, jeeps drove in. Then a tank. The IDF sealed the area. Somebody jumped onto my balcony. Somebody else banged on my door.

"Who is it?" I called out, pretending I didn't know.

"IDF! Open the door!"

I opened the door, and they pushed me down onto the floor, quickly searching me for weapons.

"Is anybody else here?"

"No."

I don't know why they bothered to ask. They started kicking in doors anyway and searching the house, room by room. Once outside, I found myself face-to-face with my friend.

"Where have you been?" Loai asked, talking harshly to me, as if I truly were what I pretended to be. "We've been looking for you. Are you trying to get yourself killed? You must have been crazy to run from your father's house last year."

A bunch of angry soldiers looked on and listened.

"We got your father," he said, "and we finally got you! Let's see what you have to say under interrogation!"

A couple of soldiers threw me into a jeep. Loai came over, leaned in so no one could hear him, and asked, "How are you doing, my friend? Is everything okay? Handcuffs too tight?"

"Everything's fine," I said. "Just get me out of here, and don't let the soldiers beat me during the ride."

"Don't worry. One of my guys will be with you."

They brought me to Ofer Military Base, where we sat in the same room in which we used to meet for a couple of hours of "interrogation," drinking coffee and talking about the situation.

"We're going to take you to Maskobiyeh," Loai said, "just for a short time. We'll pretend that you went through a tough interrogation. Your father is already there, and you'll get to see him. He is not being questioned or tortured. Then we'll take you to administrative detention. You'll spend several months there, and after that, we'll ask to extend your sentence for three more months because anybody with your status would be expected to spend a respectable time in prison."

When I saw the interrogators, even those who had tortured me during my previous stay, I was surprised to discover that I felt no bitterness whatsoever toward these men. The only way I could explain it was using a verse I had read: Hebrews 4:12 says that "the word of God is living and active. Sharper than any double-edged sword, it penetrates even to dividing soul and spirit, joints and marrow; it judges the thoughts and attitudes of the heart." I had read and pondered these words many times, as well as Jesus' commands to forgive your enemies and love those who mistreat you. Somehow, even though I was still unable to accept Jesus Christ as God, his words seemed to be alive and active and working inside me. I don't know how else I would have been able to see people as people, not Jew or Arab, prisoner or torturer. Even the old hatred that had driven me to buy guns and to plot the deaths of Israelis was being displaced by a love I didn't understand.

I was put into a cell by myself for a couple of weeks. And once or twice a day, when they weren't busy interrogating other prisoners, my Shin Bet friends came to check on me and chat. I ate well and remained the prison's best-kept secret. This time, there were no stinking hoods or crazy hunchbacks or Leonard Cohen songs (although he would one day become my favorite recording artist—weird, huh?). In the West Bank, word circulated that I was a really tough guy who gave no information to the Israelis, even under torture.

A few days before my transfer, I was moved into my father's cell. A look of relief swept over my father's face as he held out his arms for an embrace. He held me away from him and smiled.

"I followed you," I said, laughing. "I couldn't live without you."

Two others were in the cell, and we joked around and had a good time together. To be honest, I was very happy to see my dad safely behind bars. No mistakes would be made. No missiles would come from the sky.

Sometimes while he read the Qur'an to us, I just enjoyed looking at him and listening to his beautiful voice. I thought about how gentle he was when we were growing up. He never forced us to get out of bed for early morning prayers, but we all did it because we wanted to make him proud. He had given his life to Allah at a very early age and passed along that devotion to the rest of us by example.

Now I thought: *My beloved father, I am so glad to be sitting here with you. I know prison is the last place you want to be right now, but if you weren't here, your shattered remains would probably be in a little vinyl bag somewhere.* Sometimes he looked up and saw me smiling at him with love and appreciation. He didn't understand why, and I couldn't tell him.

When the guards came to transfer me out, my father and I hugged tightly. He seemed so frail in my embrace, and yet I knew how strong he was. We had been so close over the past few days that I felt as if I was being torn apart. I even found it difficult to leave the Shin Bet officers. We had developed an incredibly close relationship over the years. I looked at their faces and hoped they knew how much I admired them. They looked back at me apologetically. They knew the next stop on my journey wouldn't be so easy.

The faces of the soldiers who handcuffed me for transfer had a completely different look. To them, I was a terrorist who had escaped the IDF, made them look stupid, and evaded capture. This time, I was taken to Ofer Prison, part of the military base where I had met regularly with the Shin Bet.

My beard grew long and thick like everyone else's. And I joined the other prisoners in the daily routine. When prayer times came, I bowed and knelt and prayed, but no longer to Allah. I prayed now to the Creator of the universe. I was getting closer. One day, I even found an Arabic-language Bible stashed in the world religion section of the library. It was the whole thing, not just the New Testament. No one had ever touched it. I'll bet no one even knew it was there. What a gift from God! I read it again and again.

Every now and then, somebody would come over to me and gently try to find out what I was doing. I explained that I studied history and that since the Bible was an ancient book, it contained some of the earliest information available. Not only that, but the values it teaches are also great, I said, and I believed that every Muslim ought to read it. People were usually okay with that. The only time they got a little sore was during Ramadan, when it seemed I was studying the Bible more than the Qur'an.

The Bible study I had attended in West Jerusalem was open to everybody—Christian, Muslim, Jew, atheist, whatever. Through this group, I had had opportunities to sit down with Jewish people who came with the same purpose as I did: to study Christianity and learn about Jesus. It was a unique experience for me as a Palestinian Muslim to study Jesus with an Israeli Jew.

Through this group, I had gotten to know a Jewish man named Amnon pretty well. He was married and had two beautiful children. He was very smart and spoke several languages. His wife was a Christian and had encouraged him for a long time to be baptized. Finally, Amnon decided to do it, so the group gathered one evening to witness his baptism in the pastor's bathtub. By the time I arrived, Amnon had finished reading some Bible verses and had begun to cry very hard.

He knew that when he allowed himself to be lowered under the water, he was not only declaring his allegiance to Jesus Christ through the identification with his death and resurrection, he was also divorcing his culture. He was turning his back on the faith of his father, a professor at Hebrew University. He was abandoning Israeli society and religious traditions, destroying his reputation, and jeopardizing his future.

Not long after, Amnon received notice to begin serving his tour with the IDF. In Israel, every non-Arab citizen, male or female, over the age of eighteen is required to serve in the military—men for three years, women for two. But Amnon had seen enough checkpoint massacres to feel that, as a Christian, he could not allow himself to be placed in a position where he might be required to shoot unarmed civilians. And he refused to put on a uniform and go to the West Bank.

"Even if I could do my job by shooting a stone-throwing child in the leg instead of in the head," he argued, "I don't want to do it. I am called to love my enemy."

A second notice came. Then a third.

When he still refused to serve, Amnon was arrested and imprisoned. What I didn't realize was that Amnon was living in the Jewish section of the prison the entire time I was at Ofer. He was there because he refused to work with the Israelis; I was there because I had agreed to work with them. I was trying to protect Jews; he was trying to protect Palestinians.

I didn't believe that everybody in Israel and the occupied territories needed to become a Christian in order to end the bloodshed. But I thought that if we just had a thousand Amnons on one side and a thousand Mosabs on the other, it could make a big difference. And if we had more . . . who knows?

A couple of months after arriving at Ofer, I was taken to court, where no one knew who I was—not the judge or the prosecutors, not even my own lawyer.

At my trial, the Shin Bet testified that I was dangerous and requested that I be kept longer. The judge agreed and sentenced me to six months in administrative detention. Again, I was transferred.

Five hours drive from anywhere, in the sand dunes of the Negev Desert and very near the Dimona nuclear plant, stood the tent prison of Ktzi'ot, where you melted in the summer and froze in the winter.

"What's your organization?"

"Hamas."

Yes, I still identified myself as part of my family, as part of my history. But I was no longer like the other prisoners.

Hamas was still the majority. But since the start of the Second Intifada, Fatah had grown significantly, and each group had about the same number of tents. I was tired of pretending, and my new-found ethical code kept me from lying. So I decided to keep mostly to myself while I was there.

Ktzi'ot was serious wilderness. The night air echoed with the sounds of wolves and hyenas and leopards. I had heard stories of prisoners who had escaped Ktzi'ot, but no stories of anyone having survived the desert. Winter was worse than summer—freezing air and drifting snow and nothing but canvas to keep out the wind. Each tent had a moisture barrier across the roof. But some of the prisoners tore down pieces of it to make privacy curtains around their cots. The moisture from our breath was supposed to be trapped in that liner. But it just floated up and stuck to the naked canvas until it got too heavy. Then all that spit rained down on us throughout the night as we slept.

The Israelis virtually papered the camp with glue boards to try to keep the mouse population under control. Early one frosty morning while everyone else was still asleep, I was reading my Bible when I heard a squeaking sound, like a rusty bedspring. I looked under my cot and saw a mouse stuck to a glue board. What surprised me, though, was that another mouse was trying to save him without getting stuck himself. Was it his mate or a friend? I don't know. I watched for about half an hour as one animal risked its life to save another. It moved me so much that I freed them both.

At the prison, reading materials were pretty much limited to the Qur'an and Qur'anic studies. I had only two English-language books that a friend had smuggled to me through my lawyer. I was deeply grateful to have something to read and to strengthen my English skills, but it didn't take long for me to wear out the covers from reading the books so much. One day, I was walking around by myself when I saw two prisoners making tea. Beside them was a huge wooden box filled with novels sent by the Red Cross. And these guys were tearing up the books for fuel! I couldn't control myself. I shoved the box away from them and started scooping up the books. They thought I wanted them so I could make my own tea.

"Are you insane?" I told them. "It took me forever to smuggle in two English-language books so I could read them, and you're making tea with these!"

"Those are Christian books," they argued.

"They are not Christian books," I told them. "They're *New York Times* best sellers. I'm sure they don't say anything against Islam. They're just stories about human experiences."

They probably wondered what was wrong with the son of Hassan Yousef. He had been so quiet, mostly keeping to himself and reading. Suddenly, he was raving about a box of books. If it had been anybody else, they probably would have fought to keep their priceless fuel. But they let me have the novels, and I returned to my bed with a whole box of new treasures. I piled them around me and wallowed in them. I didn't care what anybody thought. My heart was singing and praising God for providing me with something to read while I tried to pass the time in this place.

I read sixteen hours a day until my eyes grew weak from the poor light. During the four months I spent at Ktzi'ot, I memorized four thousand English vocabulary words.

While I was there, I also experienced two prison uprisings, far worse than the one we had at Megiddo. But God got me through it all. In fact, I experienced God's presence more strongly in that prison than any time before or since. I may not have known Jesus as the Creator yet, but I was certainly learning to love God the Father.

On April 2, 2003—as Coalition ground troops raced toward Baghdad—I was released. I emerged as a respected leader of Hamas, a seasoned terrorist, and a wily fugitive. I had been tried by fire and proven. My risk of being burned had decreased significantly, and my father was alive and safe.

Once more I could walk openly down the streets of Ramallah. I no longer had to act like a fugitive. I could be myself again. I called my mother; then I called Loai.

"Welcome home, Green Prince," he said. "We missed you very much. A lot has been happening, and we didn't know what to do without you."

A few days after my return, I had a reunion with Loai and my other good Israeli friends. They had only one news item to report, but it was a huge one.

In March, Abdullah Barghouti had been spotted and arrested. Later that year, the Kuwaiti-born bomb maker would be tried in Israeli military court for killing sixty-six people and wounding about five hundred. I knew there were more, but those were all we would be able to prove. Barghouti would be sentenced to sixty-seven life terms—one for each murder victim and an extra one for all those he had wounded. At his sentencing, he would express no remorse, blame Israel, and regret only that he had not had the opportunity to kill more Jews.

"The spate of murderous terror that the accused let loose was one of the most severe in the blood-soaked history of this country," the judges said.[12] Barghouti flew into a rage, threatening to kill the judges and to teach every Hamas prisoner how to make bombs. As a result, he would serve his terms in solitary confinement. Ibrahim Hamed, my friend Saleh Talahme, and the others, however, still remained at large.

In October, my project at USAID ended, along with my employment. So I threw myself into my work for the Shin Bet, gathering all the information I could.

One morning, a couple of months later, Loai called.

"We found Saleh."

Chapter Twenty-Five

SALEH

WINTER 2003–SPRING 2006

IT WAS EASY TO KNOW where Saleh and his friends had *been*. The blood they left in their wake was unmistakable. But until now, nobody had been able to catch up to them.

That the Shin Bet had found him broke my heart. Saleh was my friend. He had helped me with my studies. I had shared bread with him and his wife, and I had played with his children. But Saleh was also a terrorist. During his imprisonment by the Palestinian Authority, he had continued his studies through Al-Quds Open University and used what he learned to become such a great bomb maker that he could even make explosives from garbage.

After Saleh's release by the PA, the Shin Bet watched to see how much time it would take him and his friends to rebuild the Al-Qassam Brigades. It didn't take long at all. The rebuilt organization wasn't big, but it was deadly.

Maher Odeh was the brains of the operation; Saleh, the engineer; and Bilal Barghouti, the recruiter of suicide bombers. In fact, the Hamas military wing consisted of only about ten people who operated independently, had their own budgets, and never met together unless it was urgent. Saleh could turn out several explosive belts overnight, and Bilal had a waiting list of candidates for martyrdom.

If I had believed Saleh was innocent, I would have warned him about what was going to happen. But when we finally connected the dots, I realized that he had been behind the Hebrew University bombing and many others. I understood that he needed to be locked away in prison. The only thing I might have done was introduce him to the teachings of Jesus and urge him to follow them as I did. But I knew he was too blinded by rage, zeal, and commitment to have listened, even to an old friend. I could, however, beg the Shin Bet to arrest Saleh and the others rather than kill them. And very reluctantly, they agreed.

Israeli security agents had been monitoring Saleh for more than two months. They watched him leave his apartment to meet in an abandoned house with Hasaneen Rummanah. And they watched him return home, where he remained for a week or so. They saw that his friend Sayyed al-Sheikh Qassem went out more frequently, but he always did what he had to do and came right back. The caution of the fugitives was impressive. No wonder it had taken us so long to find them. Once we picked up their scent, however, it was just a matter of tracking their contacts and contacts of contacts—about forty or fifty in all.

We had a lock on three of the guys on our most-wanted list, but for Ibrahim Hamed and Maher Odeh, we had only clues, nothing concrete. We had to decide whether to wait until the clues led us to them, which was a long shot, or break the spine of the Al-Qassam Brigades in the West Bank by arresting those we had already located. We decided on the latter, figuring we might even get lucky and snag Hamed or Odeh when we hauled in our net.

On the night of December 1, 2003, special forces surrounded more than fifty suspected locations at one time. Every troop available had been called in from all over the West Bank. The Hamas leaders were holed up at the Al-Kiswani building in Ramallah, and they did not respond when they were asked to surrender. Saleh and

Sayyed had a lot of weaponry, including a heavy machine gun, the type usually found welded to military vehicles.

The standoff began at 10 p.m. and continued through the night. When the shooting started, I could hear it from my house. Then the unmistakable explosion of a Merkava cannon shattered the morning, and everything was quiet. At 6 a.m., my phone rang.

"Your friend is gone," Loai told me. "I'm so sorry. You know we would have spared him if we could have. But let me tell you something. If this man—" Loai's voice broke as he tried to continue— "if this man had grown up in a different environment, he would not have been the same. He would have been just like us. He thought, he really believed, he was doing something good for his people. He was just so wrong."

Loai knew I had loved Saleh and didn't want him to die. He knew Saleh was resisting something he believed to be evil and hurtful to his people. And maybe, somehow, Loai had come to care about Saleh too.

"Are they all dead?"

"I haven't seen the bodies yet. They took them to Ramallah Hospital. We need you to go there and identify them. You're the only one who knew them all."

I grabbed a coat and drove over to the hospital, desperately hoping that maybe it wasn't Saleh, maybe somebody else had been killed. When I arrived, it was chaos. Angry Hamas activists were shouting in the street, and police were everywhere. No one was allowed inside, but because everybody knew who I was, the hospital officials let me in. A medical worker led me down a hallway to a room lined with large coolers. He opened the refrigerator door and slowly pulled out a drawer, releasing the stench of death into the room.

I looked down and saw Saleh's face. He was almost smiling. But his head was empty. Sayyed's drawer contained a collection of body parts—legs, head, whatever—in a black plastic bag. Hasaneen Rummanah had been ripped in half. I wasn't even sure it was him because the face was shaved and Hasaneen had always worn a soft brown beard. Despite media reports to the contrary, Ibrahim Hamed was not with the others. The man who had ordered these men to fight to the death had run away to save himself.

With virtually all of the West Bank Hamas leaders dead or in prison, I became the contact for the leaders in Gaza and Damascus. Somehow, I had become a key contact for the entire Palestinian network of parties, sects, organizations, and cells—including terrorist cells. And no one but a handful of elite Shin Bet insiders knew who or what I really was. It was astonishing to think about.

Because of my new role, it was my sad responsibility to organize the funerals for Saleh and the others. As I did so, I watched every move and listened for every angry or grief-filled whisper that might lead us to Hamed.

"Since the rumors are already flying," Loai said, "and you are sitting in for the leaders we've arrested, let's put out the word that Ibrahim Hamed cut a deal with the Shin Bet. Most Palestinians have no idea what's going on. They'll believe it, and he'll be forced to defend himself publicly or at least contact the political leaders in Gaza or Damascus. Either way, we may get a lead."

It was a great idea, but the agency brass nixed it because they were afraid Ibrahim would launch an attack on civilians in retaliation— as if Israel's killing his friends and arresting half of his organization hadn't made him angry enough.

So we did it the hard way.

Agents bugged every room in Hamed's house, hoping his wife or children might let something slip. But it turned out to be the quietest house in Palestine. Once we heard his young son, Ali, ask his mother, "Where is Baba?"

"We don't talk about that at all," she scolded.

If his family was that careful, how cautious would Ibrahim be? Months passed with no trace of him.

In late October 2004, Yasser Arafat became ill during a meeting. His people said he had the flu. But his condition got worse, and he was finally flown out of the West Bank to a hospital outside of Paris. On November 3, he slipped into a coma. Some said he had been poisoned. Others said he had AIDS. He died November 11 at age seventy-five.

A week or so later, my father was released from prison, and no one was more surprised than he was. Loai and other Shin Bet officials met with him the morning of his release.

"Sheikh Hassan," they said, "it is time for peace. People outside need a person like you. Arafat is gone; a lot of people are being killed. You are a reasonable man. We have to work things out somehow before they get worse."

"Leave the West Bank, and give us an independent state," my father replied, "and it will be over." Of course both sides knew that Hamas would never stop short of taking back all of Israel, though an independent Palestine might bring peace for a decade or two.

Outside Ofer Prison, I waited along with hundreds of reporters from around the world. Carrying his belongings in a black garbage bag, my father squinted in the bright sunlight as two Israeli soldiers led him out the door.

We hugged and kissed, and he asked me to take him directly to Yasser Arafat's grave before going home. I looked into his eyes and understood that this was a very important step for him. With Arafat gone, Fatah was weakened and the streets were boiling. Fatah leaders were terrified that Hamas would take over, igniting a turf war. The United States, Israel, and the international community were afraid of a civil war. This gesture by the top Hamas leader in the West Bank was a shock to everyone, but no one missed the message: Calm down, everybody. Hamas is not going to take advantage of the death of Arafat. There will be no civil war.

The fact was, however, that after a decade of arrests, imprisonments, and assassinations, the Shin Bet still had no clue who was actually in charge of Hamas. None of us did. I had helped them arrest known activists, men heavily involved in the resistance movement, all the while hoping they were the ones. We put people under administrative detention for years, sometimes based on suspicion alone. But Hamas never seemed to notice their absence.

So who was really in charge?

The fact that it wasn't my father came as a big surprise to everyone—even me. We bugged his office and car, monitored every move he made. And there was absolutely no doubt that he was not pulling the strings.

Hamas had always been something of a ghost. It had no central or branch offices, no place where people could drop by to talk to movement representatives. A lot of Palestinians came to my dad's office, shared their problems, and asked for help, especially the families of prisoners and martyrs who lost their husbands and fathers during the intifadas. But even Sheikh Hassan Yousef was in the dark. Everybody thought he had all the answers, but he was no different than the rest of us: all he had were questions.

Once he told me he was thinking of closing his office.

"Why? Where will you meet with the media?" I asked.

"I don't care. People are coming from everywhere, hoping I can help. But there is no way I can provide for everyone who needs help; it's simply too much."

"Why doesn't Hamas help them? These are the families of the movement members. Hamas has lots of money."

"Yes, but the organization doesn't give it to me."

"So ask for some. Tell them about all the people in need."

"I don't know who *they* are or how to get hold of *them*."

"But you're the leader," I protested.

"I am not the leader."

"You founded Hamas, Father. If you're not the leader, who is?"

"No one is the leader!"

I was shocked. The Shin Bet was recording every word, and they were shocked as well.

One day, I received a call from Majeda Talahme, Saleh's wife. We hadn't spoken since her husband's funeral.

"Hi, how are you? How are Mosab and the other kids?"

She started to cry.

"I don't have money to feed the children."

I thought, *God forgive you, Saleh, for what you did to your family!*

"Okay, my sister, calm down, and I will try to do something."

I went to my dad.

"Saleh's wife just called. She doesn't have money to buy food for her children."

"Sadly, Mosab, she is not the only one."

"Yes, but Saleh was a very good friend of mine. We have to do something right away!"

"Son, I told you. I don't have any money."

"Okay, but somebody's in charge. Somebody has plenty of money. This isn't fair! This man died for the sake of the movement!"

My father told me he would do what he could. He wrote a letter, sort of a "to whom it may concern," and sent it to a drop point. We couldn't track it, but we knew the recipient was somewhere in the Ramallah area.

A few months earlier, the Shin Bet had sent me to an Internet café downtown. We knew that someone using one of the computers there was in communication with Hamas leaders in Damascus. We didn't know who all these leaders were, but there was no denying that Syria was a hub of Hamas's power. It made sense for Hamas to maintain a whole organization—an office, weapons, and military camps—somewhere it could be out from under the Israeli hammer.

"We don't know who it is communicating with Damascus," Loai said, "but he sounds dangerous."

As I walked into the café, I found twenty people sitting at computers. None had beards. Nobody looked suspicious. But one of them caught my attention, though I have no idea why. I didn't recognize him, but my instinct told me to keep an eye on him. I knew it wasn't much to go on, but over the years, the Shin Bet had learned to trust my hunches.

We were convinced that, whoever this man at the Internet café was, he was probably dangerous. Only highly trusted people were able to communicate with Hamas leaders in Damascus. And we hoped that he might also lead us to the elusive, shadowy elite who actually ruled Hamas. We circulated his photograph, but no one recognized him. I began to question my instincts.

A few weeks later, I held an open house for some property in Ramallah that I had put up for sale. Several people came, but no one made an offer. Late that afternoon, after I had closed up, I got a call from a man who asked if he could still see the house. I was really very tired, but I told him to go on over and I would meet him there. I returned to the property, and he showed up a few minutes later.

It was the man from the Internet café. He told me his name was Aziz Kayed. He was clean shaven and very professional looking. I could tell he was educated, and he said he ran the respectable Al-Buraq Center for Islamic Studies. He didn't seem to be the link we were looking for. But rather than confuse the Shin Bet even more, I kept the discovery to myself.

Sometime after my encounter with Kayed, my father and I set out to visit cities, villages, and refugee camps throughout the West Bank. In one town, more than fifty thousand people gathered to see Sheikh

Hassan Yousef. They all wanted to touch him and hear what he had to say. He was still deeply loved.

In Nablus, a Hamas stronghold, we met with top organization leaders, and I figured out which of them were members of the *shurah* council—a small group of seven men who make decisions on strategic issues and daily activities for the movement. Like my dad, they were among the eldest Hamas leaders, but they were not the "executives" we were looking for.

After all these years, I could not believe that control of Hamas had somehow, somewhere along the line, slipped into unknown hands. If I, who was born and raised in the heart of the movement, had no idea who pulled the strings, who knew?

The answer came out of the blue. One of the shurah council members in Nablus mentioned the name of Aziz Kayed. He suggested that my father visit Al-Buraq and meet this "good man." My ears perked up immediately. Why would a local Hamas leader make such a recommendation? There were simply too many coincidences: first, Aziz caught my eye in the Internet café; then he showed up at my open house; and now, the council member was telling my dad he should meet this man. Was this a sign that my hunch was correct and Aziz Kayed was someone important in the Hamas organization?

Could we even be so fortunate as to have found the person in charge? As unlikely as it sounded, something inside me said to follow my instinct. I raced back to Ramallah, where I called Loai and asked him to order a computer search for Aziz Kayed.

Several Aziz Kayeds popped up, but none who fit the description. We had an emergency meeting, and I asked Loai to widen the name search to the entire West Bank. His people thought I was crazy, but they went along with me.

This time, we found him.

Aziz Kayed was born in Nablus and was a former member of the Islamic student movement. He had discontinued his activities ten years earlier. He was married with children and free to travel out of the country. Most of his friends were secular. We found nothing suspicious.

I explained to the Shin Bet everything that had happened, from the moment I stepped into the Internet café to the visit to Nablus with my father. They said that although they definitely trusted me, we simply didn't have enough to go on yet.

While we were talking, I thought about something else.

"Kayed reminds me of three other guys," I said to Loai. "Salah Hussein from Ramallah, Adib Zeyadeh from Jerusalem, and Najeh Madi from Salfeet. All three of these guys have advanced university degrees and were at one time very active in Hamas. But for whatever reason, they simply dropped out of sight about ten years ago. Now, they all live very normal lives, completely removed from political involvement. I always wondered why someone who was so passionate about the movement would just quit like that."

Loai agreed that I might be onto something. We began to study the movements of each man. It turned out that all three of them were in communication with one another and with Aziz Kayed. They all worked together at Al-Buraq. That was way too coincidental.

Could these four unlikely men be the real puppet masters running Hamas, controlling even the military wing? Could they have been flying under the radar while we had been targeting all the high-profile guys? We continued to dig, monitor, and wait. Finally our patience paid off with an enormous intelligence breakthrough.

We learned that these deadly thirtysomethings had gained total control of the money and were running the entire Hamas movement in the West Bank. They brought in millions of dollars from the outside, which they used to buy arms, manufacture explosives, recruit volunteers, support fugitives, provide logistic support, everything—all under the cover of one of Palestine's numerous and seemingly innocuous research centers.

No one knew them. They never appeared on TV. They communicated only by letters through drop points. They obviously trusted no one—as evidenced by the fact that even my father had no clue about their existence.

One day, we followed Najeh Madi from his apartment to a commercial garage a block away. He walked to one of the units and lifted the door. What was he doing there? Why would he lease a garage that far from his home?

For the next two weeks, we never took our eyes off that stupid garage, but nobody came again. Finally, the door opened—from the inside—and Ibrahim Hamed stepped out into the sunlight!

The Shin Bet waited just long enough for him to return to the building before launching an arrest operation. But when Hamed was surrounded by special forces, he did not fight to the death as he had ordered Saleh and the others to do.

"Take off your clothes and come out!"

No response.

"You have ten minutes. Then we will demolish the building!"

Two minutes later, the leader of the military wing of Hamas in the West Bank walked through the door in his underwear.

"Take off *all* your clothes!"

He hesitated, stripped, and stood before the soldiers, naked.

Ibrahim Hamed was personally responsible for the deaths of more than eighty people that we could prove. It may not be a very Jesus-like impulse, but if it had been up to me, I would have put him back in his filthy garage, locked him in for the rest of his life, and saved the state the expense of a trial.

Capturing Hamed and exposing the real leaders of Hamas proved to be my most important operation for the Shin Bet. It was also my final one.

Chapter Twenty-Six
A VISION FOR HAMAS
2005

DURING HIS MOST RECENT IMPRISONMENT, my father had had a sort of epiphany.

He had always been very open-minded. He would sit down and talk with Christians, nonreligious people, even Jews. He listened carefully to journalists, experts, and analysts, and he attended lectures at the universities. And he listened to me—his assistant, adviser, and protector. As a result, he had a much clearer, broader vision than other Hamas leaders.

He saw that Israel was an immutable reality and recognized many of the goals of Hamas as illogical and unattainable. He wanted to find some middle ground that both sides could accept without losing face. So in his first public speech following his release, he suggested the possibility of a two-state solution to the conflict. No one in Hamas had ever said anything like that. The closest they ever got to a handshake was to declare a truce. But my father was actually acknowledging the right of Israel to exist! His phone never stopped ringing.

Diplomats from every country, including the United States, contacted us to request secret meetings with my father. They wanted to see for themselves if he was for real. I served as translator, never leaving his side. My Christian friends supported him unconditionally, and he loved them for it.

Not surprisingly, he had a problem. While he spoke in the name of Hamas, he definitely did not speak from the heart of Hamas. Yet it would have been the worst possible time for him to move away from the organization. The death of Yasser Arafat had created a huge vacuum and left the streets of the occupied territories boiling. Radical young men were everywhere—armed, hate filled, and leaderless.

It wasn't that Arafat was so difficult to replace. Any corrupt politician would do. The problem was that he had completely centralized the PA and the PLO. He wasn't what you would call a team player. He had held all the authority and all the connections. And his name was on all the bank accounts.

Now Fatah was infested with Arafat wannabes. But who among them would be acceptable to the Palestinians and the international community—*and* strong enough to control all the factions? Even Arafat had never really accomplished that.

When Hamas decided to participate in the Palestinian parliamentry elections a few months later, my father was less than enthusiastic. After the military wing had been added to Hamas during the Al-Aqsa Intifada, he had watched his organization turn into an awkward creature, hobbling along with one very long militant leg and one very short political leg. Hamas simply had no idea how the governing game was played.

Being a revolutionary is all about purity and rigidity. But governing is all about compromise and flexibility. If Hamas wanted to rule, negotiation would not be an option; it would be a necessity. As elected officials, they would suddenly be responsible for budget, water, food, electricity, and waste removal. And everything had to come through Israel. Any independent Palestinian state would have to be a cooperative state.

My father remembered his meetings with Western leaders and how Hamas had rejected every recommendation. It was reflexively closed-minded and contrarian. And if it had refused to negotiate with the Americans and the Europeans, my father reasoned, what was the likelihood that an elected Hamas would sit down at the table with the Israelis?

My father didn't care if Hamas fielded candidates. He just didn't want to fill the ticket with high-profile leaders like himself who were loved and admired by the people. If that happened, he feared, Hamas would win. And he knew a Hamas victory could prove to be a disaster for the people. Events proved him right.

"There certainly exists among us concern that Israel, and perhaps others also, will impose punishments on the Palestinians because they voted for Hamas," I heard him tell a *Haaretz* reporter. "They will say 'you decided to choose Hamas and therefore we will intensify the siege over you and make your lives difficult.'"[13]

But many in Hamas smelled money, power, and glory. Even former leaders who had given up on the organization came out of nowhere to grab a piece of the pie. My father was disgusted with their greed, irresponsibility, and ignorance. These guys couldn't tell the difference between the CIA and USAID. Who was going to work with them?

I was frustrated with just about everything. I was frustrated with the corruption of the PA, the stupidity and cruelty of Hamas, and the seemingly endless line of terrorists who had to be taken out or put down. I was becoming exhausted by the pretense and risk that had become my daily routine. I wanted a normal life.

Walking along the streets of Ramallah one day in August, I saw a man carrying a computer up a flight of stairs to a repair shop. And it occurred to me that there might be a market for in-home computer maintenance, kind of a Palestinian version of the American Geek Squad. Since I was no longer working for USAID and I had a good business mind, I thought I might as well put it to profitable use.

I had become good friends with the IT manager at USAID, who was a computer wizard. And when I told him about my idea, we decided to become partners. I put up the money, he provided the technological expertise, and we hired a few more engineers, including females so we could serve women in the Arab culture.

We called the company Electric Computer Systems, and I came up with some advertising. Our ads featured a caricature of a guy carrying a computer up some stairs, with his son telling him, "Papa, you don't have to do that" and urging him to call our toll-free number.

Calls poured in, and we were suddenly very successful. I bought a new company van, we got a license to sell Hewlett-Packard products, and we expanded into networking. I was having the time of my life. At this point I didn't need the money, but I was doing something productive and having fun.

—

Since I had begun my spiritual odyssey, I'd had some interesting conversations with my Shin Bet friends about Jesus and my developing beliefs.

"Believe whatever you want," they said. "You can share it with us. But don't share it with anyone else. And don't ever get baptized, because that would make a very public statement. If anybody found out you became a Christian and turned your back on your Islamic beliefs, you could be in big trouble."

I don't think they were as worried about my future as they were about theirs if they lost me. But God was changing my life too much for me to hold back anymore.

One day, my friend Jamal was cooking dinner for me.

"Mosab," he said, "I have a surprise for you."

He flipped the channel and said with a gleam in his eye, "Check out this TV program on Al-Hayat. It might interest you."

I found myself looking into the eyes of an old Coptic priest named Zakaria Botros. He looked kind and gentle and had a warm, compelling voice. I liked him—until I realized what he was saying. He was systematically performing an autopsy on the Qur'an, opening it up and exposing every bone, muscle, sinew, and organ, and then putting them under the microscope of truth and showing the entire book to be cancerous.

Factual and historical inaccuracies, contradictions—he revealed them precisely and respectfully but firmly and with conviction. My first instinct was to lash out and turn the television off. But that lasted only seconds before I recognized that this was God's answer to my prayers. Father Zakaria was cutting away all the dead pieces of Allah that still linked me to Islam and blinded me to the truth that Jesus is indeed the Son of God. Until that happened, I could not move ahead in following him. But it was not an easy transition. Just try to imagine the pain of waking up one day to discover that your dad is not really your father.

I cannot tell you the exact day and the hour that I "became a Christian" because it was a six-year process. But I knew that I was, and I knew I needed to be baptized, no matter what the Shin Bet said. About that time, a group of American Christians came to Israel to tour the Holy Land and to visit their sister church, the one I was attending.

Over time, I became good friends with one of the girls in the group. I enjoyed talking with her, and I trusted her immediately. When I shared a bit of my spiritual story with her, she was very encouraging, reminding me that God often uses the most surprising people to do his work. That was certainly true in my life.

One evening as we were having dinner at the American Colony Restaurant in East Jerusalem, my friend asked me why I had not yet been baptized. I couldn't tell her that it was because I was an agent for the Shin Bet and involved up to my eyebrows with every political and security activity in the region. But it was a valid question, one I had asked myself many times.

"Can you baptize me?" I asked.

She said she could.

"Can you keep it a secret between us?"

She said she would, adding, "The beach is not too far away. Let's go now."

"Are you serious?"

"Sure, why not?"

"Okay, why not?"

I was a little giddy when we boarded the shuttle to Tel Aviv. Had I forgotten who I was? Was I really putting my trust in this girl from San Diego? Forty-five minutes later, we were walking along the crowded beach, drinking in the sweet, warm evening air. No one in the crowd could have known that the son of the leader of Hamas—the terrorist group responsible for slaughtering twenty-one kids at the Dolphinarium just up the road—was about to be baptized as a Christian.

I stripped off my shirt, and we walked into the sea.

On Friday, September 23, 2005, as I drove my father back from one of the refugee camps near Ramallah, he received a phone call.

"What is going on?" I heard him bark into the phone. "What?"

My dad sounded very agitated.

When he hung up, he told me it had been Hamas spokesman Sami Abu Zuhri in Gaza, who informed him that the Israelis had just killed a large number of Hamas members during a rally in the Jebaliya refugee camp. The caller insisted he had seen the Israeli aircraft launch missiles into the crowd. They broke the truce, he said.

My father had worked very hard to negotiate that truce just seven months before. Now it appeared that all his efforts were wasted. He hadn't trusted Israel in the first place, and he was furious at their thirst for blood.

But I didn't believe it. Though I didn't say anything to my father, something about the story smelled wrong.

Al-Jazeera called. They wanted my father on the air as soon as we reached Ramallah. Twenty minutes later, we were in their studios.

While they fitted my father with a microphone, I called Loai. He assured me that Israel had not launched any attack. I was livid. I asked the producer to let me see the news footage of the incident. He took me to the control room, and we watched it over and over. Clearly, the explosion had come from the ground up, not out of the sky.

Sheikh Hassan Yousef was already on the air, ranting at treacherous Israel, threatening to end the truce, and demanding an international investigation.

"So do you feel better now?" I asked him as he walked off the set.

"What do you mean?"

"I mean after your statement."

"Why shouldn't I feel better? I can't believe they did that."

"Good, because they didn't. Hamas did. Zuhri is a liar. Please come to the control room; I have something to show you." My father followed me back to the small room where we watched the video several more times.

"Look at the explosion. Look. The blast goes from bottom to top. It didn't come from the sky."

We learned later that the Hamas military guys in Gaza had been showing off, flaunting their hardware during the demonstration, when a Qassam missile in the back of a pickup truck exploded, killing fifteen people and wounding many more.

My father was shocked. But Hamas was not alone in its cover-up and self-serving deceptions. Despite what it displayed on its own news footage, Al-Jazeera continued to broadcast the lies. Then everything got worse. Much worse.

In retaliation for the phony attack on Gaza, Hamas fired nearly forty missiles at towns in southern Israel, the first major attack since Israel had completed its withdrawal from Gaza a week earlier. At home, my father and I watched the news along with the rest of the world. The next day, Loai warned me that the cabinet decided that Hamas had broken the truce.

A news report quoted Major General Yisrael Ziv, the head of operations for Israel's army: "It was decided to launch a prolonged and constant attack on Hamas," hinting, added the reporter, "that Israel was preparing to resume targeted attacks against top Hamas leaders," a practice suspended after the cease-fire.[14]

"Your father has to go in," Loai said.

"Are you asking my approval?"

"No. They're asking for him personally, and we can't do anything about it."

I was furious.

"But my father didn't launch any missiles last night. He didn't order it. He had nothing at all to do with it. It was all those idiots in Gaza."

Eventually, I ran out of steam. I was crushed. Loai broke the silence.

"Are you there?"

"Yes." I sat down. "This is not fair . . . but I understand."

"You, too," he said, quietly.

"Me, too, what? Prison? Forget it! I'm not going back. I don't care about cover. It's over for me. I'm through."

"My brother," he whispered, "do you think I want you to be arrested? It is up to you. If you want to stay out, you stay out. But this time is more dangerous than any other time. You have been at your father's side over the past year more than ever before. Everyone knows you are completely involved with Hamas. Many believe you are even part of its leadership. . . . If we don't arrest you, you will be dead within a few weeks."

Chapter Twenty-Seven

GOOD-BYE

2005–2007

"WHAT'S GOING ON?" my father asked when he found me crying.

When I didn't say anything, he suggested we cook dinner together for my mother and sisters. My father and I had grown so close over the years, and he understood that sometimes I simply needed to work through things on my own.

But as I prepared the meal with him, knowing that these were the last hours we would have together for a long time, my heart broke. I decided not to let him go through the arrest alone.

After dinner, I called Loai.

"All right," I told him. "I will go back to prison."

It was September 25, 2005. I hiked to my favorite spot in the hills outside Ramallah where I often went to spend time praying and reading my Bible. I prayed more, wept more, and asked the Lord for his mercy on me and my family. When I got home, I sat down and waited. My father, blissfully unaware of what was about to happen, had already gone to bed. A little after midnight, the security forces arrived.

They took us to Ofer Prison, where we were herded into a big hall with hundreds of others who had been picked up in a citywide sweep. This time, they also arrested my brothers Oways and Mohammad.

Loai told me secretly that they were suspects in a murder case. One of their schoolmates had kidnapped, tortured, and killed an Israeli settler, and the Shin Bet had intercepted a call the killer made to Oways the day before. Mohammad would be released a few days later. Oways would serve four months in prison before being cleared of any involvement in the crime.

We sat on our knees in that hall for ten hours with our hands cuffed behind us. I thanked God silently when someone gave my father a chair, and I saw that he was being treated with respect.

I was sentenced to three months in administrative detention. My Christian friends sent me a Bible, and I served my sentence, studying Scripture and going through the motions. I was released on Christmas Day 2005. My father was not. As I write this, he is still in prison.

———

Parliamentary elections were coming up, and every Hamas leader wanted to run for office. They still disgusted me. They all walked around free, while the only man who was actually qualified to lead his people languished behind razor wire. After all that had led up to our arrests, it didn't take much to convince my father not to partici-pate in the elections. He got word to me, asking me to release his decision to Mohammad Daraghmeh, a political analyst with the Associated Press and a good friend.

The news report broke a couple of hours later, and my phone started ringing. The Hamas leaders had tried to contact my father in prison, but he refused to talk to them.

"What's going on?" they asked me. "This is a disaster! We will lose because if your father doesn't run it will appear that he has withdrawn his blessing from the whole election!"

"If he doesn't want to participate," I told them, "you have to respect that."

Then came a call from Ismail Haniyeh, who headed the Hamas ticket and would soon become the new PA prime minister.

"Mosab, as a leader of the movement, I am asking you to schedule a press conference and announce that your father is still on the Hamas ticket. Tell them that the AP story was a mistake."

On top of everything else, now they wanted me to lie for them. Did they forget that Islam forbids lying, or did they think it was okay because politics has no religion?

"I can't do that," I told him. "I respect you, but I respect my father and my own integrity more." And I hung up.

Thirty minutes later, I received a death threat. "Call the news conference immediately," the caller said, "or we will kill you."

"Come and kill me then."

I hung up and called Loai. Within hours, the guy who made the threat was arrested.

I really didn't care about death threats. But when my father found out, he called Daraghmeh personally and told him he would participate in the election. Then he told me to calm down and wait for his release. He would deal with Hamas, he assured me.

Naturally, my father could not campaign from prison. But he didn't need to. Hamas put his picture everywhere, tacitly encouraging everyone to vote the organization ticket. And on the eve of the election, Sheikh Hassan Yousef was swept into parliament, carrying everyone else along like so many burrs in a lion's mane.

I sold my share of Electric Computer Systems to my partner because I had a feeling that a lot of things in my life would soon be coming to a close.

Who was I? What kind of future could I hope for if things kept on this way?

I was twenty-seven years old, and I couldn't even date. A Christian girl would be afraid of my reputation as the son of a top Hamas leader. A Muslim girl would have no use for an Arab Christian. And what Jewish girl would want to date the son of Hassan Yousef? Even if someone would go out with me, what would we talk about? What was I free to share about my life? And what kind of life was it anyway? What had I sacrificed everything for? For Palestine? For Israel? For peace?

What did I have to show for being the Shin Bet's superspook? Were my people better off? Had the bloodshed stopped? Was my father home with his family? Was Israel safer? Had I modeled a higher path for my brothers and sisters? I felt that I had sacrificed nearly a third of my life for nothing, a "chasing after the wind," as King Solomon describes it in Ecclesiastes 4:16.

I couldn't even share all I had learned while wearing my different hats—and hoods. Who would believe me?

I called Loai at his office. "I cannot work for you anymore."

"Why? What happened?"

"Nothing. I love you all. And I love intelligence work. I think I may even be addicted to the job. But we are not accomplishing anything. We're fighting a war that can't be won with arrests, interrogations, and assassinations. Our enemies are ideas, and ideas don't care about incursions and curfews. We can't blow up an idea with a Merkava. You are not our problem, and we are not yours. We're all like rats trapped in a maze. I can't do it anymore. My time is over."

I knew this was a hard blow to the Shin Bet. We were in the middle of a war.

"Okay," Loai said, "I will inform the agency leadership and see what they say."

When we met again, he said, "Here is the offer from the leadership. Israel has a big communications company. We will give you all the money you need to start one just like it in the Palestinian territories. It's a great opportunity and will make you secure for the rest of your life."

"You don't understand. My problem is not money. My problem is that I'm going nowhere."

"People here need you, Mosab."

"I'll find a different way to help them, but I'm not helping them like this. Even the agency can't see where it's going."

"So what do you want?"

"I want to leave the country."

He shared our conversation with his superiors. Back and forth we went, the leadership insisting that I stay as I insisted that I had to leave.

"Okay," they said. "We'll let you go to Europe for several months, maybe a year, as long as you promise to come back."

"I am not going to Europe. I want to go to the United States. I have friends there. Maybe I'll come back in a year or two or five. I don't know. Right now, I only know that I need a break."

"The United States will be difficult. Here, you have money, position, and protection from everybody. You've developed a solid reputation, built a nice business, and live very comfortably. Do you know what your life will look like in the United States? You will be very small and have no influence."

I told them I didn't care if I had to wash dishes. And when I continued to insist, they planted their feet.

"No," they said. "No United States. Only Europe and only for a short time. Go and enjoy yourself. We'll keep paying your salary. Just go and have fun. Take your break. Then come back."

"Okay," I said finally, "I'm going home. I'm not doing anything for you anymore. I'm not going to leave the house because I don't want to accidentally discover a suicide bomber and have to report it. Don't bother calling me. I don't work for you anymore."

I went to my parents' house and turned off my cell phone. My beard grew long and thick. My mother was very worried about me, often coming into the room to check on me and ask if I was okay.

Day after day, I read my Bible, listened to music, watched television, thought about the past ten years, and wrestled with depression.

At the end of three months, my mother told me that someone was asking for me on the phone. I told her I didn't want to talk to anyone. But she said the caller told her that it was urgent, that he was an old friend and knew my father.

I went downstairs and picked up the receiver. It was someone from the Shin Bet.

"We want to see you," the caller said. "It is very important. We have good news for you."

I went to the meeting. My not working had created a no-win situation for them. They could see I was determined to quit.

"Okay, we'll let you go to the United States, but only for a few months, and you have to promise to come back."

"I don't know why you keep insisting on something you know you're not going to get," I told them calmly but firmly.

Finally, they said, "Okay, we'll let you go with two conditions. First, you have to hire a lawyer and petition us through the court to allow you to leave the country for medical reasons. Otherwise, you will get burned. Second, you come back."

The Shin Bet never allowed Hamas members to cross the borders unless they needed medical treatment that was unavailable in the Palestinian territories. I actually did have a problem with my jaw that didn't allow me to close my teeth together, and I couldn't get the surgery I needed in the West Bank. It had never really bothered me much, but I figured it was as good an excuse as any, so I hired a lawyer to send a medical report to the court, requesting a permit for me to travel to the United States for the operation.

The whole purpose of this exercise was to provide a clear paper trail in the courts and show I was wrestling with a hostile bureaucracy in an attempt to leave Israel. If the Shin Bet let me go without a struggle, it would imply favoritism and people might start to wonder what I had given them in exchange. So we had to make it appear that they were making it tough on me and fighting me every step of the way.

But the lawyer I selected proved to be an obstacle. He apparently didn't think I had much of a chance, so he demanded his money in advance—which I paid him—and then he sat back and did nothing. The Shin Bet had no paperwork to generate because they received nothing from my attorney. Week after week, I called him and asked how my case was progressing. The only thing he had to do was process the paperwork, but he kept stalling and lying. There was a problem, he said. There were complications. Again and again, he said he needed more money, and again and again I paid him.

This went on for six months. Finally on New Year's Day 2007, I got the phone call.

"You're approved to leave," the lawyer declared, as though he had just solved world hunger.

"Can you meet just one more time with one of the Hamas leaders in Jalazone refugee camp?" Loai asked. "You're the only person—"

"I'm leaving the country in five hours."

"Okay," he said in surrender. "Be safe and keep in touch with us. Call once you cross the border to make sure that everything is all right."

I called some people I knew in California and told them I was coming. Of course, they had no idea I was the son of a top Hamas leader and a spy for the Shin Bet. But they were very excited. I packed a few clothes in a small suitcase and went downstairs to tell my mother. She was already in bed.

I knelt by her side and explained that I would be leaving in a few hours, crossing the border into Jordan and flying to the United States. Even then, I could not explain why.

Her eyes said it all. *Your father is in prison. You are like a father to your brothers and sisters. What will you do in America?* I knew she didn't want to see me go, but at the same time, she wanted me to be at peace. She said she hoped I would be able to make a life for myself there after being in so much danger at home. She had no idea just how much danger I had seen.

"Let me kiss you good-bye," she said. "Wake me in the morning before you go."

She blessed me, and I told her I would be leaving very early and she didn't need to get up to see me off. But she was my mother. She waited up with me all night in our living room, along with my brothers and sisters and my friend Jamal.

While I was putting all my belongings together before my flight, I was about to pack my Bible—the one with all my notes, the one I had studied for years, even in prison—but then I sensed a prompting to give it to Jamal.

"I don't have a more expensive gift to give you before I leave," I told him. "Here is my Bible. Read it and follow it." I was sure he would honor my wishes and probably would read it whenever he thought of me. I made sure I had enough cash to last me for a while, left the house, and went to the Allenby Bridge that connects Israel with Jordan.

Getting through the Israeli checkpoint was no problem. I paid the thirty-five-dollar exit tax and entered the huge immigration terminal with its metal detectors, X-ray machines, and the infamous Room 13 where suspects were interrogated. But these devices, along with strip searches, were mostly for those coming *into* Israel from the Jordanian side—not for those leaving.

The terminal was a beehive of people in shorts and fanny packs, yarmulkes and Arab headdresses, veils and ball caps, some wearing backpacks and others pushing hand trolleys stacked with luggage. Finally, I boarded one of the big JETT buses—the only public transportation permitted on the concrete truss bridge.

Okay, I thought, *it's almost over.*

But I was still a little paranoid. The Shin Bet simply did not let people like me leave the country. It was unheard of. Even Loai had been amazed that I'd gotten permission.

When I reached the Jordanian side, I presented my passport. I was concerned because while three years remained on my US visa, my passport was due to expire in fewer than thirty days.

Please, I prayed, *just let me into Jordan for one day. That's all I need.*

But all my worrying was for nothing. There was no problem at all. I grabbed a taxi into Amman and bought a ticket on Air France. I checked into a hotel for a few hours, then went to Queen Alia International Airport and boarded my flight to California via Paris.

As I sat on the plane, I thought about what I had just left behind, both good and bad—my family and friends as well as the endless bloodshed, waste, and futility.

It took a while to get used to the idea of being really free—free to be myself, free of clandestine meetings and Israeli prisons, free from always looking over my shoulder.

It was weird. And wonderful.

Walking down the sidewalk one day in California, I spotted a familiar face coming toward me. It was the face of Maher Odeh, the mastermind behind so many suicide bombings—the guy I had seen back in 2000 being visited by Arafat's armed thugs. I later exposed them as the founding cell of the ghostly Al-Aqsa Martyrs Brigades.

I wasn't completely sure it was Odeh at first. People look different out of context. I hoped I was wrong. Hamas has never dared reach into the United States to conduct a martyrdom operation. It would be bad for the United States if he was here. It would be bad for me too.

Our eyes met and held for a fraction of a second. I was pretty sure I saw a spark of recognition there before he continued down the street.

EPILOGUE

In July 2008, I sat in a restaurant having dinner with my good friend Avi Issacharoff, a journalist with *Haaretz* newspaper in Israel. I told him my story of becoming a Christian because I wanted the news to come from Israel, not from the West. It appeared in his newspaper under the headline "Prodigal Son."

As is the case with many followers of Jesus, my public declaration of faith broke the hearts of my mother and father, brothers, sisters, and friends.

My friend Jamal was one of the few people who stood by my family in their shame and cried with them. Terribly lonely after I left, Jamal met a beautiful young woman, got engaged, and was married two weeks after the *Haaretz* article appeared.

Attending his wedding, my family couldn't hold back their tears because Jamal's wedding reminded them of me, how I had destroyed my future, and how I would never marry and have a Muslim family. Seeing their sadness, even the new bridegroom started to cry. Most of the other people in the wedding cried, too, but I'm sure it was for a different reason.

"Couldn't you wait to make your announcement until two weeks *after* I got married?" Jamal asked me in a phone conversation later. "You made the best thing in my life a disaster."

I felt awful. Thankfully, Jamal remains my best friend.

My father received the news in his prison cell. He woke up to learn that his oldest son had converted to Christianity. From his perspective, I had destroyed my own future and his family's future. He believes that one day I will be taken to hell before his eyes, and then we will be estranged forever.

He cried like a baby and would not leave his cell.

Prisoners from every faction came to him. "We are all your sons, Abu Mosab," they told him. "Please calm down."

He could not confirm the news reports. But a week later, my seventeen-year-old sister, Anhar, who was the only family member allowed to visit him, came to the prison. Immediately, he could see in her eyes that it was all true. And he couldn't control himself. Other prisoners left their visiting families to come and kiss his head and weep with him. He tried to catch his breath to apologize to them, but he only wept harder. Even the Israeli guards, who respected my father, cried.

I sent him a six-page letter. I told him how important it was for him to discover the real nature of the God he has always loved but never known.

My uncles waited anxiously for my father to disown me. When he refused, they turned their backs on his wife and children. But my father knew that if he disowned me, Hamas terrorists would kill me. And he kept his covering over me, no matter how deeply I had wounded him.

Eight weeks later, the men at Ktzi'ot Prison in the Negev threatened to riot. So Shabas, the Israel Prison Service, asked my father to do what he could to defuse the situation.

One day my mother, who had been in weekly contact since my arrival in America, called me.

"Your father is in the Negev. Some of the prisoners have smuggled in cell phones. Would you like to talk to him?"

I couldn't believe it. I didn't think I would get a chance to talk to my dad until he was released from prison.

I called the number. No one answered. I called again.

"Alo!"

His voice. I could barely speak.

"Hi, Father."

"Hi there."

"I miss your voice."

"How are you?"

"I am good. It doesn't matter how I am. How are you?"

"I am okay. We came here to talk to prisoners and try to calm the situation down."

He was the same. His chief concern was always for the people. And he always would be the same.

"How is your life in the USA now?"

"My life is great. I am writing a book . . ."

Every prisoner was given only ten minutes, and my father would never use his position to get special treatment. I wanted to discuss my new life with him, but he didn't want to talk about it.

"No matter what happened," he told me, "you are still my son. You are part of me, and nothing will change. You have a different opinion, but you still are my little child."

I was shocked. This man was unbelievable.

I called again the next day. He was sick at heart, but he was listening.

"I have a secret I need to tell you," I said. "I want to tell you now, so you don't hear it from the media."

I explained that I had worked for the Shin Bet for ten years. That he was still alive today because I had agreed to have him put into prison for his protection. That his name was at the top of Jerusalem's assassination list—and that he was still in prison because I was no longer there to ensure his safety.

Silence. My dad said nothing.

"I love you," I said finally. "You will always be my father."

—

EDITOR'S NOTE: On March 1, 2010, one day before this book's release, Mosab's father disowned him. The sheikh released a letter saying that his family had renounced "the one who was once our eldest son, who is called Mosab" (Associated Press, March 3, 2010).

Despite the loss of his family and the risk to his life, Mosab continues to speak out with his message of loving your enemies.

POSTSCRIPT

IT IS MY GREATEST HOPE THAT, in telling my own story, I will show my own people—Palestinian followers of Islam who have been used by corrupt regimes for hundreds of years—that the truth can set them free.

I tell my story as well to let the Israeli people know that there is hope. If I, the son of a terrorist organization dedicated to the extinction of Israel, can reach a point where I not only learned to love the Jewish people but risked my life for them, there is a light of hope.

My story holds a message for Christians too. We must learn from the sorrows of my people, who carry a heavy burden trying to work their way into God's favor. We have to get beyond the religious rules we make for ourselves. Instead, we must love people—on all sides of the world—unconditionally. If we are going to represent Jesus to the world, we have to live his message of love. If we want to follow Jesus, we must also expect to be persecuted. We should be happy to be persecuted for his sake.

To Middle East experts, government decision makers, scholars, and leaders of intelligence agencies, I write with the hope that a simple story will contribute to your understanding of the problems and potential solutions in one of the most troubled regions of the world.

I offer my story knowing that many people, including those I care about most, will not understand my motives or my thinking.

Some people will accuse me of doing what I have done for the sake of money. The irony is that I had no problem getting money in my previous life but am living practically hand to mouth now. While it is true that my family struggled financially, especially during the long stretches when my father was in prison, I eventually became a fairly rich young man. With my government-provided salary, I made ten times the average income in my country. I had a good life, with two houses and a new sports car. And I could have made even more.

When I told the Israelis that I was done working for them, they offered to set me up in my own communications business that would earn me millions of dollars if I would only stay. I said no to that offer and came to the United States, where I haven't been able to find a full-time job and ended up practically homeless. I hope that some-day money won't be a problem for me anymore, but I've learned that money alone will never satisfy me. If money was my main goal, I could have stayed where I was and kept working for Israel. I could have accepted the donations that people have offered me since I moved to the States. But I haven't done either because I don't want to make money my priority—or give the impression that it is what drives me.

Some people may think I'm doing this for the attention, but I had plenty of that back in my own country too.

What was much harder to give up was the power and authority I had as the son of a top Hamas leader. Having tasted power, I know how addictive it can be—much more addictive than money. I liked the power I had in my former life, but when you're addicted, even to power, you are controlled more than you control.

Freedom, a deep longing for freedom, is really at the heart of my story.

I am the son of a people who have been enslaved by corrupt systems for many centuries.

I was a prisoner of the Israelis when my eyes were opened to the fact that the Palestinian people were as oppressed by their own leaders as they were by Israel.

I was a devout follower of a religion that required strict adherence to rigid regulations in order to please the god of the Qur'an and get into heaven.

I had money, power, and position in my former life, but what I really wanted was freedom. And that meant, among other things, leaving behind hate, prejudice, and a desire for revenge.

The message of Jesus—love your enemies—is what finally set me free. It no longer mattered who my friends were or who my enemies were; I was supposed to love them all. And I could have a loving relationship with a God who would help me love others.

Having that kind of relationship with God is not only the source of my freedom but also the key to my new life.

After reading this book, please do not think that I have become some kind of super follower of Jesus. I'm still struggling. The little I know and understand about my faith came from Bible studies and reading. In other words, I am a follower of Jesus Christ but am only beginning to become a disciple.

I was born and raised in a religious environment that insisted salvation was all about works. I have a lot to unlearn to make room for the truth:

> *You were taught, with regard to your former way of life, to put off your old self, which is being corrupted by its deceitful desires; to be made new in the attitude of your minds; and to put on the new self, created to be like God in true righteousness and holiness.*
>
> —EPHESIANS 4:22-24

Like many other followers of Christ, I have repented of my sins, and I know that Jesus is the Son of God who became a man, died for our sins, rose from the dead, and is seated at the right hand of the Father. I have been baptized. Yet I feel that I am barely inside the gate of the Kingdom of God. I have been told that there is much, much more. And I want it all.

In the meantime, I still struggle with the world, the flesh, and the devil. I still have misconceptions and confusion. I wrestle with what sometimes seem like invincible issues. Yet I have hope that I, like the apostle Paul who described himself to Timothy as "the worst of sinners" (1 Timothy 1:16), will become whatever God wants me to be, as long as I don't give up.

So if you meet me in the street, please don't ask me for advice or what I think this or that Scripture verse means, because you're probably already way ahead of me. Instead of looking at me as a spiritual trophy, pray for me, that I will grow in my faith and that I won't step on too many toes as I learn to dance with the Bridegroom.

As long as we continue to search for enemies anywhere but inside ourselves, there will always be a Middle East problem.

Religion is not the solution. Religion without Jesus is just self-righteousness. Freedom from oppression will not resolve things either. Delivered from the oppression of Europe, Israel became the oppressor. Delivered from persecution, Muslims became persecutors. Abused spouses and children often go on to abuse spouses and children. It is a cliché, but it's still true: hurt people, unless they are healed, hurt people.

Manipulated by lies and driven by racism, hatred, and revenge, I was on my way to being one of those people. Then in 1999, I encountered the only true God. He is the Father whose love is beyond expression, yet shown in the sacrifice of his only Son on a cross to atone for the world's sins. He is the God who, three days later, demonstrated his power and righteousness by raising Jesus from the dead. He is the God who not only commands me to love and forgive my enemies as he has loved and forgiven me but empowers me to do so.

Truth and forgiveness are the only solution for the Middle East. The challenge, especially between Israelis and Palestinians, is not to *find* the solution. The challenge is to be the first courageous enough to *embrace* it.

AFTERWORD
2011

SINCE THE RELEASE OF *Son of Hamas*, and especially since it landed on best-seller lists, people have been offering me their congratulations and support. Most authors would consider publication itself a cause for celebration, let alone best-seller status. But releasing this book has not been a big victory for me; in many ways it has been my worst nightmare. Many things have happened since this book's release that have tempered the celebration and changed my life forever.

First, the day before *Son of Hamas* was released in March 2010, I received word that my father had disowned me. As you can imagine, this was about the worst news I could have received.

Then, in May 2010, I was notified that the U.S. Department of Homeland Security had scheduled a hearing to decide whether to deport me, citing my past involvement with Hamas as a potential security threat.

But before I discuss these events, I should back up to 2008. I had come to the United States in 2007, and as I mentioned in the epilogue to *Son of Hamas*, I revealed my conversion to Christianity to Avi Issacharoff of the Israeli newspaper *Haaretz*, who wrote an article about me in late July 2008. What I didn't know was who would be reading my story.

I had known my Shin Bet handler only by the name "Captain Loai," which I knew was an alias, just as mine was "the Green Prince." Despite the customary use of code names, we trusted each other completely when we served together in the Shin Bet. We trusted each other with our lives in almost every operation, and our relationship quickly developed from fellow agents into friendship and brotherhood. But we had never had contact outside of that organization. In fact, since Loai's transfer to another district in 2004 and later dismissal from the Shin Bet in 2006, I had not heard from him at all. So I was shocked a few days after the *Haaretz* story ran to receive a personal e-mail from Gonen ben Itzhak. He revealed that he was Captain Loai!

Even though we hadn't been in contact, we were both concerned about how the other was doing. I knew Gonen was struggling with the Shin Bet leadership, and I supported him in my thoughts and prayers. Gonen was worried about me, too, even before I left Palestine. Informing on terrorist activities and involving myself in the dangerous operations of the Shin Bet is not the best way to make friends in my homeland. Gonen was afraid that he would pick up the newspaper one day and read that I had been killed.

When Gonen came across the article about my conversion, he initially saw only my picture on the cover of *Haaretz* and thought, *That's it. My friend is gone.* But then he read of my journey to the United States and the difficulties I was facing here. At first he was surprised that I had even made it out of the region; then he was worried because of the situation I faced in the United States—not having a job and practically living on the streets.

Gonen knew immediately that he had to contact me. He wrote to Avi Issacharoff asking for my e-mail address. He didn't reveal how he knew me (since I had not yet disclosed my relationship with the Shin Bet) or even that he knew me; he said only that it was his moral duty to help me. The reporter provided him with my e-mail address.

It's hard to describe the joy I felt when I received Gonen's message. After being involved in so many secret operations and keeping quiet for so long about who I really was, it was hard to develop new trust relationships with other people. And, as the *Haaretz* article revealed, things weren't going so well for me in the States. But Gonen already knew about all that had happened in the Shin Bet, and he genuinely cared about my welfare. Gonen told me about his family and about what had happened since we had parted ways in 2004. He also offered to send money—even though he didn't have much himself—in order to ease my life in America. He ended his message with, "I hope you will allow your brother the honor of helping." He called me his *brother*. I cried.

I wrote him back the next day, and we quickly resumed contact. We both knew it was against the law for a former agent and his handler to communicate outside the Shin Bet, but we were also close friends, and neither of us was working for the Shin Bet any longer. We talked on the phone several times over the next few months before Gonen flew out to America to renew our friendship face-to-face.

We met in the airport, and when we saw each other, we hugged and could not stop laughing. After all our meetings together in the Middle East—under guard, in secured locations, secret from everyone—it was incredible to meet outside that context, to meet not as representatives of Israel and Palestine, Shin Bet and Hamas, but as friends. It was amazing to think that our friendship could transcend all the barriers between us, that it could exist at all. An outside observer might note our two backgrounds and say, "Those two could never be friends." But God obviously had other plans.

Ephesians 2:14 says that Jesus himself "is our peace, who has made the two one and has destroyed the barrier, the dividing wall of hostility," and I have seen his peacemaking work in my own life through my friendship with Gonen. Our friendship is especially unlikely, and that much more incredible, considering who our fathers are. My father, as mentioned in this book, is one of the founding members of Hamas, a terrorist organization. Gonen's father was a general in the Israeli Defense Forces during the First Intifada. In fact, he was the general responsible for the West Bank during that time, which means that the permission given to arrest anyone as an administrative detention—a political prisoner, in other words—at that time would have had to be issued by Gonen's father. Gonen's father likely signed the warrant for my father's arrest on more than one occasion! And yet, out of this harsh and seemingly desolate soil, by the grace of God a great friendship was allowed to bloom.

As Gonen and I rekindled our friendship, my problems with the United States Department of Homeland Security were beginning to develop. I arrived in America on January 2, 2007, just like any other traveler might—on a tourist visa. No investigation was made into my past; no one knew of my relation to my father, to Hamas, and especially not to the Shin Bet. Airport security stopped me because I only had a few days left on my passport, but I was able to talk them into letting me pass.

Upon arriving in the States, I wanted to ask for political asylum, but I was told that I had to wait until my visa expired, which was in six months. The day my visa expired, I filed an application for political asylum. I answered the questions truthfully, but I did not disclose my connection to the Shin Bet, since I wasn't sure yet if or how I would expose my identity as a spy. I did mention that I am the son of Sheikh Hassan Yousef, that he is a Hamas leader, that I had converted to Christianity, and that I could not return to Palestine. I included letters from friends who testified that my conversion was genuine. I tried to be as honest as possible without revealing sensitive information.

A few weeks after my application for asylum was filed, the Department of Homeland Security asked me to come in for an interview. I went to their office and explained who I was and my reasons for requesting political asylum in the United States. They were shocked and probably embarrassed that they had unwittingly let someone with such an obvious connection to terrorists into the country. They couldn't understand how it had happened.

The officer at the interview seemed antagonistic toward me. He had a file folder in front of him with the details of my case. It was an imposing folder, and it looked like it included all types of media reports about my father and me and Hamas. The officer seemed overwhelmed by the details, and it appeared that he had already made his decision about me. I closed the file folder and told him, "If you have the courage, go ahead and just write 'deportation.' Send me into custody. But know that you will be responsible for whatever happens."

He didn't react, so I went on. "I love this country. I used to work for the U.S. government in the West Bank, and I have many American friends. I'm not here to abuse the system; I'm not looking to gain anything. And I'm not even trying for citizenship. I need protection. And if you still think this is a joke, that I'm just a terrorist or someone trying to take advantage of America, then let's stop pretending. You can write 'deportation' right now. But know you'll be making a big mistake and that you will be the one responsible for it."

The officer softened a little. "Please calm down; we don't want to close your file," he said, and he offered me a drink. After this confrontation, he spoke to me respectfully because he realized that I was not trying to game the system; I really was in danger and couldn't return to Palestine. "I can't tell you my personal opinion, because I'm not allowed," he said, but I could tell he believed my sincerity. "This is a very complicated case, and it will go to the courts no matter what." He suggested that I get a work permit to stay in the country while my case for political asylum was decided.

I didn't hear about my application until February 23, 2009, when, unsurprisingly, my request was denied. I suspect that the Shin Bet played a role in this, trying to hinder my asylum application so I would come back to the West Bank and continue to work for them. The Department of Homeland Security wrote that I was "barred from a grant of asylum because there were reasonable grounds for believing [I] was a danger to the security of the United States and because [I] engaged in terrorist activity."

There were court hearings after this. I tried to explain my situation, that I was not the enemy, nor was I a threat to American security. When the court demanded evidence to support this, I filed a draft of *Son of Hamas*. I sat down with the Department of Homeland Security's attorney and told her, "Listen, I love this country, and I want to stay here. This is my full story. I didn't include it on the application, but I was a Shin Bet agent for many years. I saved the lives of many Americans, Israelis, and Palestinians, and I did it because of my principles. I've never been a terrorist. I grew up in an environment that encouraged terrorism, but I rebelled against it. I was never involved in any killings. Please, read my story." I had hoped that what I described in the book would make it clear where I stood, that it would be apparent that, far from being a security risk and a terrorist, I was trying to protect the freedoms the Department of Homeland Security was also seeking to defend. My presence in the United States seemed logical, given my background of helping the Shin Bet disarm terrorism in the Middle East and specifically the protection I gave the USAID workers while I was employed there.

I thought my book would be able to stop the long court process. Instead, it was used against me and quoted out of context. For example, a Homeland Security senior attorney cited that in chapter 18 of this book, I admit to transporting Hamas members to safe houses. My reaction? *Of course I did!* As a result, I was able to conduct a secret operation with Shin Bet that eventually led us to the terrorists responsible for, among other things, bombing the Hebrew University cafeteria in July 2002—a tragedy that counted five American citizens among the dead. By providing these Hamas members with shelter, we kept them under Shin Bet supervision and control, and we were eventually able to bring them to justice.

If Homeland Security had read the rest of my book, they would have known I also worked with forty Americans on the USAID water project in the West Bank. Who took care of their security? Who warned them not to come to Ramallah if there was going to be an Israeli military incursion or if there would be shooting? Who protected their offices? I wasn't being paid to do that. I did it because of a Christian morality that taught me to love, not hate.

Reading through these accusatory documents, I thought, *Was my behavior that of someone who is a threat to Americans?*

I received notice in May 2010 that a deportation hearing was scheduled for June 30, 2010, because actions I had performed while undercover in Hamas were seen as evidence of my "true" sympathies. It was so frustrating to have my testimony turned against me like that!

Here I should back up once again. Shortly before *Son of Hamas* was first published, in late February 2010, my friend Avi Issacharoff wrote another article about me for *Haaretz*, revealing my identity as a Shin Bet agent. Avi was somewhat skeptical of my story, so I suggested that he interview Gonen about it. (I had just seen Gonen and his wife in December 2009, though he was in the dark about the details of the book—he only knew that I was publishing one.) Gonen agreed to the interview, but he and the reporter thought it best to conceal Gonen's real name. Gonen confirmed the details of *Son of Hamas* and talked about our friendship. Avi Issacharoff, after his interview with Gonen, called me and said, "Man, I'm shaken. This is crazy!" But I was thankful that Avi believed me and that my story was given more credibility through Gonen's corroboration.

But Gonen took a huge risk in confirming my story. He was still living in Israel, and the consequences for his revelation could have been huge. The Shin Bet contacted Gonen after his interview ran in *Haaretz*, and they told him they were considering pressing charges against him for revealing his identity. They warned him not to communicate with me again. The penalty Gonen faced for exposing his identity and confirming my revelation of their secrets was eight years in prison. Furthermore, if he was sent to prison, he would be unable to provide for his family. He was also just finishing up law school in Israel; a charge like the one the Shin Bet was threatening Gonen with under Israeli law would have precluded him from practicing law in Israel. And there was the further risk of embarrassing Gonen's father, a well-respected, retired general in the Israel Defense Forces.

And here we are brought back to the looming deportation hearing. My attorney asked me if I knew anyone who could testify on my behalf, but I said I didn't. I knew what Gonen faced if he were to testify, and he had already risked so much for me. If he testified, he would not be able to keep his identity a secret. Even though I faced the danger of deportation (and the inevitable death sentence that entailed), I could not willingly endanger my friend's life and livelihood. I prayed that God would somehow bring resolution to this trial.

Gonen was aware of the situation I faced. Since my story had come out, Gonen and I had been talking every day. He knew all the facts. I was not even considering asking him to testify on my behalf; that would be an impossibility. But Gonen insisted, "I'll come."

"You can't!" I told him. "You can't expose your identity. That would be a big problem!"

But Gonen said, "It doesn't matter. This is very important, and I will come."

Just a few days before my trial, the Shin Bet renewed their warning to Gonen that he was not to see or contact me in any way. Failure to comply would surely result in a lengthy prison sentence.

Three days after this meeting, Gonen flew to the United States to testify in my deportation hearing. (Incidentally, Gonen was also in his last semester of law school, and two of his final exams fell on the day of my trial.)

Gonen joined me in Washington, DC, where we "went public" together for the first time at a dinner sponsored by the Endowment for Middle East Truth. Sarah Stern, the president of that incredible organization, introduced us to senators, congresspeople, and other influential figures on Capitol Hill who were eager to lend their support to our cause. My story and the threat of deportation I faced began to gain momentum among political leaders.*

The deportation hearing was scheduled to take place at 8:00 a.m. Gonen was waiting with a security guard in an adjacent courtroom. As the judge entered into the court record the documents and motions that had been introduced since my last hearing, I sat next to my attorney, thinking about how I would answer all the questions I was sure would be asked and expecting to have to defend myself tooth and nail. The judge called Gonen in, signaling that the hearing was about to begin. But before Gonen could enter the courtroom, something completely unexpected happened: the Department of Homeland Security's senior attorney announced that the Department no longer opposed my request for asylum.

The court was adjourned, and I didn't realize quite what was happening. As people filed out of the courtroom, my lawyer explained what had happened. I couldn't believe it! The judge granted me asylum, pending a routine background check, and that was that. After

*I am especially grateful to U.S. Representative Doug Lamborn (CO), who circulated through the House of Representatives a letter that was cosponsored by twenty-one other members of Congress, asking Department of Homeland Security Secretary Janet Napolitano to give "full consideration . . . to Mr. Yousef's views and conduct in recent years, particularly his cooperation with Shin Bet at significant risk to his own safety and life." Signatories included Representatives Frank Wolf (VA), Trent Franks (AZ), Cynthia Lummis (WY), Bill Posey (FL), Kenny Marchant (TX), John Kline (MN), John Shadegg (AZ), Joe Wilson (SC), Daniel Lungren (CA), John Boozman (AR), Michele Bachmann (MN), Marsha Blackburn (TN), Bill Shuster (PA), Joseph Pitts (PA), Lynn Jenkins (KS), Rob Bishop (UT), Jeff Fortenberry (NE), Dana Rohrabacher (CA), Robert Aderholt (AL), Mike Pence (IN), and Aaron Schock (IL). Tzachi Hanegbi, Chairman of the Foreign Affairs and Defense Committee of the Knesset (Israeli Parliament), MK Einat Wilf, and other committee members also wrote a very kind letter thanking me for my "actions to strengthen the security of Israeli citizens and Palestinian residents from 1998 to 2007." I also owe a debt of gratitude to R. James Woolsey, former director of the CIA, who wrote a letter stating that my deportation "would be such an inhumane act it would constitute a blight on American history."

nearly three years of red tape and wondering what would happen, I was now at peace in the United States. I no longer had to worry about deportation. As I left the courthouse, I thanked God for his wonderful grace toward me and for all those he had used to bring about this verdict.

This verdict was, of course, great for me, but Gonen's fate was still undecided. We discussed the possibility of his remaining with me in the United States, but he said, "I want to go back. If they arrest me, they arrest me. I'll know that I did the right thing." He went back to Israel, and he was not arrested. He received four letters from the Shin Bet reprimanding him, but no action was taken. Just like when we were working for the Shin Bet, Gonen saved my life again, and I will always be grateful. (By the way—the legal exams he missed by coming to my defense? He was able to reschedule them, and he passed with a high score.)

But as great as it is to have been granted political asylum, there will always loom the shadow of estrangement from my family. My family members are the ones who should share my joy and sorrow, with whom I should celebrate victory and mourn defeat, but I have been disowned. The shame brought on my family by my decision to go public can never be scrubbed clean. I have broken their hearts and ruined their lives. Who will marry my sisters now? How can my brothers return to their schools?

I knew ahead of time the dangers of telling my story, but that does not lessen the pain I feel now. Yet in spite of this pain, I still hold on to hope that they have not disowned me from their hearts. I hope that, through the grace of God, we will someday be reunited as a family.

I am happy to be in the United States, but I miss my family and my country. Still, while I had more money and power in the West Bank, the anonymity of living in such a large country has its advantages. Despite my being on TV and being a best-selling author, many people, even in my U.S. hometown, don't recognize me here. In that respect, going public with my story hasn't changed much in my life. People will ask me what I do, and I'll respond, "I'm a farmer. I've been looking for a job on an organic farm, but I can't find a job."

Of course, then some of those same people will see me on the news or will read my book, and they'll say, "Hey, I thought you said you were a farmer! You're not a farmer!" I just smile and respond, "But I am a farmer. I plant and harvest ideas. I'm an idea farmer." And the people who recognize me keep quiet. Not many people know where I live, and almost nobody knows my address or the city I am in. I try to keep a low profile as much as possible. While many people have expressed support since I came out with my story, it's still hard to know what people are thinking in their hearts, and after the work I did with the Shin Bet, I'm used to not trusting others—even those who may be worthy of my trust.

While publishing *Son of Hamas* has changed my surroundings quite a bit, it has not changed who I am. I still have to work at following and trusting God, and the more I understand about the person of Jesus Christ, the more I realize how much I don't know. I don't understand God, and I am not trying to—there's no way I possibly could even if I tried with all my might. All I can say is that I feel him. I feel his work. God is not a drug in my life, and he is not just a hanger on which I place all my blames and sorrows. God is my inspiration, my leader, my teacher, my guide. I am not a "religious person," and I don't think I will go back to "religion" no matter what. I have rules, I obey rules, and sometimes when I feel I'm weak in an area of my personal life, I'll say, "Okay, I want to put a rule for my life here, because I have to." But I am not a religious person. If I go to church on Sunday, I go because I want to. I don't go there to socialize; I go there to worship. And if I'm not there, I'm worshiping somewhere else.

I find that worship can take place anywhere. For example, I was scuba diving just a few days ago, and I was on the bottom of the ocean. I bowed my knees eighty feet underwater in the Pacific Ocean. That was worship! It reminded me of what Philippians 2:10 says we can expect in the future: "That at the name of Jesus every knee should bow, in heaven and on earth and under the earth." I like to connect and commune with my Lord in a different way, not in a traditional way, not in a religious way—in a way I can connect with him and feel his love. If I fail, I know it's my mistake. If I succeed, I know it's his blessing. And that's how I like to keep it. I am not following people.

I am sometimes disappointed in the church, especially here in the West. I am eager for a new generation to lead it and recognize their responsibility toward the other side of the world and the major problems we are facing, like the problem of Islam. We have huge responsibilities as Christians, and the problems look controversial, but we can't back down just to be "politically correct." I don't know why it's so easy for us as followers of Jesus Christ to understand the real nature of Islam and to speak the truth about it, and yet do nothing about it, or do something too late for it to matter. The church, it seems, is ready to act after everybody else has started to act, and that's not how it should be. In my personal story, I witnessed members of Congress and Jewish leaders trying to save my life, while the church that was supposed to be standing by me came late. That was frustrating to me, not because I didn't get enough support from the church, but because it showed me the reality of the church today, that we're so often behind what others are doing.

It's not about me or even just about politics. As the Christian church, we're supposed to be one body, and so we should be standing together at the forefront of all major humanitarian issues— whether related to the economy, politics, education, or human rights. Spiritually, they're all tied together under Jesus' mission. We need to listen to what *he* is saying—not to what this leader or that leader is saying—and to follow his teaching and principles. Jesus wasn't afraid to speak out for others, and we shouldn't be either.

I don't mean to come down too hard on the church. I am grateful for the many people who encouraged me and prayed with and for me, some of whom didn't even know me. I'm not saying I don't appreciate the support I did receive. What I am saying is that prayer is not a substitute for action. We are to pray, yes, but as the book of James says, our faith must be accompanied by actions. It's not enough to pray. Praying can become irresponsible, even lazy, if we use it as an excuse for not acting. Just as the devil can tempt us to set up false images of who God is, I believe he can tempt us to mistake the true nature of prayer. There are many things that God would have us Christians accomplish, and I think it is our responsibility to accomplish them.

For me, this has meant speaking out against Islam, the religion of my family and culture. As you can imagine, my message has not always been welcome. In some cases, people are shocked that I should speak out about a subject that is often taboo in public discourse. Others are confused and don't know how to respond. Still others— even some from the Muslim community—have encouraged me to continue speaking my message. What I am doing is starting a conversation and trying to get others to join in. I am especially hopeful about the next generation of Muslims. They seem to be more open-minded. My goal is to wake them up. I want them to understand that they are not doomed by the realities of the religion, political systems, and regimes of the region they were born in. They can fight the faith they have known, change their futures, and ultimately change their destinies.

Soon *Son of Hamas* will be released as a free e-book download in Arabic. I am thrilled about this release, since it coincides with my goal of starting a conversation. From experience I know that many will take things out of context, disbelieve the book, or write it off altogether. I'm amazed at how the media, on both sides of an issue, can skew people's minds and opinions, and they so often get it wrong! For example, I could not believe how often the TV news reports about the Shin Bet operations I was involved in misstated the facts! I would talk to the people of my city and get their opinions on what happened, and they didn't know the facts either. The facts seemed clear as day to me, but all the noise surrounding the issue obscured the truth. So I know there will be many who misunderstand or choose not to understand what I have to say. But I also know that some will read my book and their lives will be changed as they consider my encounter with Jesus Christ and his gospel of peace. My prayer is that they, too, will embrace Christ's command to love their enemies. There is hope for peace in the Middle East, but it does not begin with political solutions or negotiations; it begins with the changing of individual hearts.

As I look to the future, I am thankful to have a friend like Gonen at my side. We have overcome the odds together in so many ways. We stayed alive in dangerous circumstances, became friends despite our cultural and faith divides, and reunited miles and years later with a shared mission. In a culture where sometimes it seemed that everyone was using everyone else and you never knew whom you could trust, we became brothers. My Homeland Security hearing, when we stood together in that courtroom, was just one more chance to beat the odds. And we are not done yet. We will continue to use all our strength and ability to work toward peace in the Middle East.

I don't know what I will face next, but I am confident of God's leading. Gonen asked me a while back, "Brother, do you think this is an accident? Why did we meet in the first place? Why did we do what we did? How were you, among all the thousands who couldn't, able to leave the Shin Bet? How were you able to come to the United States and write a book? How are we talking on the phone right now and doing all these things? Do you think this is an accident? There is no logical mind that could say this is an accident!" When I look at the events of the past year with my encounters with the Department of Homeland Security, of the past three years living in the United States, of the ten years before that with the Shin Bet, and of my youth and childhood spent under the shadow of Hamas, it is impossible for me not to see the hand of God guiding me along to where I am. And, Lord willing, I will continue to follow his guiding hand in the rest of the time I have. The events of this last year have shown me again that friendship and love are stronger than agency, policy, and tradition. No matter what happens, I will continue to speak out with firm conviction that unconditional love for the "other" side and forgiveness for those who have hurt us are the only principles that will lead to healing and a better way for us all.

THE PLAYERS

MOSAB'S FAMILY

Sheikh Yousef Dawood – His paternal grandfather

Sheikh Hassan Yousef – His father; cofounder and leader of Hamas since 1986

Sabha Abu Salem – His mother

Ibrahim Abu Salem – His uncle (mother's brother); a cofounder of the Muslim Brotherhood in Jordan

Dawood – His uncle (father's brother)

Yousef Dawood – His cousin, son of Dawood, who helped him purchase inoperative weapons

Mosab's brothers – Sohayb (1980), Seif (1983), Oways (1985), Mohammad (1987), Naser (1997)

Mosab's sisters – Sabeela (1979), Tasneem (1982), Anhar (1990)

KEY PLAYERS (IN ORDER OF APPEARANCE)

Hassan al-Banna – Egyptian reformer and founder of the Muslim Brotherhood

Jamal Mansour – Cofounder of Hamas in 1986; assassinated by Israel

Ibrahim Kiswani – Mosab's friend who helped him purchase inoperative weapons

Loai – Mosab's handler in the Shin Bet

Marwan Barghouti – Secretary-general of Fatah

Maher Odeh – Hamas leader and head of Hamas security wing in prison

Saleh Talahme – Hamas terrorist and Mosab's friend

Ibrahim Hamed – Head of Hamas security wing in the West Bank

Sayyed al-Sheikh Qassem – Hamas terrorist

Hasaneen Rummanah – Hamas terrorist

Khalid Meshaal – Head of Hamas in Damascus, Syria

Abdullah Barghouti – Bomb maker

THE OTHERS (IN ALPHABETICAL ORDER)

Abdel Aziz al-Rantissi – Hamas leader; leader of the deportee camp in Lebanon

Abdel-Basset Odeh – Hamas suicide bomber, Park Hotel

Abu Ali Mustafa – Secretary-general of PFLP; assassinated by Israel

Abu Saleem – Butcher; Mosab's crazy neighbor

Adib Zeyadeh – Covert leader of Hamas

Ahmad Ghandour – Early leader of Al-Aqsa Martyrs Brigades

Ahmad al-Faransi – Aide to Marwan Barghouti

Ahmed Yassin – Cofounder of Hamas in 1986; assassinated by Israel

Akel Sorour – Friend of Mosab and fellow prison inmate

Amar Salah Diab Amarna – First official Hamas suicide bomber

Amer Abu Sarhan – Stabbed three Israelis to death in 1989

Amnon – Jewish convert to Christianity and fellow prison inmate with Mosab

Anas Rasras – Maj'd leader at Megiddo Prison

Ariel Sharon – Eleventh prime minister of Israel (2001–2006)

Avi Dichter – Head of Shin Bet

Ayman Abu Taha – Cofounder of Hamas in 1986

Aziz Kayed – Covert leader of Hamas

Baruch Goldstein – American-born physician who slaughtered twenty-nine Palestinians in Hebron during Ramadan

Bilal Barghouti – Cousin of Hamas bomber Abdullah Barghouti

Bill Clinton – Forty-second president of the United States

Captain Shai – Israel Defense Forces officer

Daya Muhammad Hussein al-Tawil – French Hill suicide bomber

Ehud Barak – Tenth prime minister of Israel (1999–2001)

Ehud Olmert – Twelfth prime minister of Israel (2006–2009)

Fathi Shaqaqi – Founder of Palestinian Islamic Jihad and initiator of suicide bombings

Fouad Shoubaki – PA chief financial officer for military operations

Hassan Salameh – Friend of Yahya Ayyash, who taught him how to make bombs to kill Israelis

Imad Akel – Leader of Al-Qassam Brigades, Hamas military wing; killed by Israelis

Ismail Haniyeh – Elected Palestinian prime minister in 2006

Izz al-Din Shuheil al-Masri – Sbarro pizza parlor suicide bomber

Jamal al-Dura – Father of twelve-year-old Mohammed al-Dura, who Palestinians say was killed by IDF soldiers during a demonstration by Palestinian security forces in Gaza

Jamal al-Taweel – Hamas leader in the West Bank

Jamal Salim – Hamas leader killed in assassination of Jamal Mansour in Nablus

Jamil Hamami – Cofounder of Hamas in 1986

Jibril Rajoub – Head of security for the Palestinian Authority

Juma'a – Gravedigger in cemetery near Mosab's childhood home

King Hussein – King of Jordan (1952–1999)

Kofi Annan – Seventh secretary-general of the United Nations (1997–2006)

Leonard Cohen – Canadian singer and songwriter who wrote "First We Take Manhattan"

Mahmud Muslih – Cofounder of Hamas in 1986

Majeda Talahme – Wife of Hamas terrorist Saleh Talahme

Mohammad – Founder of Islam

Mohammad Daraghmeh – Palestinian journalist

Mohammed al-Dura – Twelve-year-old boy allegedly killed by IDF soldiers during a Fatah demonstration in Gaza

Mohammed Arman – Member of Hamas terrorist cell

Mosab Talahme – Oldest son of terrorist Saleh Talahme

Muhammad Jamal al-Natsheh – Cofounder of Hamas in 1986 and head of its military wing in the West Bank

Muhaned Abu Halawa – Member of Al-Aqsa Martyrs Brigades

Najeh Madi – Covert leader of Hamas

Nissim Toledano – Israeli border policeman killed by Hamas

Ofer Dekel – Shin Bet officer

Rehavam Ze'evi – Israeli tourism minister assassinated by PFLP gunmen

Saddam Hussein – Iraqi dictator who invaded Kuwait in 1990

Saeb Erekat – Palestinian cabinet minister

Saeed Hotari – Dolphinarium suicide bomber

Salah Hussein – Covert leader of Hamas

Sami Abu Zuhri – Hamas spokesman in Gaza

Shada – Palestinian worker killed by mistake by an Israeli tank gunner

Shimon Peres – Ninth president of Israel, who assumed office in 2007; has also served as prime minister and foreign minister

Shlomo Sakal – Israeli plastics salesman, stabbed to death in Gaza

Tsibouktsakis Germanus – Greek Orthodox monk murdered by Ismail Radaida

Yahya Ayyash – Bomb maker credited with advancing the technique of suicide bombing in the Israeli-Palestinian conflict

Yasser Arafat – Longtime chairman of the PLO, president of the PA; died in 2004

Yisrael Ziv – Israeli major general for the IDF

Yitzhak Rabin – Fifth prime minister of Israel (1974–1977; 1992–1995); assassinated by right-wing Israeli radical Yigal Amir in 1995

Zakaria Botros – Coptic priest who has led countless Muslims to Christ, via satellite television, by exposing the errors in the Qur'an and revealing the truth of Scripture

GLOSSARY

abu – Father of

adad – Number

adhan – Muslim call to prayer, five times a day

Al-Aqsa Martyrs Brigades – Terrorist group, formed during the Second Intifada out of various resistance groups, that carries out suicide bombings and other attacks against Israeli targets

Al-Aqsa Mosque – Islam's third holiest site from which Muslims believe Mohammad ascended into heaven; located on the Temple Mount, Jews' holiest site and believed to be the location of the ancient Jewish Temples

Al-Fatihah – The opening sura (passage) of the Qur'an, read by the imam or religious leader

Al-Jazeera – Arab satellite television news network; based in Qatar

Allah – Arabic word for God

Allenby Bridge – Bridge across the Jordan River between Jericho and Jordan; originally built by British General Edmund Allenby in 1918

baklava – Rich pastry made with layers of dough, filled with chopped nuts and sweetened with honey

Black September – Bloody confrontation between the Jordanian government and Palestinian organizations in September 1970

Caliphate – Islamic political leadership

Democratic Front for the Liberation of Palestine (DFLP) – Secular Marxist-Leninist organization opposing the Israeli occupation of the West Bank and Gaza

dinar (dee'-nahr) – Official currency of Jordan, used throughout the West Bank in addition to the Israeli shekel

emir – Arabic for chief or commander

Ezzedeen Al-Qassam Brigades (Eza-deen' al Kas-sam') – Military wing of Hamas

Fatah – Largest political faction of the Palestine Liberation Organization

fatwa – Legal opinion or decree concerning Islamic law issued by an Islamic scholar

feda'iyeen **(fedai-yeen')** – Freedom fighters

Force 17 – Yasser Arafat's elite commando unit

hadith **(hah'-dith)** – Oral traditions of Islam

hajj – Pilgrimage to Mecca

Hamas – Islamic resistance movement in the West Bank and Gaza, listed by the United States, European Union, and others as a terrorist organization

Hezbollah – Islamic political and paramilitary organization in Lebanon

hijab – Head covering or veil worn by Muslim women in some cultures

IDF (Israel Defense Forces) – Israel's military force, including ground forces, air force, and navy

imam – Islamic leader, usually of a mosque

intifada – Rebellion or uprising

Islamic Jihad – Islamic resistance movement in the West Bank and Gaza, listed by the United States, European Union, and others as a terrorist organization

jalsa – Islamic study group

jihad – Literally means "struggle" but interpreted by militant Islamic groups to call for armed struggle, even terrorism

Kalashnikov – Russian AK-47 assault rifle; invented by Mikhail Kalashnikov

Knesset – Legislative branch of the Israeli government

Ktzi'ot – Israeli tent prison in the Negev where Mosab spent time

Kurds – Ethnic people group, most of whom live in Kurdistan, which covers parts of Iraq, Iran, Syria, and Turkey

Labor Party – Socialist/Zionist left-wing political party of Israel

Likud Party – Right-wing political party of Israel

maj'd **(mah-jeed')** – Hamas security wing

Maskobiyeh (mahs-koh-bee'-yah) – Israeli detention center in West Jerusalem

Mecca – Islam's holiest site, located in Saudi Arabia, where the prophet Mohammad founded his religion

Medina – Islam's second holiest site; the burial place of Mohammad located in Saudi Arabia

Megiddo – Prison camp in northern Israel

Merkava – Combat tank, used by the Israeli Defense Forces

minaret – Tall spire of a mosque from which a Muslim religious leader calls the faithful to prayer

mi'var – At Megiddo, a processing unit where prisoners stayed before being moved into the camp population

Molotov cocktail – A petroleum bomb, usually a gasoline-filled glass bottle with a rag wick, that is ignited and thrown at a target.

mosque – Muslim place of worship and prayer

Mossad – National intelligence agency of Israel, comparable to America's Central Intelligence Agency

mujahid (moo-jah-ha-deed') – Muslim guerilla soldier

Munkar and Nakir – Angels believed to torment the dead

occupied territories – The West Bank, Gaza, and the Golan Heights

Operation Defensive Shield – Major military operation conducted by the Israel Defense Forces during the Second Intifada

Oslo Accords – The 1993 agreements reached between Israel and the Palestine Liberation Organization

Ottoman Empire – Turkish empire that lasted from about 1299 to 1923

Palestinian Authority (PA) – Formed in 1994, according to the terms of the Oslo Accords, as the governing body of the West Bank and Gaza

Palestine Liberation Organization (PLO) – Political/resistance organization, led by Yasser Arafat from 1969 to 2004

Popular Front for the Liberation of Palestine (PFLP) – Marxist-Leninist resistance organization in the West Bank and Gaza

Qur'an (kor-ahn') – The holy book of Islam

rakat (*rak'ah*) – Islamic set of prayers and postures

Ramadan – Month of fasting to commemorate the receipt of the Qur'an by Mohammad

sawa'ed – Agents for the Hamas security wing in the Israeli prison camps; threw balls containing messages from one section to another

Scud – Ballistic missile developed by the Soviet Union during the Cold War

sharia – Islamic religious law

shaweesh – A prisoner chosen to represent other inmates with the Israeli prison administrators; a "trusty"

sheikh (shake) – Muslim elder or leader

Shi'a – Islam's second largest denomination after Sunni

Shin Bet – Israeli intelligence service, comparable to America's Federal Bureau of Investigation

shurah **council** – In Islam, a panel of seven decision makers

shoter (sho-tair') – Hebrew for Israeli prison guard or police officer

Six-Day War – Brief war in 1967 between Israel and Egypt, Jordan, and Syria

Sunni – Islam's largest denomination

sura – Chapter in the Qur'an

Temple Mount – In Old Jerusalem, the location of Al-Aqsa Mosque and the Dome of the Rock, the oldest Islamic building in the world; also believed to be location of First and Second Jewish Temples

wudu – Islamic ritual purification

TIME LINE

1923 – End of the Ottoman Empire

1928 – Hassan al-Banna founds the Society of the Muslim Brothers

1935 – The Muslim Brotherhood is established in Palestine

1948 – The Muslim Brotherhood takes violent action against the Egyptian government; Israel declares its independence; Egypt, Lebanon, Syria, Jordan, and Iraq invade Israel

1949 – Hassan al-Banna is assassinated; Al-Amari refugee camp established in the West Bank

1964 – Palestine Liberation Organization founded

1967 – Six-Day War

1968 – Popular Front for the Liberation of Palestine hijacks an El Al 707 and diverts it to Algiers; no fatalities

1970 – Black September, in which thousands of PLO fighters are killed by Jordanian troops, as Jordan expels the PLO

1972 – Eleven Israeli athletes killed by Black September at the Munich Olympics

1973 – Yom Kippur War

1977 – Hassan Yousef marries Sabha Abu Salem

1978 – Mosab Hassan Yousef is born; thirty-eight people are killed in a Fatah attack on Israel's Coastal Highway north of Tel Aviv

1979 – Palestinian Islamic Jihad founded

1982 – Israel invades Lebanon and drives out the PLO

1985 – Hassan Yousef and his family move to Al-Bireh

1986 – Hamas founded in Hebron

1987 – Hassan Yousef takes a second job, teaching religion to Muslims at the Christian school in Ramallah; beginning of the First Intifada

1989 – Hassan Yousef's first arrest and imprisonment; Amer Abu Sarhan of Hamas murders three Israelis

1990 – Saddam Hussein invades Kuwait

1992 – Mosab's family moves to Betunia; Hassan Yousef is arrested; Hamas terrorists kidnap and murder Israeli police officer Nissim Toledano; Palestinian leaders are deported to Lebanon

1993 – Oslo Accords

1994 – Baruch Goldstein kills twenty-nine Palestinians in Hebron; first official suicide bombing; Yasser Arafat returns triumphantly to Gaza to set up Palestinian Authority headquarters

1995 – Israeli prime minister Yitzhak Rabin assassinated; Hassan Yousef is arrested by the Palestinian Authority; Mosab buys illegal, inoperative guns

1996 – Hamas bomb maker Yahya Ayyash is assassinated; Mosab is arrested and imprisoned for the first time

1997 – Mosab released from prison; Mossad unsuccessfully attempts to assassinate Khalid Meshaal

1999 – Mosab attends a Christian Bible study

2000 – Camp David Summit; Second Intifada (also known as the Al-Aqsa Intifada) begins

2001 – French Hill suicide bombing; Dolphinarium and Sbarro pizza parlor suicide bombings; PFLP secretary-general Abu Ali Mustafa assassinated by Israel; Israeli minister of tourism Rehavam Ze'evi assassinated by PFLP gunmen

2002 – Israel launches Operation Defensive Shield; nine killed in Hebrew University attack; Mosab and his father are arrested and imprisoned

2003 – Western Coalition forces liberate Iraq; Hamas terrorists Saleh Talahme, Hasaneen Rummanah, and Sayyed al-Sheikh Qassem are killed by Israel

2004 – Death of Yasser Arafat; Hassan Yousef released from prison

2005 – Mosab is baptized; truce ends between Hamas and Israel; Mosab's third arrest and imprisonment; Mosab released from prison

2006 – Ismail Haniyeh elected Palestinian prime minister

2007 – Mosab leaves the occupied territories for America

ENDNOTES

1. No one has ever had this information before. In fact, the record of history is already filled with numerous inaccuracies about the day that Hamas was born as an organization. For example, Wikipedia inaccurately claims that "Hamas was created in 1987 by Sheikh Ahmed Yassin, Abdel Aziz al-Rantissi and Mohammad Taha of the Palestinian wing of Egypt's Muslim Brotherhood at the beginning of the First Intifada. . . ." This entry is accurate regarding only two of the seven founders, and it is off by a year. See http://en.wikipedia.org/wiki/Hamas (accessed November 20, 2009).

    MidEastWeb says, "Hamas was formed about February 1988 to allow participation of the brotherhood in the first Intifada. The founding leaders of Hamas were: Ahmad Yassin, 'Abd al-Fattah Dukhan, Muhammed Shama', Ibrahim al-Yazuri, Issa al-Najjar, Salah Shehadeh (from Bayt Hanun) and 'Abd al-Aziz Rantisi. Dr. Mahmud Zahar is also usually listed as one of the original leaders. Other leaders include: Sheikh Khalil Qawqa, Isa al-Ashar, Musa Abu Marzuq, Ibrahim Ghusha, Khalid Mish'al." This is even less accurate than the Wikipedia entry. See http://www.mideastweb.org/hamashistory.htm (accessed November 20, 2009).

2. The PLO's first high-profile plane hijacking had occurred on July 23, 1968, when PFLP activists diverted an El Al Boeing 707 to Algiers. About a dozen Israeli passengers and ten crew members were held as hostages. There were no fatalities. But eleven Israeli athletes were killed four years later in a PLO-led terrorist attack at the Munich Olympics. And on March 11, 1978, Fatah fighters landed a boat north of Tel Aviv, hijacked a bus, and began an attack along the Coastal Highway that killed about thirty-five people—and wounded over seventy others.

    The organization had had an easy time recruiting from among the Palestinian refugees who made up two-thirds of Jordan's population. With money flooding in from other Arab countries in support of the cause, the PLO became stronger and better-armed than even the police and the Jordanian army. And it wasn't long before its leader, Yasser Arafat, was in striking distance of taking over the country and establishing a Palestinian state.

King Hussein of Jordan had to act quickly and decisively or lose his country. Years later, I would be amazed to learn through an unforeseeable relationship with the Israeli security service that Jordan's monarch had entered into a secret alliance with Israel at this time—even as every other Arab country was committed to its destruction. It was the logical thing to do, of course, because King Hussein was unable to protect his throne and Israel was unable to effectively patrol the long border between their two countries. But it would have been political and cultural suicide for the king had this information ever leaked out.

So in 1970, before the PLO could grasp any more control, King Hussein ordered its leaders and fighters out of the country. When they refused, he drove them out—with the aid of weapons provided by Israel—in a military campaign that came to be known among Palestinians as Black September.

Time magazine quoted Arafat as telling sympathetic Arab leaders, "A massacre has been committed. Thousands of people are under debris. Bodies have rotted. Hundreds of thousands of people are homeless. Our dead are scattered in the streets. Hunger and thirst are killing our remaining children, women and old men" ("The Battle Ends; The War Begins," *Time*, October 5, 1970).

King Hussein owed a great debt to Israel, which he would try to repay in 1973 by warning Jerusalem that an Arab coalition led by Egypt and Syria was about to invade. Unfortunately, Israel did not take the warning seriously. The invasion came on Yom Kippur, and an unprepared Israel suffered heavy and unnecessary losses. This secret, too, I would learn one day from the Israelis.

Following Black September, PLO survivors fled to southern Lebanon, which was still reeling from a deadly civil war. Here the organization initiated a new power grab, growing and gaining strength until it virtually became a state within a state.

From its new base of operations, the PLO waged a war of attrition against Israel. Beirut was too weak to stop the endless shelling and missile attacks against Israel's northern communities. And in 1982, Israel invaded Lebanon, driving out the PLO in a four-month campaign. Arafat and a thousand surviving fighters went into exile in Tunisia. But even from that distance, the PLO continued to launch attacks on Israel and amass an army of fighters in the West Bank and Gaza.

3. "Arafat's Return: Unity Is 'the Shield of Our People,'" *New York Times*, July 2, 1994, http://www.nytimes.com/1994/07/02/world/arafat-in-gaza-arafat-s-return-unity-is-the-shield-of-our-people.html (accessed November 23, 2009).

4. Leonard Cohen, "First We Take Manhattan" copyright © 1988 Leonard Cohen Stranger Music, Inc..

5. Israeli Ministry of Foreign Affairs, "Suicide and Other Bombing Attacks in Israel Since the Declaration of Principles (September 1993)"; The Palestinian Academic Society for the Study of International Affairs, Jerusalem, "Palestine Facts – Palestine Chronology 2000, http://www.passia.org/palestine_facts/chronology/2000.html. See also http://www.mfa.gov.il/MFA/MFAArchive/2000_2009/2000/11/Palestinian%20Terrorism-%20Photos%20-%20November%202000.

6. Further confirmation of this connection would come the following year when Israel invaded Ramallah and raided Arafat's headquarters. Among other documents, they would discover an invoice, dated September 16, 2001, from the Al-Aqsa Martyrs

Brigades to Brigadier General Fouad Shoubaki, the PA's CFO for military operations. It requested reimbursement for explosives used in bombings in Israeli cities and asked for money to build more bombs and to cover the cost of propaganda posters promoting suicide bombers. Yael Shahar, "Al-Aqsa Martyrs Brigades—A Political Tool with an Edge," April 3, 2002, International Institute for Counter-Terrorism, IDC Herzliya.

7. Leonard Cole, *Terror: How Israel Has Coped and What America Can Learn* (Bloomington: Indiana University Press, 2007), 8.

8. "Obituary: Rehavam Zeevi," BBC News, October 17, 2001, http://news.bbc.co.uk/2/hi/middle_east/1603857.stm (accessed November 24, 2009).

9. "Annan Criticizes Israel, Palestinians for Targeting Civilians," U.N. Wire, March 12, 2002, http://www.unwire.org/unwire/20020312/24582_story.asp (accessed October 23, 2009).

10. European Union, "Declaration of Barcelona on the Middle East," March 16, 2002, http://europa.eu/rapid/pressReleasesAction.do?reference=PRES/02/930&format=HTML&aged=0&language=EN&guiLanguage=en.

11. An interesting sidenote about Colonel Jibril Rajoub: This man had taken advantage of his position as protective security chief in the West Bank to build his own little kingdom, making his officers bow and scrape as though he was heir to a throne. I have seen his breakfast table groan under the weight of fifty different dishes, prepared just to show everyone how important he was. I have also seen that Rajoub was rude and careless and that he behaved more like a gangster than a leader. When Arafat rounded up as many Hamas leaders and members as he could back in 1995, Rajoub tortured them without mercy. Several times, Hamas had threatened to assassinate him, prompting him to buy a bulletproof, explosion-proof car. Even Arafat didn't have anything like it.

12. Associated Press, "Palestinian Bombmaker Gets 67 Life Terms," MSNBC, November 30, 2004, http://www.msnbc.msn.com/id/6625081/.

13. Danny Rubinstein, "Hamas Leader: You Can't Get Rid of Us," *Haaretz*, http://www.haaretz.com/hasen/pages/ShArt.jhtml?itemNo=565084&contrassID=2&subContrassID=4&sbSubContrassID=0.

14. "Israel Vows to 'Crush' Hamas after Attack," Fox News, September 25, 2005, http://www.foxnews.com/story/0,2933,170304,00.html (accessed October 5, 2009).

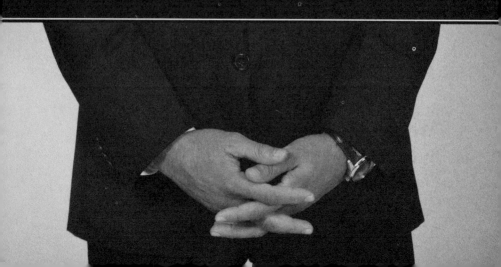

ABOUT THE AUTHORS

Mosab Hassan ("Joseph") Yousef is the son of Sheikh Hassan Yousef, a founding leader of Hamas, internationally recognized as a terrorist organization and responsible for countless suicide bombings and other deadly attacks against Israel. An integral part of the movement, Mosab was imprisoned several times by the Israeli internal intelligence service. After a chance encounter with a British tourist, he started a six-year quest that jeopardized Hamas, endangered his family, and threatened his life. He has since embraced the teachings of Jesus and has been granted political asylum in America.

Ron Brackin has traveled extensively in the Middle East as an investigative journalist. He was in Bethlehem, Ramallah, Gaza, and Jerusalem during the Al-Aqsa Intifada. He was on assignment in Baghdad after the fall of Iraq and more recently with the rebels and refugees of southern Sudan and Darfur. He has contributed articles and columns to many publications, including *USA Today* and the *Washington Times*. Ron has also served as a broadcast journalist and a congressional press secretary in Washington.